D1731344

Trends in Linguistics

State-of-the-Art Reports

edited by

W. Winter

University of Kiel, Germany

11

CONTEMPORARY HEBREW

by

HAIIM B. ROSÉN

1977

MOUTON

THE HAGUE · PARIS

ISBN 90 279 3106 2

Printed in Hungary

FOREWORD

The invitation extended to me by Professor Werner Winter to contribute a volume on Contemporary Hebrew to the *Series Critica* was a welcome occasion to try to reassess our knowledge of this language sixteen years after I had attempted, in my *Ha-'ivrit šelanù*, to open this field to up-to-date linguistic research. I have endeavoured here not only to sketch a picture of Israeli Hebrew as a representative of a specific type of language organism, but also to supply the mould into which the material facts of this language must be cast in order to arrive at an adequate description of its working mechanism. This will be found amalgamated with a history of scholarly advance and achievement; the reader will have to judge whether my efforts to depict the relative impact of my own contribution with the amount of balanced objectivity required in a survey such as the present one have been successful.

It is my pleasant duty to acknowledge gratefully the financial assistance granted by the Department of General Studies of the Israel Institute of Technology of Haifa for the purpose of compiling the bibliography. Sincere thanks go to Mrs. Sarah Munster, assistant at the Department of Linguistics of the Hebrew University, who located, with penetrating understanding of the subtleties of the subject matter, all flaws of English expression; those that remain are my own responsibility.

Jerusalem, May 1971   H. R.

TABLE OF CONTENTS

TRANSCRIPTION

The transcriptional equivalences that apply between Latin characters and unpointed (unvocalized) script in Israeli Hebrew forms
are marked (+) below.

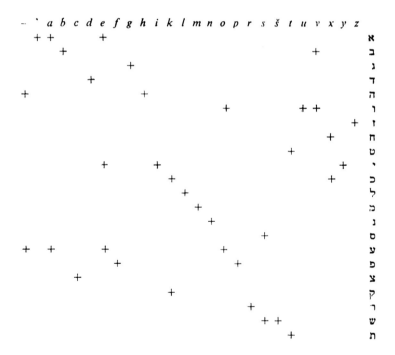

Note that c is a dental affricate (German z), x an unvoiced postvelar fricative (*ach*-sound).

For the value of the accent signs ' and ' see § 3.7.3.

The representation of Biblical Hebrew forms is by one-to-one transliteration:

א ב ג ד ה ו ז ח ט י כ ל מ נ ס ע פ צ ק ר שׁ שׂ ת
ʼ b g d h w z ḥ ṭ y k l m n s ʻ p ṣ q r š ś t

ִי וּ ֵי וֹ ֵ ֲ ֹ ִ ֶ ַ ֻ ֱ ָ ֳ ְ ־ (dāḡēš)
î û ê ô ē ă ō i e a u ĕ ā ŏ – ·

E.g. בְּדָבְּרְכֶם bᵉḏabᵉrkem

1 NAME AND IDENTITY

1.1 THE UNIQUENESS OF CONTEMPORARY (ISRAELI) HEBREW

The uniqueness of Contemporary or Israeli Hebrew is adequately described by characterizing it as a language the very existence of which is part of the national self-identification of the community that uses it; a language created by intended rebirth; a language whose creation as a vehicle of communication was an ideological act and also the result, at least in part, of scholarly research; a language scientifically studied and analysed within some seventy years following its emergence, but given a name of its own in scholarship only as a result of the recognition, by virtue of that same scholarly study, of its historical autonomy.

1.2 NAMES PROPOSED

1.2.1 Neo-Hebrew

Any designation of this language, which contains the element 'new' (such as Neo-Hebrew, *néo-hébreu, neuhebräisch*) is inadequate, simply because such names were used, prior to the formation of Israeli Hebrew (IH), for Mishnaic and later for mediaeval rabbinical Hebrew, which were, at the time, the only known layers of postbiblical Hebrew. Following the emergence of Israeli Hebrew, the historical incision can no longer be made so as to create a division between what was biblical and what came after, but rather to set aside from Israeli Hebrew whatever preceded it in history (BERGSTRÄSSER 1928: 47). It will serve our purpose well if we unite BIBLICAL HEBREW and what was termed, mainly by Protestant scholars up to half a century ago, NEUHEBRÄISCH[1] under the common name of CLASSICAL HEBREW, a name that very suitably depicts the position these layers occupy in the mind of the speaker of Contemporary Hebrew versus his own language. What Hebrew has in common with other languages whose history involves a layer termed *classical* is the not insignificant fact that the present-day language is named as a modification of a more comprehensive designation.[2]

While the designations of the type *néo-hébreu* are useless, for the reasons stated, the names involving the adjective *modern* are no more suitable, although they have the one advantage of opposing current Hebrew to classical language (AEŠCOLY 1937: 4). In two respects, "modern" Hebrew is different from other languages which bear that title: it is not just the nth stage in the evolution of Hebrew (ROSÉN 1952b: 5; 1958c: 65-6), because for the purposes of historical linguistics, it would not suffice to state the chronological succession of *états de langue*, but one would also have to determine in what way the preceding *états de langue* have supplied language material to their successor; for Hebrew the situation is different from all other "modern" languages in that any given item stemming from an "ancient" stage is not necessarily channelled

---

[1] BERGSTRÄSSER (1928: 46-7) has the division into *Althebräisch, Mittelhebräisch*, and *Neuhebräisch*; this matches his terminology for the other living Semitic languages, where the current form is always called *Neu-*, while the earliest attested one bears a name with *Alt-*. It is precisely this analogy which we must consider out of place.

[2] A singular confusion has led to terminological difficulties in Soviet usage. Following Byzantine ecclesiastical usage, "Jews" are "Hebrews" in Russian, as a consequence of which early Zionist usage represented 'Jewish-national' as *'ivri*, and Russian еврейский stands for what is ethnically connected with Jews: as the designation of a language, еврейский язык is 'Yiddish'. For the Hebrew language, древнееврейский 'Old-Hebrew' had to be used, which, of course, is not the counterpart of еврейский. Soviet linguists have practically no other way than using the native forms of the language names: иврит, идиш (cf., e.g., ZAND 1965). In German-speaking countries, it was customary for some time to call the current language *'ivrit* to distinguish it from *hebräisch*, the Holy Tongue. We feel that the use of the native designation *'ivrit* in any of the European languages would place Israeli Hebrew among the non-European native speech forms that do not rank as languages of civilization within the European cultural conscience.

through, or even present in, chronologically intermediate stages. The second reason for the inadequacy of the term *modern* is that Contemporary Hebrew is by no means more modern (in terms of *Weltbild*) than previous literary language; it is not by virtue of the revival that modern thought can be moulded into Hebrew (irrespective, of course, of the linguistically irrelevant introduction of technical terms at whatever moment the civilizatory necessity arose); this is why authors who use the term *modern* waver as to when "modernism" became apparent and whether it was coincident with revival (cf., e.g., COHEN – ZAFRANI 1968: 14; THORNHILL 1951: 103).

1.2.2 Modern Hebrew

MODERN HEBREW is a convenient rendering of the Hebrew term that is still preferred by those who wish to imply by nomenclature that current Hebrew is not a linguistic entity commanding some autonomy towards everything that preceded it: *'ivrit xadaša*, literally 'New Hebrew' (cf., e.g., ORNAN 1968a: 1). Now, while this is wanted to match linguistic terminology for languages conventionally termed *Modern = Neu-*[3] (*xadaša* is the adjective used for 'Modern Greek', *'Neuhochdeutsch'*, etc.), it was not conceived as such: in his programmatic article on "Ancient Hebrew and New Hebrew", J. KLAUSNER (1929: 10) makes it apparent that what he has in mind is the emergence of a "new" language, in the sense that it contains previously nonexistent expressional tools; the dogmatic position taken by KLAUSNER over many years was, moreover, that Hebrew must continue the use of expressions found in the later layers whilst discarding whatever was discarded by the latter.[4]

---

[3] *'Ivrit xadaša* has never been used, to my knowledge, in the sense of *'Neuhebräisch'*.

[4] Cf. BENDAVID (1965: 250). It is worthwhile to quote, in this context, a little known forerunner of KLAUSNER's (ROSENBERG 1893: 146): "Shall we use Biblical or postbiblical language? or shall new forms and expressions be introduced? The closest related language, Aramaic, shows that current language (neo-Aramaic) is the result of great changes, even metamorphoses in the course of millenia. Consequently, Biblical Hebrew, which is a closed period, cannot become a *Volkssprache* any more than Ancient Greek, Gothic, Church Slavonic, etc.; the revival of Hebrew is feasible only by further developments, that is change: whatever lives, changes."

This is not the case; so we do not recommend the term *'ivrit
xadaša* any more than we do *Modern Hebrew*.

1.2.3 Spoken Hebrew

Other early attempts at naming the language use the fact that it is
spoken as its distinguishing mark. True, the revival converted Hebrew
from an "unspoken" language into a spoken one, and formal writing
was, on average, closer to classical language than common oral usage;
however, the characteristics that made Israeli Hebrew stand apart from
Classical Hebrew linguistically – structurally, functionally – were
present in contemporary writing as much as in contemporary speech
See *1.4.1*.

1.3 DESIGNATIONS IN LINGUISTICS

1.3.1 Israeli Hebrew

It must have been precisely the non-chronological ("unhistorical",
"untraditional") nature of the term ISRAELI HEBREW that aroused
opposition to it as the expression of a certain viewpoint within
Hebrew studies. At this writing, almost twenty years after having
introduced the name,[5] I can find no purely or preponderantly
linguistic treatment of the language using any other. Only where
the discussion is tainted "ideologically", and written in Hebrew,
are other terms sometimes propagated.

Israeli Hebrew was not meant as a geographical designation;[6]
I think there was some emotional load in that term when it was finally
adopted: the name of Israel symbolized the culmination of the
materialization of the aspirations to nationhood in the field of
language as well as in the realm of territorial independence. There
is no other way to circumscribe what is meant by *Israeli Hebrew*
than to say that it is the national language *(Staatssprache)* of

---

[5] Cf. VRIEZEN (1956: 6), BLANC (1956b: 188), KUTSCHER (1957: 38). The term
first appears in writing in ROSÉN (1952b: 4–5).
[6] So interpreted by ULLENDORFF (1957: 251–2), probably in the light of
occasional "Palestinian Hebrew" or "Spoken Hebrew of Palestine" found
in earlier discussions (SPIEGEL 1930: 17; CHRISTIE 1931: 5).

Israel, the first language of nearly a million Jewish natives of Israel, largely monolingual, and the second, but prestige language of close to two million multilingual speakers (the non-native Jewish and part of the non-Jewish population of Israel).[7]

1.3.2 Contemporary Hebrew

CONTEMPORARY HEBREW would be an innocent term that would avoid all issues; it has the disadvantage of being historically unstable (we cannot speak of the "Contemporary Hebrew of the thirties") and of calling to our minds other "contemporary languages" *(Gegenwartssprachen)* that derive their right to this title by their giving expression to notional, conceptional, and intellectual frames of "modern times", but are not quite essentially different from non-contemporary shapes of the same language of a generation ago. In some respects, Israeli Hebrew is, in fact, such a "contemporary" language, but it is not only this aspect which we have to discuss linguistically. TÉNÉ has had the useful idea of employing for his treatise the noncommittal title of "Contemporary Hebrew" (TÉNÉ 1968), while discussing therein a language termed *Israeli Hebrew.* We shall follow this lead. That *Contemporary Israeli Hebrew* would, at the least, be highly pleonastic, needs, I feel, no further explanation.

1.4 NONSYNONYMOUS DESIGNATIONS

SPOKEN HEBREW, CHILDREN'S HEBREW, or NATIVE (ISRAELI) HEBREW are not synonyms of Israeli Hebrew, and their use for anything which these terms do not mean, must be objected to.

---

[7]   A statistical survey up to 1954 may be found in BACHI (1955). – Slight variations of the term *Israeli Hebrew* risk, in our opinion, being somewhat misleading. Concerning "Native Israeli Hebrew" (TÉNÉ 1969: 61) see below, *1.4.3.* The use of *Israeli* without *Hebrew* attached to it is objectionable, more so if it is itself modified by various subdividing adjectives (BLANC 1957a: 400; 1964a: 135-7; e.g., "General Israeli"), since an allusion that Israeli Hebrew was not really, fundamentally and intrinsically Hebrew, would taint scholarship with ethnico-cultural ideological attitudes, which we had better not allow to distort our insights.

2*

1.4.1 Spoken Hebrew

There is no diglossy in Israel, although – of course – differences are noticeable between spoken and written usage. We do not think that these stylistic differences are more profound than their analogues in most nations, at any rate they do not justify considering the spoken form of Israeli Hebrew as a separate linguistic entity. It is true that the full revival of Hebrew was achieved by its conversion to a spoken language;[8] Hebrew was "revived as a spoken language" (KUTSCHER 1956: 32), but neither was revival identical with spokenness nor was the reintroduction of speech sufficient for the revival. Israeli Hebrew clearly has at least two layers, one spoken and one written (ORNAN 1968:1–2), and many will find this primary division insufficient. Consequently nothing warrants the adoption of the term Israeli Hebrew exclusively for the spoken style (as proposed by MORAG 1959: 247; modified 1967: 639); if this is done, we are left with no specific term for written contemporary usage, and the impression is created that the latter needs no term of its own, owing to its intrinsic similarity to Classical Hebrew. RABIN (1958b: 248) advocates the recognition of a "Modern Literary Hebrew", but then, is non-literary writing a form of spoken language or a language of no standing? An extreme position was taken by BEN-ḤAYYIM (1953: 50, 54) who, in this highly polemical publication outright opposed "spoken" to "cultured" language, ascribing practically all deviations from classical grammar to the former. This had been the habit of quite a few scholars prior to the stabilization of descriptive research, and in studies conducted up to the mid-fifties, one can find numerous observations made on contemporary usage, but spoken of as though they were exclusive characteristics of colloquial Hebrew, since it was commonly accepted that written language was (or, at least, was supposed to be) quasi-pure Classical Hebrew.

1.4.2 Children's Hebrew

There is Hebrew CHILDREN'S LANGUAGE, which should be, and to some extent has been, studied (H. M. COHEN 1951: 91–97; BAR-ADON 1959 and 1963a, b) in contrast with adults' language; but again, up to the fifties, perfectly common features of Israeli Hebrew were presented by various authors, reluctant to admit the use of non-

---

[8] Although attempts at speaking Hebrew were made prior to the revival (cf. RABIN 1958a: 7; 1969: 34; 1970).

classical language in the mouths or pens of educated adults, as though they were children's style. Most of the published work of that period ostentatiously devoted to the description of children's Hebrew contains little more than unordered enumerations of linguistic phenomena that were, at that time as at any other, distinctive of Israeli Hebrew. Two authors (BARLES 1937: 185–90; AVINERY 1946: 145) have gone as far as ascribing takeovers from foreign languages to children's speech or considering loan translations as one of its characteristics. AVINERY (1946), devoting an entire chapter (pp. 144–80) to "The language of our children", lists, amongst other things, the following fundamental features of Israeli Hebrew (of all age groups) as characteristic of children's speech: adverbial use of masculine singular adjective forms (see *6.4.2.1*); the univerbated compound *'af 'iš* 'not a man' (*le-'af-'iš* 'to nobody'; *6.5.2*); determinated status of superlatives with *haxi-* use of *klum* 'rien' with no formal negation in a verbless sentence (*8.3.2*); and finally the use of the *'et*-case ('accusative') in construction with the kernel *yeš l-* '*alicui est* ..., have' (p. *5.5.3*), even examining "children's usage" in the light of some biblical attestations of 'unsyntactical' *'et-* (cf. ROSÉN 1966: 214–6). Similarly, familiar style features (such as *še-* + potential tense '*que...* + subjonctif'; see note *181*) were discussed along with typically journalese expressions under the heading "On children's and popular language" by the late Y. PERETZ (1943: 296–300; 1944: 58–9), a fighter for the non-recognition of Contemporary Hebrew as a linguistic entity in its own right.

1.4.3 Native Hebrew

The distribution of age groups in the Jewish population of Palestine during the first half of the present century was such that children were distinct from adults not only by their age, but generally speaking, by the fact of being natives. There is even a popular designation for native-born children: *Sabras*. This created the risk of identifying children's speech with native speech, and of lumping both together in contrast to the language of adult immigrants. Some authors discussed phenomena observable in "Sabra Hebrew"[9] and conveniently left open the question whether what was meant was the language of native children, of children in general, or of natives of any age: what we ordinarily find discussed in such studies are common Israeli Hebrew features, irrespective of the birthplace or the age of the speaker.

Of course, recent immigrants are recognizable as such either by a deficient knowledge of Hebrew or by more pronounced linguistic habits hailing from their primary tongues; however, once the linguistic integration of any one of these speakers is completed, once he has mastered Hebrew to the same degree as the old settlers and has minimized his foreign accent, from that moment on his speech is distinguishable neither from that of other immigrant groups nor from that of adult natives,[10] or at least there are enough features common to all immigrant groups and natives alike to constitute a complete language system, precisely the one we call Israeli Hebrew. Moreover, there is no assimilation of language habits to those of the native born; on the contrary, the few phonetic characteristics or slang usages that can be identified as peculiar to native youth are usually abandoned once the subject concerned reaches what can be termed mature age,[11] and the native starts talking ordinary standard Israeli Hebrew. No characteristics have been noted of a specifically native language on either the syntactic or morphological levels; there are lexical slang features that must be properly identified as language of school children, adherents to youth movements, or soldiers – age groups that are naturally preponderantly native. There seems to be one subphonemic phenomenon that is really exclusively ascribable to young native speakers: the materialization of /r/ with the cardinal value of a voiced postvelar fricative, and its consequent position in the

---

[9] E.g. PATAI (1953) (in fact this is a list of how the sabras "pronounce the letters").
[10] The broad distinction between Oriental and non-Oriental phonetic styles (*3.3.1*) has nothing to do with being a native or a recent immigrant.
[11] S. Z. KLAUSNER (1955: 213) has the facts right, but their linguistic evaluation wrong. Terminology does not play any role here (*pace* BLANC 1956b).

phonemic grid diffierent from that of standard IH /r/ (apical
vibrant). The first to observe this was WEIMAN (1950: 19). On the
other hand, the highly syncopated and slurred speech of many
youngsters, that very frequently reduces dramatically the number of
syllables and vocalic or consonantal phonemes made audible in a
word group, must be relegated to the realm of style and cannot
serve as a basis for constituting a specific phonemic system of
"native Israeli Hebrew".

We are, consequently, somewhat at a loss as to what NATIVE
HEBREW is. According to BLANC (1957b: 33), who introduced the
term, it is a synonym of "Israeli Hebrew", and he later made it
abundantly clear that the distinction between native and non-native
was one that applied to the speakers, not to the language (BLANC
1964: 133):

> A distinction [...] can [...] be made between non-native speakers
> [...] and native speakers, whose speech bears no direct relation to
> their forebears' native language.

The "native sound system" (BLANC 1968: 243–247) differs by
nothing from the Israeli Hebrew one, and can conveniently be
retermed "native General Israeli sound system" (BLANC 1968:
243–7), without a "non-native General Israeli sound system" being
in existence. The former can be heard only from speakers born after
1915, which is again a sociological (rather: statistical) truism. The
predilection of some authors for "native" Hebrew must have been
called forth on socio-statistical grounds:

> The essential socio-linguistic feature of contemporary Hebrew is
> the emergence of native speech, and its growing stabilization. (TÉNÉ
> 1969: 50).

Misinterpreting "native Hebrew" as a type of language runs the risk
of a resultant search for features of "non-native Hebrew" and of
suggestions like that of MORAG (1967: 643) that liturgical Hebrew
words in traditional spelling pronunciations used by members of
various communities in a way corresponding to their habits prior

to their acquisition of current and living Israeli Hebrew represented
a non-native form of Israeli Hebrew speech. Summarizing our
abstention from recommending the use of the adjective *native* in
discussions of the linguistic features of Israeli Hebrew, we must
reiterate that what few phonetic traits there are of nativeness in
Hebrew speech tend to disappear in the course of the young natives'
integration in adult society, in the same way as foreign traits
stemming from the immigrants' primary languages are being con-
scientiously obliterated in the course of that same process of integration. One could even say, to sum up, that most young sabras
had, *sit uenia uerbo*, a slight "native accent".

1.5 SEMITIC FEATURES OF ISRAELI HEBREW

We cannot appropriately conclude a chapter on the identity of
Israeli Hebrew without expressly stating our view that it is a Semitic
language.

1.5.1 Its genealogical and typological "character"

To recall that the question of the Semitic identity of Israeli Hebrew
is one concerning its genealogical, and not its typological relationship is to solve the problem.[12] Israeli Hebrew is a language in which
inherited (Hebrew, Semitic) means of expression have been assigned
to the materialization of a given (European, primarily Slavo-
Teutonic) categorial system. The first assignments of the nature
indicated constituted the "revival" of the language. I do not quite
see how things can be viewed any differently; the *innere Form* of
Israeli Hebrew is different from that of biblical or postbiblical
language, it cannot be Semitic, since there is no such thing as the

---

[12]   "La parenté génétique [...] consiste dans le fait que chaque élément d'une
langue est relié par une fonction à un élément d'expression d'une autre."
– "La parenté typologique [...] consiste en ce que des catégories de chacune
d'entre elles sont liées par une fonction à des catégories de chacune des autres."
(HJELMSLEV 1963: 158)

"internal form" of a language family, and the culture represented by Israeli Hebrew is hardly the property of any other known Semitic language, living or dead. Maybe there will never be another living language as fascinating for the linguist as Israeli Hebrew because of the striking disparateness of its genealogical and its typological relatives.

1.5.2 Lacunae in the phonemic system

Intuitively constructed formulas to this effect have been not uncommon in the characterization of Israeli Hebrew ever since BERGSTRÄSSER (1928: 47) spoke about

ein Hebräisch, das in Wirklichkeit eine europäische[13] Sprache in durchsichtiger hebräischer Verkleidung ist.

A "genuinely Semitic" Hebrew was an ideal orthoepists and most purists were trying to achieve, interpreting this notion, however, in the shape of a Brockelmann-style Arabocentric protolanguage. It was not borne in mind that "typically" Semitic distinctions such as t : t have not been preserved in oral traditions of Hebrew other than in Arabophonic environments. The lacunae in the sound inventory of Israeli Hebrew in comparison to reconstructed Hebrew have nothing to do with the allegedly diminished Semitic character of the language: losses analogous to the merger of *h and *h and the continuation of both by h (which again merges with a fricative allophone of the unvoiced velar), to the non-distinction of c and ' (where non-syllabic glottal articulations are lost, but their "reflexes" preserved in the form of vocalic shadings and quantity), to the non-distinction of "emphatic" (velarized?) stops from their non-emphatic counterparts, or the disappearance of q through merger with other phonemes, and finally to the loss of quantitative distinctions

---

[13] Inappropriate terms in this context are: *Indo-European* (genealogical, misses the point), *Europeanized* (this implies a process, but Israeli Hebrew was not less European at first and more European later, it was created as European as it is now).

in the consonantal sphere – all these can be paralleled from quite a few dead and living Semitic languages and they are no indication of the genealogical affinity of a language.

We need not go into the notoriously circular question of exactly what set of characteristics defines a language as belonging to a given genealogical entity, in our case Semitic (cf. ULLENDORFF 1958). The morphological system of Israeli Hebrew tallies with that of Biblical Hebrew to an extent hardly ever experienced with different stages of the same language. Despite some surface alterations, the systemic image is not changed; moreover, essentially Semitic morphological processes are maintained even where a clash is created between Israeli Hebrew and its typological relatives that would favour other types of expressional means.

1.5.3 Morphological features

While the root is hardly productive any more, there is a lexeme which structurally corresponds exactly to a root – the radical (6.1.2): to derive, e.g., adjectives from *seder* 'order', *šapaàt* 'flu', or *mišmaàt* 'discipline', a discontinuous morpheme is extracted from the nouns after the optional elimination of the postformatives: *s-d-r*, *š-p-a*, *m-šm-a*; these morphemes have three positions, just as Semitic roots, but are not necessarily identical with the roots. The derived adjectives 'orderly', 'flu-stricken', and 'disciplined' would be derived from the motivating morphemes by one common pattern morpheme (6.1.3), *me-u-a-*: *mesudar*, *mešupaa*, *memušmaa*. This is as typically Semitic as can be.

Typically Semitic again is the personal suffixation of nouns: *roš-i* 'my head', *ktivat-i* 'my writing'.[14] Employing a more circumlocutory expression of (quasi-)possessive relations, since late

---

[14] Of course, apparent suffixation can also be created, e.g., in Indo-European, with clitic possessives; cf. Mod.Gk. *to spíti mu* 'my house'; but there the clisis is not forcibly linked to the noun (*i kalí su aderfí* 'your beautiful sister'). An Indo-European language in which true personal suffixation of nouns is found, is Persian; this engenders a *Sprachbund* feature with Turkish, Arabic, and – of course – Hebrew.

Biblical Hebrew (*ha-ktiva šel-i*, literally 'the writing of me'), Israeli Hebrew makes ample use of the possibilities of developing functional contrasts between the two constructions (*2.6.3, 7.1.5*). The use of the freely movable genitival *šel*-forms does not render Israeli Hebrew less Semitic than Biblical Hebrew, the principal reason being that the forms of direct personal suffixation to the noun are not at all going out of use or being "replaced" by the more analytical ones.

Determination is a morphological category, in that the determinative element is not freely movable. Determination consequently can, and does, as in other Semitic languages, enter relations of syntactic concord that can serve as expressions of nexus: *ha-sefèr ha-gadol* (sentence-part nexus) 'the big book' versus *ha-sefèr gadol* (sentence nexus) 'the book is big'.

1.5.4 Syntactic properties

In syntax, a very notable Semitic feature of Israeli Hebrew is the structure of the relative clause which centres around a freely movable "retrospective" pronoun (*ha-sefèr[1] še-kara'tì[2] bo[3]* 'the book[1] [subordinator]-I have read[2] in it[3]' = 'the book in which I have read')[15]. Explicit subordination is not compulsory and can be replaced by juxtaposition of the retrospective pronoun to its antecedent: *ha-sefèr bo kara'tì*. There is no tendency whatsoever to infringe on this structure.

True to its Semitic nature, Israeli Hebrew distinguishes verbal from verbless ('nominal') sentences, and the latter can be subdivided into sentences with and without subject-predicate concord

---

[15] In many dialects of Yiddish, relative clauses are structured exactly as Hebrew ones: the introductory element (*voz*) is invariable (a "general subordinator"; cf. *8.5.1*) and is followed at some point of the clause by a retrospective pronoun (e.g. *im* 'him') in gender-number concord with the antecedent. Such a construction is, of course, not of German origin and doubtless constitutes one of the Hebraisms in Yiddish; however, for the purpose of assessing the 'Semitic' features of Israeli Hebrew, it must be borne in mind that here again the ancient feature was preserved thanks to the support of what appeared to be the usage in Yiddish.

	Hebrew	Russian	
	GENDER-NUMBER CONCORD	PERSON-NUMBER CONCORD	
Verbal (con-cord com-pulsory)	Ha-baxur ʾoved Ha-baxura ʾovedèt Ha-baxurim ʾovdim	Мальчик работает Девица работает Мальчики работают	'The young man works' 'The young lady works' 'The young men work'
	PERSON-NUMBER CONCORD	GENDER-NUMBER CONCORD	
Verbless (with concord)	Ha-baxur ʾavad Ha-baxura ʾavda Ha-baxurim ʾavdu	Мальчик работал Девица работала Мальчики работали	'The young man worked' 'The young lady worked' 'The young men worked'
	Ha-baxur yafe Ha-baxura yafa Ha-baxurot yafot	Мальчик красив Девица красива Девицы красивы	'The young man is handsome' 'The girl is pretty' 'The girls are pretty'
(without concord)	Ha-baxur Ha-baxura } babayit Ha-baxurim Ha-baxurot	Мальчик Девица } дома Мальчики Девицы	'The young man is 'The young lady is } at home' 'The young men are 'The young ladies are

(8.1.2). As in most Semitic languages, a tense-mood uncharacterized copula is not a morphological entity, and its function is taken over by concord (ROSÉN 1965). But here we arrive at a peculiar collision between adopting a genealogical or a typological view of the position of a language in relation to others. I would not dispute too strongly an opinion according to which sentence nexus is less an indication of genealogical affiliation than of typological affinity. Here we are faced with a rare historic coincidence, namely that the very Indo-European language that exerted the strongest typological influence on revived Hebrew happened not only to possess the same type of sentence structure and nexus, but also to assign pattern functions quite analogously to Hebrew, as shown on p. 28.

The maintenance of the Semitic syntactic feature was supported by the characteristics of the substrate. But this must not be taken as symptomatic. Once the system of Israeli Hebrew was integrated and consolidated (about a generation after the "revival"), with whatever Semitic features were rooted and whatever European traits absorbed in it at that time, it became self-supporting and self-perpetuating as probably the only living Occidental language in the Middle East.

2 THE STUDY OF CONTEMPORARY HEBREW

2.1 STAGES OF DEVELOPMENT

There is historical development in the study of revived Hebrew. The observable stages of evolution range from sheer wondering over the fact of the renaissance to full-fledged structural description of the language as though no rebirth had ever taken place. These stages appear in chronological succession, each one adding a new aspect or feature of which scholars have become aware; it is as though the more important components of Israeli Hebrew had one by one reached their turn for scholarly discussion, and complete description of the language system is the chronologically final stage. This makes it necessary for the reader to bear in mind constantly that many things in the previous stages were said without an all-embracing picture of the Israeli Hebrew system underlying them; atomism is the major shortcoming in this scholarly field prior to the first publications of structural analysis.

Cf. the research report in RABIN (1970b: 329-39).

2.2 FIRST PART OF THE CENTURY: VIEWS ON THE REVIVAL

2.2.1 Forerunners

In the initial stage, it is difficult to distinguish eagerness to revive from enthusiasm over revival achieved. The earliest publication dealing with living Hebrew in Palestine that has come to my notice is ROSENBERG's not precisely dated *Hebräische Conversations-Grammatik* (ROSENBERG 1900), probably so named in accordance with the other beginners' grammars in the renowned Hartleben library, which must have considered such a book necessary for the completeness of its series. While the author mentions the use of Hebrew

in der Correspondenz und im mündlichen Verkehr bei den Juden im
Oriente und in Rußland (ROSENBERG 1900: 1)

and his "freudige Überraschung" to find, in 1893, that

die Schulkinder [. . .] in allen Lehrgegenständen, sowie im Privatgesprä-
che fließend und correct hebräisch sprachen und schrieben (ROSENBERG
1900: 2),

the Hebrew he teaches in his little book has little to do with our own
usage; it is, in all respects, artificial classical language, and one must
wonder whether it in fact reflects the usage of those schoolchildren.
Probably not, since ROSENBERG already notes the existence of
various "schools" in relation to language policy (purists – for
Biblicizing language, Talmudists – for incorporation of postbiblical
material in the modern language, whilst he himself was aware of the
"anachronism" of wishing to use biblical language, because "the
images of a language are in every case taken from the *Culturleben*
and the *Weltanschauung* of a. people", but drew no conclusions
therefrom; cf. *2.2.7*). Still, many of the features apparent in his
conversation exercises (features that are clearly unclassical, but out
of ignorance rather than as a result of linguistic evolution) recur in
printed texts (mainly in newspapers) up to the late twenties or
thirties, and may therefore be authentic; they may thus provide
interesting testimony for diachronic (*sic!*) research within living
Hebrew, at least to the extent that they corroborate phenomena
observed in authentic Palestinian texts. Such research will show
that the grossly unclassical and largely imported features of early
living Hebrew are in a steady recession (!) up to the late forties
(cf. ROSÉN 1969a: 108–9).

2.2.2 Study of the revival phenomenon

Already in the wake of World War I, E. M. LIPSCHÜTZ attempted
to view the REVIVAL PHENOMENON historically;[16] the first of a num-

---

[16] In the sense of its "internal" history. The external history of the revival
has been often related; see, e.g., now RABIN (1969) and SIVAN (1969).

ber of studies united in his book of 1920 bears the title "Vom lebendigen Hebräisch – Ein sprachgeschichtlicher Versuch" (LIPSCHÜTZ 1920: 1–47). There are sober fundamentals in this study: the notion of a "living" language is discussed (LIPSCHÜTZ 1920: 10–1), the problem of *innere Sprache* (LIPSCHÜTZ 1920: 10) is raised with respect to revived Hebrew, and LIPSCHÜTZ is perfectly aware of the notional sieve through which transmitted Hebrew words must have passed, particularly in case their transmission goes through a non-Hebrew Jewish form of language (as Yiddish; LIPSCHÜTZ 1920: 9–10); it is probably out of his own experience that the author ascribes "die Wandlungen jedes Wortes" to his own generation ("Die neueste Entwicklung [...] ist nicht älter als 30 bis 40 Jahre."; LIPSCHÜTZ 1920: 18). Unfortunately this study was forgotten; I do not think its ideas were taken up until I recalled (ROSÉN 1955a: 83–84) its *Leitmotiv*

Jedem, der die Sprache meistert, sind alle ihre Werdestufen gegenwärtig (LIPSCHÜTZ 1920: 19),

a principle without which the functional integration of *tota Hebraitas*[17] into one language system would have never been understandable. However well-conceived, BERGSTRÄSSER's qualification of Hebrew as a "transparently Hebrew-disguised European language", is part of a totally negatively characterized brief rejection of "present Hebrew", which – to his mind – was a "Scheinlösung", because no "sicheres Sprachgefühl" had yet been established (BERGSTRÄSSER 1928: 47). One can feel how reluctantly BERGSTRÄSSER had accepted current Hebrew to scholarly respectability by including a sample of it amongst his survey of Semitic languages; his *Sprachprobe* (BERGSTRÄSSER 1928: 57–59), however, is no such thing at all: while it has the outward appearance of a transcription, it is merely a presentation, in Latin characters, of a text (part of a 1925 speech by the then British High Commissioner of Palestine at the inaugura-

---

[17]   *Thesaurus totius Hebraitatis et veteris et recentioris*: thus reads the Latin title-page of BEN-YEHUDA's dictionary; it is this work more than anything else that constitutes the revivors' achievement in the renaissance of Hebrew (cf. BEN YEHUDA 1908-59).

tion of the Hebrew University), to which Tiberian vocalization has been very meticulously applied. Such diametrically opposed attitudes may have been amongst the factors that encouraged Joseph KLAUSNER to add the dimension of historical perspective to many of his essays on revived Hebrew, of which we can here refer only to his influential article "Ancient Hebrew and New Hebrew" (J. KLAUSNER 1929). KLAUSNER'S dogmatic position on language policy (*2.5.3*) is in contrast to that of LIPSCHÜTZ, but directs him towards a much more lenient attitude towards "unauthentic" phraseology and a more intensive search in the "source" texts for antecedents of deviant grammatical features; those that can be "attested" are termed *"mistakes"*, but in quotes (but those that cannot are still real mistakes), a historistic attitude pervades everything, and the parallel of the Greek *Sprachenkampf* is invoked for the first time (J. KLAUSNER 1929: 11–2).[18]

The introductory chapter ("The miracle of Hebrew reborn") of SPIEGEL'S book on the Hebrew literary renaissance (SPIEGEL 1930) well reflects the romanticizing pioneer spirit of those times. Hebrew has "liberated itself from books" (SPIEGEL 1930: 16–7, where slang features are already mentioned) and its innovations are called its "conquests"

---

[18] Interestingly enough, not this, but another parallel was invoked by the great classical scholar J. VENDRYES (1951: 90–1), that of Sanskrit and Latin; this is inappropriate, since Hebrew was not revived as a language of religious cult, nor was the revival essentially secularization (although some vocabulary items hailing from cult terminology were secularized; cf., e.g., AVINERY (1964: 37–8), ROSÉN (1958c: 68) and literature quoted there), and moreover, because no revival ever took place in Sanskrit and Latin, and what really interested VENDRYES were the chances of Irish (cf. particularly VENDRYES 1933: 9–11). This piece of VENDRYES' testifies to the amount of misunderstanding with which the revival of Hebrew met with linguists other than Hebraists. (On these misunderstandings, in particular concerning the comparison of revived Hebrew with "Living Latin", cf. TUR-SINAI 1951: 30–1). About a year after the publication of VENDRYES (1951), the author inquired of me whether living Hebrew was, in fact, a reality. (I must have been the first "revived", albeit not native, speaker he had met.) In 1956, WHATMOUGH (1956: 28) still holds that the revival of Hebrew runs counter to historical principles and is therefore an "unsuccessful experiment", but Marcel COHEN (in an essay written in 1939, but not published until 1970) considers the revival of Hebrew "un cas unique, dans notre horizon historique, de révivification d'une langue morte, qui pose de nombreux problèmes linguistiques." (M. COHEN 1970: 25; similarly D. COHEN 1968: 1293.)

by AVINERY (1946), who in some two hundred concisely written pages includes, *inter alia*, a discussion of some of the more obvious facts that we have come to recognize as characteristic of Israeli Hebrew, – such as features of children's language (*1.4.2*) and foreignisms. While AVINERY generally tends to include not too many of the "innovations" in the category of "mistakes" (he uses "attestation" criteria analogous to those employed by J. KLAUSNER), his relegation of them to layers outside the "normal", or average, never permits their being viewed in systemic simultaneity with the "authentic" forms. Functional analysis, according to any type of structural attitude, is impossible at this stage; consequently, many of the "innovated" features will be found functionally misjudged and, what is more important, those features that are not formally "innovated" are still considered as being authentic "source" Hebrew[19] and functioning the same way as their (philological) antecedents;[20] no emergence of an autonomous linguistic system is recognized.[21]

2.3 THE EARLY THIRTIES: STUDY OF FOREIGN ELEMENTS

2.3.1 Foreign "influences" and innere Form

The first "ingredient" other than linguistic heritage to be noticed in revived Hebrew was FOREIGN ELEMENTS, as we should prefer to call them for the time being rather than *influences*. The beginning of their scientific treatment coincides with the entry, on the literary stage, of trained linguists, and with the appearance, in the scope of Hebrew usage, of a new substratum, the German linguistic system. It may have been the clash between the phenomena occasioned by the German and those brought forth by the previously exclusively

---

[19] A general appreciation of the ideology apparent at that period concerning what constitutes "authentic" Hebrew will be found in ROSÉN (1969: 92–4, 106–9).
[20] The same attitude pervades AVINERY's (1964) encyclopedic collection of previously published *Einzelstudien*.
[21] These rudimentary views on facts of language have persisted to this very day in one field, lexicography. Only plans exist for synchronic, strata-organized dictionaries. E. LEVENSTON's Hebrew-English *Megiddo-Dictionary* (Tel-Aviv, 1968) is the only one I know of, in which some semantic order is introduced on the level of Israeli Hebrew. Attempts at drawing up a "basic" or "foundation" word list for didactic purposes, have been made in RIEGER (1953) and in MEHLMAN – ROSÉN – SHAKED (1960).

operative Slavic-Yiddish substrate components that made the students of Hebrew foreignism-minded and aware of the fact that pre-1930 living Hebrew had not been "pure" either. Irene GARBELL, Moscow-born and educated in Germany, produced in her Berlin thesis *Fremdsprachliche Einflüsse im modernen Hebräisch* (GARBELL 1930) in fact a rather comprehensive survey of features that set current Hebrew off from classical layers, attributing, of course, all differences to foreign influences. Significantly enough, morphology does not appear here, but it is a remarkable achievement that she organized her material in two principal parts, "Übernahme von fremdem Material" and "Beeinflussung der inneren Sprachform"; it is this second part that opens a way to the core of what constitutes a truly linguistic study of Israeli Hebrew. Loan translations and syntactic features (in the broadest sense) are exemplified and discussed (GARBELL 1930: 34–45, 53–70). The greater part of loanwords are rightly assigned to "European" rather than to any particular language (GARBELL 1930: 26–9). Certain information that can no longer be considered valid (e.g. the widespreadness of Slavic characteristics) is illustrative of what Hebrew looked like in the late twenties.

None of the studies subsequently published on "foreign influences" are really comparable in scope and insight with that of GARBELL. This holds in particular for TUBIELEWICZ's monograph that purports to discuss the "influence of European languages" (TUBIELEWICZ 1956), but is, in fact, a nostalgic survey of lost beauties of Hebrew, unreliable because of factual mistakes due to misinformation. In this vein, all deviations from Classical language are judged to be Europeanisms, and this includes substandard features and genuine mistakes (TUBIELE-WICZ 1956: 349–50).

2.3.2 Yiddish and Slavic elements

The several studies on the Yiddish "influence" on Israeli Hebrew have very much concentrated on Yiddish contributions to familiar colloquial style (Slavo-Yiddish formational suffixes, idioms), cf., e.g., W. CHOMSKY's (1957: 193–5) account, which treats this particular aspect exclusively. This kind of Yiddish-originating elements in Israeli Hebrew can only very reluctantly be classed as "influences on the language"; they stay

marginal and have, in fact, only one function: that of stylistic characterization, and their position in and towards Hebrew is very largely
comparable to the one they occupy in Jewish styles of other languages
(as of American English, where, e.g., the -nik suffix used in American-
English formations occupies precisely the same position and has the
same emotional value as in Israeli Hebrew). Practically all writers on
Yiddishisms in Israeli Hebrew have to some extent stressed these
linguistically quite irrelevant Yiddish elements in substandard or informal styles. Once this course was taken, it seemed easy to "discover" the
thus "established" Yiddish "influence" in a series of features where, at
some stages of research, no better explanation could apparently be
thought of. LARISH (1933: 84) includes the penult stress of certain
Israeli toponymics amongst Yiddishisms (see *3.7.5*); likewise ZAND
(1965), who, while ascribing to Yiddish the status of a "substrate",
devotes the larger part of his paper to the alleged Yiddish origin of the
inventory of Israeli Hebrew initial consonant clusters (cf. *3.6.1*). An
attempt at identification of genuine structural interference of Yiddish
IN Israeli Hebrew was made by BLANC (1965) (not ON Israeli Hebrew,
because, I presume, these Yiddish elements were not a contributing
factor to the creation of Israeli Hebrew, but were operative in modifying
its shape after it had been created); after mentioning the customary
lexical items and idioms, he goes on to deal with

Yiddish 'aspectoid' distinctions that are found in the Yiddish verb and
are suspect of having engendered, or helped to engender, similar distinctions now found in the Hebrew verb (BLANC 1965: 190–2)

(as *šatak* 'was silent': *hištatek* 'became silent'; *'amad* 'was standing':
neemad 'stood up, came to a halt'), but even here no clear lines are
drawn between cases in which the coexistence of a Yiddish *Sprachbewußt-
sein* only stabilized vaguely existing relations, those in which the
Yiddish-type form relation is stylistically characterized, and lastly
those, in which, in fact, Yiddish contributed categorial distinctions to
the central (standard) system of Israeli Hebrew.

The vagueness that results from terming contact features of every
nature INFLUENCES led Dorothea MÜLLER-OTT to the ill-con-
ceived conclusion that all Slavic-originating formational processes
apparent in Israeli Hebrew have gone through Yiddish (MÜLLER-
OTT 1965)[22]. Here again, the line successfully drawn by GARBELL

---

[22]   The article, which is principally devoted to *kibucnik* and its kin, is unreliable
because of its numerous faulty forms and misjudged features.

(1930) (see above) between the expressional level and the *innere Sprachform* is obliterated, and the fundamental nature of the Slavic structural element present in so essential a portion of the Israeli Hebrew categorial system goes once more undetected. Not until MASSON's thesis was the nature of Slavic formational influences recognized as "transpositions" (MASSON 1968: 145),

c'est à dire emprunter à une autre langue certaines structures mais non les morphèmes qui y figurent,

and the sample list (MASSON 1968: 147–9) given for denominal derivation shows the striking preponderance of Slavic models: *gumiya* 'rubber band' : *gúmi* 'rubber' = резинка : резина; *kapit* 'tea spoon' : *kaf* 'spoon' = ложечка : ложка. However, it still remains to be said that it is neither a morpheme (as -*nik*) nor affixation as such that testifies to Slavic character; rather, it is the choice between derivation and composition (резинка *vs. rubber band*) for the expression of this particular notional relation, a choice in which Israeli Hebrew has most obviously calqued on Russian.

Cf., e.g.. *1.5.4. 4.2.2, 4.3.1, 8.3.*

2.4 INCLUSION OF FORMS OF SPECIAL LANGUAGE

The next step in widening the scope of language material accounted for in the study of living Hebrew was the inclusion of FORMS OF SPECIAL LANGUAGE: child language and, later, slangs. A collection of items of what genuinely was children's usage was published by RIVKAY in 1932; but as to subsequent authors on the subject, we have already mentioned (*1.4.2*) the attitude that dictated their inclusion of unclassical language features, irrespective of whether they were or were not present in adults' speech (or even writing), in what purported to be descriptions of "children's language". (It was as though such usages could be condoned and "acknowledged", if they came from the mouth of children, but not, if from adults.) Children's language can now be distinguished from children's slang, thanks to the studies conducted on the former by BAR-ADON (1959) and on slang by SAPPAN (1963).[23] *Slang* had earlier been a tendentious synonym of *informal colloquial* or even non-classicizing standard. SAPPAN contrasts slang to the "standard stratum" (that is "usage corresponding to the usual [stylistic; H. R.] level", and not "the one complying with rules of normative grammar")[24] (SAPPAN 1963: 9). However, I can see no substantiation for his thesis that Hebrew slang preceded standard language in the introduction of numerous new means of expression; rather, it seems to emerge from SAPPAN's own materials (SAPPAN 1963: 67–77) that slang does no more than overstep the limits set by standard speech for the employment of given expressional means (such as suffixal derivation, and the like). I think the author has not succeeded in his endeavour to show that the status – mainly on the diachronic level – of slang versus commonly accepted standard is in Hebrew largely the same as in other language societies. His thesis is tantamount to saying that whatever is "new" (i.e. unclassical) in Israeli Hebrew, came from, by and through Hebrew slang; this would have left the "revival" immaculate, but, unfortunately, it is precisely this that is – to say the least – unsubstantiated by factual evidence.

2.5 THE MID-FORTIES AND THE FIFTIES: VIEWS ON LIVING HEBREW

2.5.1 Appreciation of facts of language

The subsequent stage of scholarly activity, extending from the middle forties to the middle fifties, was not so much one of fact-finding as one of FACT-APPRECIATION. Almost first in that period was a collection of "new" language features that pretended not to

---

[23] Followed by SAPPAN (1965; a slang dictionary) and SAPPAN (1969).
[24] In the original: "[. . .] and not the normative stratum"; numerous authors on current Hebrew have the habit of speaking of "spoken" vs. "normative Hebrew".

be one: an article, published by MORAG in the professional quarterly
of the Teachers' Union (MORAG 1947), assembling the "unclassical"
phenomena previously discovered in "children's language" or found
to be results of "foreign influence" as well as numerous others, but
branding them in their totality as "depravations of language" and
recommending "ways for their eradication" (although the latter
were nothing else but alternative forms, more classical on the surface). Morag had found the ground prepared by an increasing mis-
take-awareness (in retrospect, rather language-policy-awareness) on
the part of the professional grammar teacher (*grammar teacher* and
linguist seemed to be synonymous at that time in common parlance).
Mention must be made, however, of the fact that a few years earlier,
grammarians' voices had been raised in an attempt to fortify a
defence line by sanctioning part of what was considered as an infringement of grammar on the grounds of (more often than not very
precarious) attestation in classical sources; AVINERY (1943) took a
stand in this direction (followed by a similar outlook in W. CHOM-
SKY 1958), chiefly directed against the stringency advocated by
J. KLAUSNER (*2.2.2*) in the observation of rules of classical (albeit
postbiblical) grammar.

2.5.2 Semiprofessional occupation with language and evolutional views

The semiprofessional public had always been keenly interested in
questions of language improvement, and numerous weekly "language corners" were devoted to that subject in all communications
media, including the broadcasting service, which was a highly sensitive spot, since announcers were directed to propagate an extremely
puristic style of speech sharply contrasting with even educated
usage. It was about that time that I became involved in public discussion of language matters in a not altogether futile attempt at lay-
ing the traditional inertia open to criticism: the monotonous line of
the broadcast fault-correcting "language corners" was broken by
the insertion of about monthly talks on "Language Processes",
later published in three consecutive series (ROSÉN 1952a, 1953a,

1956a). Since many of my co-workers in the field have agreed in considering them as the turning point in scholarly attitude towards living Hebrew it may not be out of order to review here in brief what their general idea was.

This was an attempt at more "sanctioning", not by attestation, but on grounds of "general linguistic principles", showing that numerous formal differences between common usage and the classical antecedents might be interpreted as the result of diachronic change (hence the title of the series), and were therefore justifiable in view of the fact that Hebrew was accepted as a living, that is, changing language, and that changes had their laws. On the surface, this was historical explanation, but it must be admitted that some missionary zeal at sanctioning was at the back of the linguist's mind. The really new thing was the introduction, into the study of contemporary Hebrew, of some general linguistics: analogy[25], de-synonymization, dissimilation, assimilation, rephonemicization, etc. etc., all diachronic, and preponderantly atomistic at that, systemic analysis being almost entirely absent. But all this diachronistic attitude led to one *ceterum censeo:* correctness is not a diachronic notion. Without intending to do so, I succeeded in making *normative* an improper word. What I had really meant to do, was to prepare the ground for a descriptive systemic grammar of Israeli Hebrew, a grammar which had to be different from that of any preceding shape of Hebrew.

2.5.3 The clash between descriptivism and normativism

It is not correct that the violent reaction – welcoming adherence and venomous rejection – that followed the "modern" linguistic approach to Israeli Hebrew became apparent only after the materialization of the plan of describing the language grammatically (ROSÉN 1955a); the *Kulturkampf*-like discussion, which – in its final stages – widely exceeded the limits of the scholarly community, had already passed through its initial stage in the early fifties.[26] While I wish to stress that the fire has

---

[25] Cf., *inter alia*, the summarizing presentation by BAR-ADON (1962).
[26] The term *Classical Hebrew* now re-emerges by contrast (VRIEZEN 1956), after it had not been taken up after AEŠCOLY (1938; cf. p. 000).

gone out long ago, it is worthwhile to recapitulate some of the more important arguments raised at the time:

(1) There is no uniform shape of spoken Hebrew, and any attempt at description has to be aimed at a given group of speakers circumscribed by the linguist for this purpose (e.g., BEN-HAYYIM 1955: 337). (We held against this that, in theory, every structural description is a description of an idiolect, and we have only to be aware of the criteria according to which the idiolect concerned is selected for description: we had selected a rather widely used form of speech that showed no, or very few, signs that could serve as identifying marks of the (ethnic, social, etc.) group to which the speaker belonged.)

(2) There is no standard that could serve as a base for linguistic description (e.g., BEN-HAYYIM 1955: 337; BENDAVID 1965: 303–25). – In the earliest descriptive discussion the "standard" notion had been used abundantly to set it off against "norm" to which more classicistic criteria were applicable. Unfortunately, "standard" had been represented (by myself and others) as being a feature of speakers (or groups of speakers), and BEN-HAYYIM's (1955: 52) rejoinder that numerical majority (or social weight) was no really adequate criterion for assigning status to a language form had been virtually called for, as well as his near cynicism in putting the question "who", in fact, talked "Hebrew". The circumscription of a group of standard speakers (persons holding secondary education, or civil servants) was finally replaced (ROSÉN 1955a: 139; cf. p. xii) by a definition of standard feature (rather than standard speaker), defined by the absence of identifying marks (see above under (1)).[27]

(3) Language description (in the case of Hebrew at least) is prejudicial to conducting a healthy language policy.[28] Admittedly, the appearance of the first purely descriptive studies on features of Israeli Hebrew had been particularly welcomed by scholars of a pronounced leave-your-

[27] One and the same speaker is liable to reveal features of various stylistic levels or shades, according to the situation or discourse. However, heterogeneous stylistic variants will hardly ever participate in one given utterance; sociolinguistic gimmicks hardly serve the purpose (e.g., BLANC 1968: 242; four highly doubtful sentences, that vary at three or more points, are made up and then checked for reality with a learned friend): this leads to a notion of features marking style levels, including the "standard" one, while it must be obvious that standard style must be the unmarked term of all stylistic contrasts.
[28] On the whole complex of questions see now ROSÉN (1969; in particular pp. 92–4, 106–11).

language-alone attitude;[29] but it would be an unfair distortion to say that descriptivism was a deathblow to the notion of 'mistakes' and 'corrections' (so BEN–ḤAYYIM 1955: 56) or to the distinction of written and spoken styles. Quite to the contrary, even the explanation (and, admittedly, justification) of deviations from classical usage as "natural" language processes (ROSÉN 1952a, 1953a, 1956a) explicitly upheld the notion of 'mistake', and only set a new boundary between what was a 'mistake' and what was not.[30] The "interference" in language, on scientific grounds, objected to by BEN–ḤAYYIM (1955: 48), could not be an impediment to *Sprachpflege* (advocated, amongst others, by BEN–ḤAYYIM 1955: 65); it could only result in providing a new basis for language cultivation. It was just those stringent formal procedures of structural descriptivism that made the sober and objective distinction of stylistic levels possible. While the new descriptive movement never aimed at "handing down rulings on language"[31], without its lovingly probing into every functional distinction, however subtle, emerging in the new system, neither language education of native speakers nor scientifically devised teaching of Hebrew as a second language would ever have become possible.

2.6 DESCRIPTIVE LINGUISTIC RESEARCH

2.6.1 Structural approach to Israeli Hebrew

The onset of the following, and in a way final, stage in the history of research into Israeli Hebrew, is, I think, more significantly marked by the establishment, in 1953, of a department of linguistics

[29] In a very stimulating series of semi-popular articles published by BLANC under the anagrammatic pen-name of KABLAN in the avant-guarde literary bi-weekly *Masa'* during 1952 and 1953; BEN–ḤAYYIM took to trying to refute "Kablan" in that same periodical (no. 19/54, 27 Aug. 1953), after the former had strongly criticized his 1953 polemics against "modern" linguistic research into Israeli Hebrew (*Masa'* 17/52, 30 July 1953).
[30] The descriptivist never demanded that features discovered by him should be adhered to as norms. (Unhappy, or tendentious, misinterpretation by BEN–ḤAYYIM [1955: 52] of the Hebrew expression for 'must' in a sentence "such and such a form *must* occur in such and such a case" as meaning 'has to', instead of, what was meant, '*muß*', i.e. 'can be predicted'.)
[31] Accusation by BEN–ḤAYYIM (1955: 52). "Handing down rulings" was explicitly objected to as a matter of language policy (ROSÉN 1958a: 23 = 1966a: 29, citing BLOOMFIELD 1933: 500).

in the Hebrew University of Jerusalem than by the publication of any particular scholarly study. DESCRIPTIVE LINGUSTIC RESEARCH had found its natural habitat in that department, and teaching in Israeli Hebrew linguistics could here be initiated; and what turned out to be as important in the development of this discipline as in many others in the broader domain of linguistics, the academic respectability thus achieved had an immense impact on the creation of a school that was in a position to treat Israeli Hebrew analytically, and synchronically, of course, as a complete, autonomous, and coherent system of language. There had been some earlier statements on Israeli Hebrew of a structural and descriptive character[32], and the 1950 study by WEIMAN (a "structural sketch" of Israeli Hebrew phonemics and morphemics devised in order to lay the foundation for the identification of foreign elements; WEIMAN 1950) had precipitated a series of reviews and discussions that laid open the basic positions taken by Israeli scholars on the subject (BLANC 1953, (GOSHEN-)GOTTSTEIN 1951, ROSÉN 1955b, BEN-ḤAYYIM 1955).

2.6.2 Systemic description

To describe Ha-ʾivrit šelanù (ROSÉN 1955a), which has been often regarded as some sort of turning point or pathway into the present phase of Israeli Hebrew linguistic research, I find it expedient to enumerate what reviewers[33] have considered, approvingly or not, but with a remarkable amount of unanimity, to be the more noteworthy contributions of that book. Its *pièce de resistance* is a complete phonological (ROSÉN 1955a: 138–87) and morphological

---

[32] RABIN's *Hebrew reader* (1944, but not published until 1949) should here be mentioned. The explanatory notes contain many a valuable observation, e.g. on *kax* or *ze* as "empty antecedent" representing a sentence content (RABIN 1949: 57, 71), on *le-* as an equivalent of a genitival construction (RABIN 1949: 31); however, the great bulk of these observations refer to phenomena of current language as "tendencies" or "idiomatic usages".

[33] ULLENDORFF's inaugural lecture (ULLENDORFF 1957) draws a faithful picture of the scholarly situation as it existed at the time my 1955(a) book appeared; SEGAL (1958) dwells on the historical aspects that come out in chapters 1–4; BAR-HILLEL (1957) demands that the introduction on the essence of morphological analysis (ROSÉN 1955a: 193–8) be rewritten;

(ROSÉN 1955a: 188–245) structural description of Israeli Hebrew; the former is more TROUBETSKOYAN than not, leading into morphophonemics by a study of boundary signals (ROSÉN 1955a: 178–84), but is so strongly based on *Lautabsicht* (that I thought could in every case be revealed from morphological relations) and orderedrule neutralizations, that the whole thing inadvertently got a kind of CHOMSKYist shape (undetected, of course, at the time, but dogmatically objected to as "introduction of overlapping" and "levelfusing"; BLANC 1956d: 797–8) which I have later thought better to remould into simpler structural terms (ROSÉN 1962a: 1–11). The morphological part widens the scope of the study of dependent morphemes by embracing a series of adnominal and adverbal modifiers (like *m'od* 'very' and *dey* 'quite') arranged in categorial paradigms; a technique of establishing categories by interlacing distributional criteria is used for the first time (a morpheme A that is mutually exclusive with B and C, which are not mutually exclusive of each other, and a morpheme D, that is exclusive of C and E, but not of A, establish three different categories, any two (and, in other cases, more) of which can be covered by one portmanteau morpheme); semantic values of dependent morphemes are assessed accordingly (ROSÉN 1955a: 206–7, 212, 214–5; cf. ROSÉN 1966a: 265–76). In another section (ROSÉN 1955a: 237–42), living formational types are set off from ones that are no longer productive, and the semantic values of the former are assessed.

The chapters of ROSÉN 1955a that surround the one presenting the descriptive grammar are, in a way, preparatory to it. The method of structural analysis had to be presented to the Israeli reader; this

---

BLANC (1956d: 795), while welcoming my "tearing down the wall of fancy and folklore erected by some of the normativists around the 'inferiority' of modern usage as compared to the 'superiority' of their own recommendations", condemns nonadherence to the "established" school of phonemic analysis (see below). I have mentioned only the more noteworthy ones of the review articles; reviews published in Hebrew almost exclusively emphasized the language-policy aspect of the book, the ensuing *Sprachenkampf* discussion spreading over the daily press in a not too delicate style (on the part of traditionalist opposition).

had the side-effect of the shortcomings of the book or "undesirable" (that is, untraditional) results of the descriptive analysis being ascribed, by its opponents, to the method itself. Structural linguistics became taboo with traditional Hebraists; and it was not until the late sixties, when some of them adopted the generativist approach, that they acceded to the treatment of Hebrew by "modern" methods: the pre-selection of facts necessary for generativist treatment that considers only "acceptable" or "well-formed" utterances, was a welcome corrective for the deviations from established norms revealed by structural analysis. The components of Israeli Hebrew were traced back to their historical antecedents (ROSÉN 1955a: 53–82), but the paramount feature in the historical development of Israeli Hebrew was stressed: very frequently, in cases in which A' had succeeded A of an earlier layer of Hebrew, both A and A' coexisted in Israeli Hebrew, differentiated either functionally or stylistically; this was shown (ROSÉN 1955a: 83–106) to be the one phenomenon that was responsible more than any other one for the historical uniqueness of Israeli Hebrew, and it was from here that the conclusion was drawn that no feature or element of Classical Hebrew surviving in Israeli Hebrew must on any account be deemed to function in Israeli Hebrew in the same way as in its classical predecessors.[34] A first attempts was made (ROSÉN 1955a: 122–35) to circumscribe Israeli Hebrew typologically.

2.6.3 Syntax

Syntax, that had been missing from ROSÉN 1955a, was the topic to which soon afterwards 'Ivrit tova (ROSÉN 1958a) was devoted. The book centres around two chapters which treat the two fundamentals of syntagmatics: adnominal and adverbal adjuncts. As the operational basis of syntagmatic analysis the notion of (immediate) constituents is presented and discussed in a preparatory chapter (ROSÉN 1958a: 49–82 = 1966a: 55–94); the problem of the type

---

[34] The inverse is also true (cf. ULLENDORFF 1957: 261–2). The structural study of Israeli Hebrew has permitted some insight into its differences from Biblical Hebrew, which led to some discoveries concerning the latter.

'inorganic chemist' *(xima'i 'i-'orgániy)* is thoroughly discussed and decomposition into the immediate constituents *(xim- +
'i-'orgániy) + -a'i* '(anorganic+chem)+-ist', or, analogously *'orex-
+(din+pliliy)* '(criminal+law)+-yer', established. Already the 1957 edition (ROSÉN 1957: 77–8) states clearly that an "inorganic chemist is not a chemist who is inorganic", and foreshadows the doctrinary issue of *the late Churchill*,[35] while in the 1966 edition the inability of these expressions to undergo a predicative transformation *(tipeš gamur* 'a perfect idiot' → *tipeš hu gamur* 'an idiot is perfect' [*sic!*] and not in the inverse direction) is explicitly stated. The view is expressed that

it is the nonexistence of a [predicative] form in the *Sprachschatz*, that is in the linguistic memory of the hearer, that constitutes the mark of the constituent-structure of the expressions concerned, i.e. of their semantic nature" (ROSÉN 1966a: 89).

It is this basic approach of viewing composite expressions as syntagms made up of constituents that derive their status as such from their being variables in a given selection (substitution) class, that led to the more important findings in the two principal chapters (the third and the fourth) of ROSÉN (1958a). What has proved more fruitful and stimulating to subsequent research than any other result arrived at in the book, is the distinction established between governed object and ungoverned adverbial complement (ROSÉN 1958a: 83–112 = 1966a: 95–124) both marked by the presence of a preposition which, however, is variable in the latter case, and invariable in the former,[36] so that the constituent structure of, e.g.,

---

[35] WINTER (1965), against which MOTSCH (1967) takes a defensive position. At the time of writing *'Ivrit tova*, I was inexcusably unaware that the immediate-constituent solution had already been reached by JESPERSEN (1911- 2: 293. ("The combination *sound sleeper* besides being an adjective + a substantive can also be analyzed as a derivative in *-er* from the combination *sound sleep*. [. . .] *A Quarterly Reviewer* [. . .] could not be analyzed as a reviewer who is quarterly."). Cf. JESPERSEN (1937: 21; "Irregular junction"): "An adjunct may be virtually a subjunct (tertiary) to some *adjectival or verbal idea contained in the primary* [emphasis by me; H. R.]: [. . .] *an utter fool, a perfect stranger*, [. . .] *ein starker Trinker.*" Cf. JESPERSEN (1937: 22).
[36] For a parallel distinction suggested for German, see *7.1.4* with note *158*.

(*hištamaštì be-*)+*sefèr* 'I used + a book' would be as shown, while three constituents would be present in *katavtì be-sefèr* 'I wrote in a book', due to the substitutability of the preposition *be-* in the latter by, e.g., *'al-* 'on'. When a small list of prepositions could be drawn up that occur in governed status, 'case' was proposed as their class feature (see *7.1.4*), and meaning was denied to them wherever they were governed.

As to nominal groups, a noteworthy result of their study was the identification of a paradigm of adnominal constructions (ROSÉN 1958a: 113–80 = 1966a: 125–94; cf. ROSÉN 1957) and the examination of the semantic relations prevailing between its members. This led, amongst other results, to the discovery of a previously un-revealed category in Hebrew – possession, the members of which are appurtenance (inalienability) and non-appurtenantive possession (alienability), formally distinguished by the morphosyntactic nature of the syntagmatic link between a noun and its determinant noun or (suffixed) personal pronoun: *sifri* (*-i* '1st pers. sg.') 'my book, i.e. the book written by me' : (*ha-*)*sefèr šel-i* 'my book, i.e. the book written by me' or '(the)/a book owned by me'.[37] (cf. *7.1.2*) That same categorial distinction was later brought to light in additional types of syntactic oppositions: exocentric adjectival compounds (ROSÉN 1961: 24–6), and the use of the "article" *ha-* as a possessive morpheme for the indefinite person (*man, on;* – cf. *7.2.2*; ROSÉN 1966b: 126–30).[38]

---

[37] While I had (ROSÉN 1958a: 141 = 1966a: 153) clearly presented the semantic relations between the two terms of this binary opposition exactly as shown here, the explicit expressions *terme marqué* and *terme non-marqué* were used only with reference to other types of occurrence of the *šel-* vs. construct state construction (ROSÉN 1958a: 153 = 1966a: 186; 1957: 331). ORNAN must have been reluctant to admit the existence of paradigmatic relations between syntactic constructions, when, at several instances (e.g. ORNAN 1968: 26–30), he assembled occurrences of the unmarked term (in our case the *šel-* construction) that referred to what could be expressed by the marked term (i.e. appurtenance), in order to refute my statements.

[38] It is also present in what corresponds to the *accusativus graecus* construction, N(oun)$_1$ +N/Adj. +*be-*(prep.) +N(oun)$_2$ (personal characteristic) +-pers.suff. (agreement with N$_1$): *talmid mecuyan be-xišron-o* (*kišaron* 'talent') 'a student of great talent'; see *7.1.4*.

2.7 THE SIXTIES: CONSOLIDATION

2.7.1 Monographic studies

During the brief period of consolidation following the appearance of ROSÉN (1955a) and ROSÉN (1958a), an (astonishingly) small number of *Einzelstudien* were devoted to matters of grammatical description (still fewer to lexical questions). Determination (including the emergence of an *article partitif*) was discussed in ROSÉN (1961), vowel length examined by TÉNÉ (1962); in a review of ROSÉN 1958a, FRAENKEL (1960) questioned some details of immediate-constituent analysis, while later (FRAENKEL 1966) he suggested to complement it by more attention to suprasegmentals. Adverb formation is introduced into the scope of morphology (cf. *6.4.2.1* below) in a study mainly centering around adjectives and their classification (ROSÉN 1962b); the latter subsequently served as the starting point for a survey on nominal compounds (ROSÉN 1966b), preceded by KADDARI (1965) and followed up quite recently by MASSON (1969). Another late addition to studies on particular questions was R. MIRKIN (1968) on aspect in participial formations, intended to modify ROSÉN (1956b) (cf. *7.2.1* below). Comparatively few of these studies (e.g. BAR-ADON 1966; see *8.4.2*) led into blind alleys.[39]

2.7.2 Integration and didactic application

The 1962 *Textbook of Israeli Hebrew* (ROSÉN 1962a) includes a descriptive grammar (complete, in full detail, except for pattern syntax), whose individual paragraphs are arranged in a didactically determined sequence. It incorporates features, the analysis of which had not been achieved earlier, such as certain mechanisms of unvocalized reading (ROSEN 1962a: §§ 12.7, 14.6, 15.1, 18.2, 34.4, 41.6), paired plurals versus duals (§§ 35.1–2), syntax of nominalizations (§§ 45.5, 7–8; 51.6), transformational relations between verb

---

[39]   This is the appropriate place to mention some of the unpublished dissertations treating specific subjects in Israeli Hebrew, that began to be written about that time: TÉNÉ, *La phonologie de l'hébreu contemporain selon l'usage d'un unilingue* (TÉNÉ 1961); SIVAN, *Patterns and trends of linguistic innovations in Modern Hebrew, Introduction and part 1: The verb* (SIVAN 1964): ORNAN, *The nominal phrase in Modern Hebrew with particular reference to the prose writings of N. H. Bialik* (ORNAN 1964; Part 1 published as ORNAN 1965); likewise BAR-ADON (1959), and MASSON (1968).

stems (§§ 44.1–3), radicals as motivating elements of stem formation (§ 42.1), and deictic properties of pronouns (§§ 36.2, 40.3, 42.4,
44.5); the glossary presents, for the first time, to my knowledge,
nominal and verbal items alike by their stems rather than by their
roots.

2.7.3 Descriptive syntactic analysis and syntactic categories

The syntactic description of Israeli Hebrew naturally came last;
it forms the final, but major portion of the second edition of *'Ivrit
tova* (ROSÉN 1966a: 195–302). Since practically all of the statements
on syntax made in the present survey will be based on that analysis
we shall only have to state here how that syntax is presented and
how its findings were arrived at, a point that is not wholly irrelevant
in present-day linguistic science.

The syntax of ROSÉN (1966a: 197–302) is a non-generative categorial pattern syntax, in which the Israeli Hebrew sentences are
said to be based on one of a tentative number of twenty-one patterns,
the forms of which are of the type, e.g., *ze* + noun/m.sg.adj. +
adverb; or (subject) noun + *hu* + adj./(pred.)noun + adverb; or
na+inf.; etc. These patterns are not expressible in terms of each
other, and they are assumed to form a paradigm, so that a meaning
can be attached to each one of the patterns (e.g. pattern meanings
for the various types of nominal sentences are established as
'classification' versus 'identification' versus 'comment'). The order
properties of each pattern are studied, and relative succession of
the constituents semantically interpreted, where appropriate. The
possibilities of constituent deletion are examined. The constitutive
variables of each pattern are of the types: finite verb group, infinitive group, noun, adjective, impersonal (*5.6.1-2* below), and
adverb, and each type admits specified expansions and substitutes.
These, however, are not generatively described as representing
semantic components or transformed kernels, but distributionally
identified by the "interlacing mutual exclusion" technique (*2.6.1*;
7.1.2), on the basis of which it can be stated what categories are
covered by each given expansion; e.g., the adjective modifier

4

legámre 'entirely' is said to express gradation, evaluation, quantifica-
tion, and comparison. Substitutes are analogously assigned to
modificatory categories; e.g., the pronominal substitute of an
adjective *kaze* 'such' is said to be characterized by determination,
degree, contrast, comparison, and relativity (since no such further
modification otherwise admissible with adjectives would be admissible in modification of the substitute *kaze*). Finally, pattern
substitutes are termed "transformations"[40], a term the purport of
which is correspondingly restricted (ROSÉN 1966a: 287–95).

2.7.4 Patterns and constituents

That this approach and this style of analytical presentation can
very usefully serve the purposes of linguistic description, is shown
by RUBINSTEIN's penetrating *Verb phrase* (RUBINSTEIN 1970a), a non-
generative grammar taking account of pattern transformations.[41]
The syntactic behaviour of Israeli Hebrew verbs is treated, as it
would appear, exhaustively; the treatment is strongly reminiscent
of the syntax volumes of Jespersen's *Modern English grammar*
(JESPERSEN 1911–), which did not, however, serve as the direct

---

[40]   A regrettable omission is the absence of a statement on substitutes in that
paragraph (such as the statements in paragraphs dealing with constituent
substitutes) concerning over what modificatory categories (of the "sentence
expansions"; ROSÉN 1966a: 265–6) every one of the substitutes extends. It would
have been easy to use the mutual exclusion technique in order to make nontrivial
statements such as that the pattern substitute 'nominalization' extends over, that
is, already implies, 'qualification' (*'ulay* 'perhaps', etc.), but not over 'generalizing
extension' (*gam* 'also').

[41]   This study widely surpasses RUBINSTEIN (1968; *The nominal sentence*),
where, it is our duty to say, the author fails to obtain some results achieved in
ROSÉN (1966a: 209–25, 230–55). RUBINSTEIN's presentation is, at least on the
surface, generative (the introduction [pp. 11–51] is an intelligent first
exposition in Hebrew of generative theory); amongst other consequences
of this Procrustean procedure, there is RUBINSTEIN's failure to state in what
conditions each one of the nominal sentence patterns occurs (cf. ROSÉN 1966a:
233–4, 247–52) and, as a result, the impossibility of establishing, in view of
neutralizations, the environments of significant oppositions between the patterns
and their purport (cf. *8.1.4* (x)–(xii)). After this book, RUBINSTEIN abandoned
the generative approach and embarked on "non-generative transformational
grammar".

model: verbs are classed by their syntactic behaviour, but no *a priori* semantic subcategorization is attempted. Since the entire study is based on the author's attestation files, it can serve as a syntactic lexicon of verb constructions (unfortunately, there is no index). What appears to be the most important achievement of the book is the discovery that the transformability of a given type of pattern is by no means predictable, but depends on the lexical identity of the verb; no semantic characterization of the verb permits us to predict whether a sentence containing it can undergo a stated transformation; partial overlapping of the semantic ranges of two verbs will come to light by their occurring in an identical construction[42], which is, however, not subject to the same transformation in both cases:

Ra'iti			considered		
		'oto ke-fakid tov 'I			him as a
Higdarti			defined		good clerk'

but ont:

Ra'iti			considered	
(but not:		*ki hu pakid tov* 'I		that he was
(*Higdarti*)			(defined)	a good
				clerk'*.

RUBINSTEIN (1970a: 23) considers this a "theoretical difficulty"; it is, in fact, the pendant, in verbal syntax, of the situation which

---

[42]   The disposition of the material in RUBINSTEIN (1970a) shows that the author still considers semantic subcategorization (of the verb) economic for syntactic description, but to depict his approach faithfully, it should suffice to quote his opening paragraph on "verbs of taking": "The following sentences have been assembled exclusively on grounds of a formal criterion: that there are two objects in the sentence. Still, they indicate clearly that there is a relation between meaning and structure, while verbs occurring in the following sentences differ from each other semantically, they nevertheless have a common [*supply*: element of; H. R.] meaning. It is this meaning that is relevant for the two-object structure" (RUBINSTEIN 1970a: 151).

we have sketched above *(2.6.3)* for nominal syntax, when discussing the *tipeš gamur* 'perfect idiot' construction. Here as well as
there (to summarize what was said in ROSÉN 1966a: 91–3),

> the nonexistence of a given transform marks the constituent structure
> of the expression concerned, that is its semantic nature;

RUBINSTEIN has not shown the sentences concerned to be of
different constituent structure:

   ra'iti+ ('oto ke-fakid tov) versus *(higdartì+'oto)+ke-fakid tov,*

although otherwise he acknowledges the existence of "objects that
are sentences" (cf. RUBINSTEIN 1970a: 93) in the type 'I considered
him as a good clerk', but not in the one with 'define'[43]. Different
types of objects characterize, for RUBINSTEIN, different types of
transitivity; but transitivity is not, in itself, formally defined, as a
consequence of which, according to him,

> the verbs *'išen* 'smoked', *kara'* 'read', *šata* 'drank' and others are
> transitive as well as intransitive verbs; in *haya šoxev 'al-mitato me'ašen
> ve-kore'* 'he used to lie on his bed smoking and reading' they have to
> be considered intransitive verbs (RUBINSTEIN 1970a: 46).

But the case is different for 'drinking': in *hu kore'* 'he reads' we have
ellipsis ("dropping", RUBINSTEIN 1970a: 34) of the object, the
identity of which can by no means be predicted and which does not
exclude any 'readable' thing, but in *hu šote* 'he drinks' we have no
ellipsis, but a zero (covert) object, which, while it cannot be defined
accurately, would seem to exclude anything like milk or soda water.
Considerations of this sort, which are civilization-conditioned as
much as grammatical, tend to impart to our syntactic descriptions
the full amount of necessary consistency.

We have dwelt at some disproportionate length and detail on these
comprehensive descriptive studies, in order to underline that solid
knowledge about the grammatical structure of Israeli Hebrew had been

---

[43]   For a comparable situation in English (*I believe the man+ to be honest – I
believe +that John teaches French*) see now BOLINGER (1967).

achieved by the second half of the sixties. Consequently, any attempts at compiling grammatical manuals or reference grammars without due account being taken of the results of the analysis[44] were bound not to be too successful.

2.8 METHODS TO STUDY HEBREW VERSUS HEBREW TO STUDY METHODS

While some twenty years ago descriptive research was engaged in consolidating a method to be employed for the study of Hebrew, in recent years there have been signs of employing Hebrew for the study of a method. Although the earliest use made of Hebrew to examine how linguistic methods work was aimed at demonstrating distributional componential analysis (HARRIS 1948), I am here referring, of course, to the several recent attempts to reformulate some of the known facts of Israeli Hebrew in generativist metalanguage. It is a curious coincidence that this shade of linguistic occupation has been welcomed precisely in circles which had, at the time of the "struggle over linguistics" (2.6.1), vehemently opposed "modern" linguistic research into Israeli Hebrew. I cannot help finding an explanation for this surprising fact in the notion of acceptability and wellformedness that is at the outset of generative presentation: this notion can be interpreted on grounds of any desired criterion in terms of language policy; as a matter of fact, *wellformed* in current generative work on contemporary Hebrew is commonly synonymous with puristically *normative*. Consequently, apart from all other known characteristics of generative theory,[45] all types and strata of

---

[44] COHEN – ZAFRANI's *Grammaire de l'hébreu vivant* was not published until 1968, but obviously written much earlier, since it is stated in its preface (vii) that ROSÉN (1955a) was still "la seule description réalisée" at that time. The book contains an interesting structural-descriptive phonology of Israeli Hebrew (COHEN – ZAFRANI 1968: 19–50), based on the earlier descriptions; otherwise it is a students' grammar, in which stylistic qualifications of the forms mentioned are rare (vulgarisms are mentioned without it being stated that they are such, but non-puristic variants are hardly adduced along the classicizing forms exhibited; different strata of language are mixed) and syntactic function is sometimes confused with morphological characterization. There could have been achieved more at the time of publication.

[45] Generative research into Israeli Hebrew syntax has singularly refrained from making use of whatever potentials generative theory may have for studying the semantic effects of the introduction of a transformation, although distributional analysis yields significant results in this respect. E.g., REIF's unpublished thesis of 1968 contends that there is no way of stating or predicting the

Hebrew are quite frequently fused together (because an *a priori* notion of wellformedness does not prevent that con-fusion),[46] so that quite a few achievements of the stringently synchronic-systemic approach go unheeded.[47]

If the purpose of those studies has been to show what generative grammar can contribute to the recognition and interpretation of the features of a given language, then this purpose has been spectacularly achieved. The question whether the (admittedly very few) generativist studies hitherto conducted on Israeli Hebrew have helped to discover at least some facts of language beyond those analyzed and described by categorial structural grammar, must – also concerning Hebrew – be answered with an emphatic and unqualified "no". Looking forward to future developments, it is, in the considered judgment of the present writer, structural corpus analysis that will have to be encouraged as a means to elucidate what still has to be brought out about the facts of current Hebrew.

---

semantic differences between the construct-state "nominalizations", although, I think, I have clearly shown (ROSÉN 1957; 1958a: 137–73 = 1966a: 149–87) what that way was.

[46] In this type of studies, it cannot be stated when, where, and how two 'well-formed' sentences coexist in – *sit uenia uerbo* – a corpus; but precisely the corpus notion is indispensable for us in the particular situation in Hebrew, where different kinds of strata maintain a unique sort of coexistence, as in part mutually superimposed corpora. To develop "machine aids for translation" (PRICE 1969a), it may be necessary to list forms originating from all conceivable periods of Hebrew and all possible current literary styles, but one wonders what semantic information can be retrieved from such a machine if it is nowhere said what set of forms constitute a 'system'. On the other hand, the grammatical information given is distressingly primitive: adjectives, for instance, it is said "are words that are found in the syntactic constructions: (a) Noun + Adjective, (b) Noun + (Root) *hyh* ('is') + Adjective "(PRICE 1969: 233). By this definition *šam* 'there' is an adjective: cf. *Hatalmid šam mafria* 'The pupil there is disturbing (the lesson).' and *Hatalmid haya šam* 'The pupil was there.' But then, of course, the author demands that adjectives should have attributes like gender (m., f.) etc. Furthermore, adjectives "do not have a construct declension" (!), obviously because there is only a neatly defined class of those that have (see below, *6.4.2.1*), but that class includes precisely those three words that are given by PRICE as the examples for adjectives (*tov* 'good', *yafe* 'nice', *gadol* 'big'). This is one case out of innumerable ones.

[47] Reference is commonly made to school-grammars, and never – not even by way of rejection – to a work of structural corpus analysis. This also goes for the several "algorithms" aimed at computer programming for the generation of words (PRICE 1969b, CHOUEKA 1969, SAMUELSDORFF 1964).

3 PHONOLOGY

3.1 PHONETIC DATA

Phonetic data are available in BLANC (1957b, 1964a [texts]), and GARBELL
(1955: 26), and instrument-based data in TÉNÉ (1961, 1962). Details on
pronunciation in relative narrowness in BLANC (1964b: 17–22) are directed at the English-speaking student; WEINBERG (1966) presents features
of Israeli Hebrew phonetics (the approach is not structural, but in terms
of graphemes reproduced).

3.2 THE SHAPE OF ORALLY TRANSMITTED HEBREW

3.2.1 Community pronunciations and Schulaussprache

The oral transmission of Hebrew in the Jewish communities supplied, towards the onset of the revival, a variety of ways of repro-
ducing the graphemes of pointed Hebrew writing. The more important differences between these styles of spelling pronunciation lay
in the reproduction of the central vowel phonemes, in certain
monophthongizations and diphthongizations, in the maintenance
or loss of spirant alternants of non-emphatic stops and of emphatic
(velarized, laryngealized?) articulations as such. While the loss or
maintenance of phonetic distinctions in each community was
decisively regulated by the phonetic habits of the host populations,[48]

---

[48] In Jews' languages, the Hebrew element immediately to be affected by
the basic phonemic properties of other languages was the stock of Hebrew
vocabulary immerged in the special Jewish language; it must be assumed that
some, at least, of the features of the pronunciation of Hebrew actually constituted a transfer from the pronunciation of Hebrew words in Ladino, Yiddish,
Judaeo-Arabic, etc. Cf. GARBELL (1930: 15–6), ZAND (1965: 232), according
to WEINREICH (1960: 25, 57).

none of the numerous pronunciation traditions must be credited with more authenticity or even with the preservation of more, or more important, distinctions than the rest. The Ashkenazi (Central and Eastern European) community, aware of the nonauthenticity of its own varied traditions, at the time of the revival and for its purposes, began to consider as prestige style another pronunciation system, which, in fact, had less phonemic distinctions than its own; that style became termed *Sephardic* by way of contrast, although neither the Sephardi nor any one of the extra-European community traditions had that phonetic shape (GARBELL 1930: 14; 1955: 27; MEDAN 1955; MORAG 1959c: 251). The pseudo-Sephardic pronunciation had no distinction that had been lost from the Ashkenazi traditions, and had less distinctions in the following respects:

Graphemes	$o˙$ $ō$ $ǎ$ $å$ a	$ṭ$ $t˙$ t s $ś$
Ashkenazic	/oy/ /aw/ | /o/ | /a/	/t/ | /s/
Sephardic	/o/ | /a/	/t/ | /s/

This kind of *Schulaussprache*, current in Hebrew-speaking circles at the beginning of this century, enjoyed moreover the reputation of being "scientific" and more "authentic" (cf. e.g., CHRISTIE 1931: 5) due to its essential consistency with the Christian theological *Schulaussprache* based largely on LXX and Vulgate transcriptions (with some shortcomings due to misinterpretations and to deficiencies of Hellenistic and Vulgar Latin spelling, as, e.g., the interpretation of $ϑ$ and all $δ$'s, $γ$'s, $β$'s, and b's as stops) as well as on Humanists' Hebrew, which was a phonetic Latinization of the Sephardi tradition prevalent in the Italian renaissance.

3.2.2 Emergence of a phonetic koiné

This pseudo-Sephardic *Schulaussprache* became, as the inter-community pronunciation in Palestine in the latter part of the last century, the basis of revived Hebrew. Its success must be ascribed to the fact that it bore the characteristics of a *koiné* in relation to the previous community pronunciations (ROSÉN 1958c: 61-2);[49] distinctions that were not maintained in all community pronunciations disappeared from the *koiné: ḥ : x* (or *ḥ : x*); *q : k; ṭ : t; ʿ : ʾ* (all these are exclusively extra-Ashkenazic distinctions given up in favour of the second member of each pair); *å : a; γ : g;* and *δ : d* are distinctions present only in part of the "Oriental" traditions given up in favour of the second member of each pair; *s* and *t* acquired a position consistent with the one valid in the majority of Oriental styles *(3.2)*.[50] A phonemic distinction common to all community traditions is maintained irrespective of different actualization: *ṣ : s* versus *[ts] : s;* the latter (German-Yiddish tainted) shape is maintained.

3.3 THE PHONEMIC SYSTEM

3.3.1 The Israeli Hebrew phonemes

Consequently the PHONEME GRID[51] is poorer in oppositions than that of any one of the "traditions" and, of course, than what we can

---

[49] "Gemeinaussprache" of a "Zwischenstämmekreis" (LIPSCHÜTZ 1920: 24–5); "gemeinsame Aussprache" (PLESSNER 1931: 804). It can be gathered from information, *inter alia*, in ROSENBERG (1900: 6–7, 10, 12) that at his time, speech had not yet been altogether koinéized and community pronunciations were still in living use in Palestine. ZAND's (1965: 230–5) "phonetic *koiné*" is differently conceived and based not on phonological relations, but on preponderance of articulatory similarity considering Yiddish dialect areas and certain Hebrew pronunciation traditions.

[50] This presentation of the genesis of the Israeli Hebrew phonemic grid in terms of phonological processes seems more refined than the somewhat simplistic emphasis laid on "la fondamentale non-semiticità linguistica dei parlanti ebraico" (GARBINI 1964: 188); according to GARBELL (1940: 15), "kann keineswegs behauptet werden, daß die Indogermanisierung des hebräischen Lautsystems eine Erscheinung ist, die mit der modernen Sprachrenaissance in Beziehung steht".

infer for biblical and post-biblical Hebrew. It follows that since
the graphemic shapes are preserved, the spelling has become
"historical" or "archaic". The phonemic system of the "Oriental"
community style is closer to the written shape in that it retains the
oppositions *ḥ* : *x* and ’ : ‘.[52] Otherwise, socially levelled pronunciation styles have no influence on the phoneme inventory; in one
case (/r/ and /ʀ/, see below), the position and valeur of a phoneme
is merely different according to the style represented ("native"
versus standard; cf. above *1.4.3*), in other cases the characteristics
of pronunciation styles are subphonemic.

3.3.2 Questions of analysis

3.3.2.1 Vocalic length

Few, and only theoretical, problems are presented by the phonemic
grid. While VOCALIC LENGTH is concomitant with phonemic stress (TÉNÉ
1962), there exist isolated pairs in which a significative opposition is
expressed by a difference in vowel quantity: [laxé·n] 'therefore' : [laxén]
'to you (f.pl.)'; [natá·ti] 'I planted' : [natáti] 'I gave'. In the first case,
[laxé·n] is the marked term, and [laxén] is enclitic (cf. below *5.5.3*),
unless it occurs in sentence-initial position, in which case its syllable
prominence is not phonemically operative. [natá·ti] must, by system
symmetry, be interpreted as /natáati/ (ROSÉN 1952b: 6; 1955a: 242):[53]

> *noter* 'keeps watch' : *natar* 'kept watch' : *natarti* 'I kept watch'
> *notea* 'plants'   : [natá(·)] 'planted' : [natá·ti] = *nataati*

---

[51] WEIMAN (1950: 8–27; with complete array of minimal pairs); ROSÉN
(1955a: 145–51; minimal pairs); TÉNÉ (1968: 986, 990; 1969: 52); COHEN –
ZAFRANI (1968: 26, 36; unsubstantiated statements concerning the existence,
in the Hebrew speech of recent arabophonic immigrant groups, of an opposition
k : *q*, and of a fortis : lenis materialization of the contrasts *p* : *b*, etc.).
[52] With complete consistency only in the old vocabulary stock that corresponds to Hebrew learning. In words acquired, or innovated, in Israel, "vocal
spelling" is liable to waver.
[53] Other suggestions (two phonemes /ɛ/ : /e/, not recommended by BLANC
1964: 137; pertinent vowel length, RABIN 1940) add phonemic entities to the
grid and are therefore uneconomical in view of the extremely low functional
load of the oppositions involved.

3.3.2.2 Monophonematic evaluation of composite articulations

The question of MONOPHONEMATIC EVALUATION of a composite articulation arises in the case of /c/ = [ts]/[dz], and is decided on grounds of pattern symmetry: [tsaxak] 'laughed' and [raxats] 'washed' = /caxak/ and /raxac/. Cf. *daxak* 'pushed' and *raxav* 'rode (on horseback)', for verbal stems have neither initial nor final consonant clusters; [tsarix] : [tsrixim] 'must (m.sg.) : must (pl.)' = /carix/ : /crixim/ (no other native tripartite consonant articulations occur initially); but pattern symmetry may also demand biphonematic valuation: [tsisa] 'fermentation': *tasas* 'fermented'=*gsisa* 'dying agony' : *gasas* 'be dying' yields *tsisa* for [tsisa]. Native [tš] is, by all considerations, biphonematic, and the same holds also for foreign names and loans even where [tš] and [dž] would require monophonematic evaluation in the original languages, since foreign pattern symmetry cannot count for Israeli Hebrew phonemic analysis: [tš] is biphonematic in *tšok* 'choke (of an automobile)'.[54] Thus the occurrence, as such, of [tš] is no marker of foreignness.

3.4 EXTRASYSTEMIC AND MARGINAL PHONEMIC FEATURES

3.4.1 Phonematic indicators of foreignness

It will be recalled that it was the theoretical study of INDICATORS OF FOREIGNNESS (or extrasystemicity) that gave the impetus for the synchronic description of Israeli Hebrew (WEIMAN 1950), and Israeli Hebrew has remained unique in its position as an excellent means for the clarification of all methodological problems involved. There is probably no other living language with such a proportion of bilingual, even native bilingual, speakers on the one hand, and of speakers aware of a word's foreignness (i.e. homophony in Hebrew and another language) on the other hand. While the physical facts concerning any one of the forms in question are beyond doubt (which may be good enough for some approaches), their structural status cannot be formulated without serious probing into the very foundations of our analysis. A description will state that *f* occurs initially only outside some central layer of vocabulary that may be

---

[54] Different approach: BLANC (1964: 136) and GARBINI (1964: 189).

circumscribed negatively by its not containing names *(fílip)*, foreign loans, whether absorbed or not (*fílim* 'film', *fotosintéza* 'photosynthesis'), and slang expressions (*fileax* 'snatched'). If this obvious fact (which is one among numerous similar ones) is deprived of its singular status by refusing to let etymological considerations guide us in structural descriptive analysis, no phonemic analysis is, in fact, possible. If we hold that words such as those quoted must be included in the "corpus" on the basis of which Israeli Hebrew phonology is formulated, we shall no longer be able to say that the opposition $p : f$ is neutralized initially (and the archiphoneme represented by [p]) – or, if one prefers, that the limited distribution of /f/ does not include initial position; nor shall we be able to lay the phonological foundation for the fact that, in verbal inflection, prefix-bearing forms with stem initial /f/ correspond to prefixless ones with /p/ (*lefazer* 'to disperse' – *pazer* 'disperse [imp.]'). We might wish to recuperate these losses by making analogous statements in morphophonology, but then what statement within the framework of phone distribution can be made at all if every single one of them can be easily refuted by some "absorbed" family name or "well-known" foreign loan?[55] It would not even be possible to state what were the maximum number of components and admitted structure of an internal consonant cluster *(rekonstrúkcya)*. Moreover, we would lose a convenient possibility not only for making interesting statements, but also for formulating fundamental facts of linguistic awareness. WEIMAN who, in his introductory paragraphs on method, referred to the question of why the Viennese say *telefǒ* (TROUBETZ-KOY 1939: 205-6 = 1949: 245-6) could only derive from this phenomenon the existence of foreignness markers in a language, but was unable at his time to present similar phenomena from Israeli Hebrew, to show how speakers introduced extrasystemic phonological features into words known to be foreign; the quite current forms *fantomíma, fornográfya* (with speakers who would never utter *fazer*), *termofílim* 'Thermopylae' make it quite obvious that

---

[55] Surveys of criteria of foreignness: WEIMAN (1950: 64–5) ROSÉN (1955a: 147–76, *passim*).

initial /f/ is not just another consonantal phoneme, but – on the basis of a synchronic etymological sentiment – a marker of un-Hebrewness, which the analyst has a duty not to obliterate.

3.4.2 Marginally situated lexical entities

Phonology must be a description of relations (distributional features, neutralizations, allophonic variations, sequential groupings) observable in a layer of vocabulary that excludes all MARGINALLY SITUATED LEXICAL ENTITIES – not only because there is always some marginal entity that precludes a phonological statement from being made, but mainly because the marginality marked by the phonological deviation is operative in motivating other formal features. These features (we are principally concerned with stress phenomena that apply to marginal lexical entities; cf. below *3.7.3*) cannot be adequately described except in correlation to the phonological deviations, e.g.: a stem ending in /p/ or /b/ retains the stress of the unsuffixed form even where suffixes are added that otherwise attract stress (cf. *3.7.3*):

rasáp (army acronym for) 'Company Sergeant Major' – f.sg. *rasápit* – m.pl. *rasápim*, f.pl. *rasápiyot*;
xabúb (from Arabic) 'darling, honey' – pl. *xabúbim*;
the same for a stem with initial /f/: *fílim*, pl. *fílmim*. This cannot mean anything else than that the speaker is aware (by "etymological" sensitiveness, bilingualism, or phonemic consciousness) of the marginality of such words, and "knows" that a form with initial /f/ is not the same as any other one.

3.4.3 Phonological treatment and characterization of extra-Hebraic vocabulary

Where a phone of a foreign or otherwise marginal form is not at all part of the native (central) sound inventory, two attitudes are possible: maintaining the extrasystemic phone ([wálla·] interjection, from Arabic) or approximation by a native phone (*vádi* for *wa·di* 'wadi'). In cases where the foreign phone is an allophone of an Israeli Hebrew phoneme, some significant ways of treatment may occur:

(1) If the position of the phone corresponds to Israeli Hebrew (central) allophonic distribution, mimicry is the likely treatment, but it is also possible to substitute another member of that same Israeli Hebrew phoneme in order to "overestrange" the loan. For instance, /e/ contains, *inter alia*, the allophones [e·] or [eʸ] and [ɛ]; the latter occurs in Engl. *special*, but for its absorption into Israeli Hebrew in the sense of 'special cab', another, distributionally "wrong" and consequently more "typically English" allophone of /e/ is selected: [spe·šl] or [speʸšl] (almost homophonous with *spatial*): the selection of [spe·šl] or [spɛšl] may be stylistically indicative of the educational level of the speaker.

(2) If the position of the foreign phone contradicts Israeli Hebrew (central) allophonic distribution, it is most likely to be preserved. /š/ has the allophone [ž] (in assimilatory conditions) and [š] (free allophone). In [garáž] and [žakét] 'jacket', [ž] occurs in contradiction to distributional behaviour, precisely as [e·] in [spe·šl].

Should it be assumed that, by virtue of such cases, Israeli Hebrew has the phonemes /ē/ (vs. /e/), or /ž/ (vs. /š/), or that it has them only in foreign words? It would be stretching the notion of 'phoneme' too far if either were to be contended. What is foreign is the occurrence in a stated position, but not the phone as such. Admittedly, we cannot transcribe [žaket] phonemically unless we risk confounding it with /šaket/ 'quiet', but should one adapt language features to help one overcome one's shortcomings? The spoken chain contains features that are phonemically neither analysable nor transcribable, only phonetically recordable;[56] it is precisely by these features (as are, *mutatis mutandis*, and on the morphological level, Engl. *receive, perceive, conceive*) that lexical layers are characterized.

3.4.4 *Abnormal phoneme groupings*

"ABNORMAL PHONEME GROUPINGS"[57] or rather phoneme sequences that would, in non-marginal words, constitute a positive boundary signal, are among the most common indicators of lexical marginality. A final sequence -VCt #, where $V \neq a$, does not occur in centrally situated words (e.g., -iCt- would indicate a boundary

---

[56] BLANC's (1956c: 799) cavalier objections miss the subtler points of methodology: already in his review of WEIMAN (1950) he had refrained from going below the articulatory surface (BLANC 1953: 88), and his fundamentally different approach is not devoid of superficiality.

[57] As *ntsy* in Engl. *intelligentsia*; cf. TROUBETZKOY (1939: 228–30 = 1949: 274–6).

-iC ≠ t-), but can be attested from *spórt* and *koncért* (*koncerèt* appearing in children's language). A rule stating that non-final clusters of more than two consonants other than with two non-occlusives surrounding one occlusive (*-ntr-* in *psantran* 'pianist' and *-lgr-* in *tilgref* 'telegraphed') are initially inadmissible or else compulsorily materialized with vocalic anaptyxis before the third component is not upheld in marginal words *(transkrípcya, špríc)* and marks them as such; otherwise, such consonantal articulations in immediate succession constitute a boundary signal ([*-špr-*] = /*-š* ≠ *pr-*/ as in *'iš pratiy* 'private person').

3.5 THE PHONOLOGICAL STRUCTURE OF ISRAELI HEBREW IN DIACHRONIC VIEW

3.5.1 Loss of a junctural distinction: pausal versus contextual

The PHONOLOGICAL STRUCTURE of Israeli Hebrew may be conceived of as the immediate result – whether as a diachronic reality or otherwise – of the loss of the junctural distinction of pausal versus contextual forms in Tiberian Biblical Hebrew. Apart from a handful of forms[58], the form taken over is the contextual one. The principal difference between the overall phonemic system of Tiberian Hebrew and the contextual subsystem is that the feature of spirancy (distinguishing [p] from [f], [b] from [v], etc.) would have to be considered as allophonic (in non-emphatic environment) in the overall system, but as pertinent within the limits of the contextual subsystem, where the juncture feature 'contextuality' that entails

---

[58] Nouns with the pattern *CóCi* (*yófi* 'beauty', *koši* 'difficulty', Biblical Hebrew contextual forms *ypi·*, *qši·*), intermittently with the pattern *CéCi* (*lexi* 'cheek', but *kli* 'tool, container', Biblical Hebrew pausal form *k·éli*) (AVINERY 1932: 56; 1964: 133). Also in idiomatically frozen Biblical reminiscences: *laavod befarèx* 'be enslaved in hard labour' (contrast: *'ᵃvodat-perèx* 'hard labour'). – Verbs of the pattern *-CaCea(x)* (*yešaleax* 'will send away' or *yitparea* 'will behave unruly') correspond to Biblical Hebrew forms in *-aC·ēᵃḥ* and *-aC·eᵃˁ* that are compulsory *in pausa*, but vary with *-aC·aḥ* and *-aC·aˁ* in contextual position. The Israeli Hebrew successors of the latter (such as *yešalax*) are high-level puristic style. Cf. AVINERY (1964: 133-4).

spirancy in certain cases can no longer be taken into account (ROSÉN 1961b). This is very concisely why, e.g., [p] and [f] are an allophonic pair in Biblical Hebrew, while they are two distinct phonemes in Israeli Hebrew. In the parallel cases, the analogous phonemic split has not resulted in the addition of a phoneme, but in rephonemicization, since the allophones concerned became grouped with those of other phonemes:

$$/[k]+[x]/ : /\d{h}/ \; > \; /k/ : /[x]+[\d{h}]/$$
$$/[b]+[v]/ : /w/ \; > \; /b/ : /[v]+[w]/^{59}$$

Even within the limits of the contextual subsystem, the functional load of the plosive : spirant opposition was extremely low, and spirants and (non-emphatic) stops could contrast only in one type of environment (V_1C—V_2, where C is not one of the plosives-spirants, and V_1 is not a "long" vowel). Since in all other environments the occurrence of a plosive or spirant, respectively, was still predictable, redundancy of the conditioning factor and the feature of plosiveness or spirancy, respectively, was the result in those environments. One very important conditioning factor was consonantal length ("gemination") concomitant with what is usually considered as vocalic length, but also concomitant with non-spirancy (in traditional pronunciations, at least), in a way that, e.g., for C = voiced labial, $C\cdot$ (long consonant) was only [b·], never [v·].

Sequences occurring		Sequences not occurring	
(*i* for any short, *ē* for any "lengthened" vowel, *d* excepted)		($C \neq$ laryngeal)	
	different nucleus quantity		different consonant quantity
[—iC·V́—]	[—ēC·V́—]		[—iCV́—]
[—ēCV́—]	[—iCV́—]		[—ēC·V́—]
[—i·CV́—]	[—iCV́—]		[—i·C·V́—]
[—í·CV·#]	[—íCV·#]		[—í·C·V·#]
[—ēCVC#]	[—íCVC#]		[—ēC·VC#]
[—ēCV·#]	[—íCV·#]		[—ēC·V·#]^{60}

Since there can be no contrastive pair depending solely on the opposition of consonantal quantity, the loss of this feature incurred by most of the pronunciation traditions did not result in any functional loss, but only in the phonemic split of articulatorily different vowel allophones: [—ēCV́—] : [—iC·V́—] > [—eCV́—] : [—iCV́—] and the like, that is, the opposition became loaded on vowel timbre and was no longer borne by prosodic differences.

As a result, while previously the contrastive environments for the plosive: spirant contrast were few, they now became very numerous: [—i·CV́—] : [—iC·V́—] > [—iCV́—]; this was a merger unless C = /p f b v k x/, cases in which, e.g. [—i·fV́—] : [—ip·V́—] > [—ifV́—] : [—ipV́—]. Oppositions of the type /p/ : /f/ have by now become heavily loaded. If it is taken into account that, in the Israeli Hebrew *koiné*, *å* (that could graphemically take the position of a "short" as well as of a "lengthened" vowel) and *a* ("short" vowel) have merged ([—åfV́—] : [—ap·V́—] > [—afV́—] : [—apV́—]), and that in some of the pairs of phonemes /b/ : /v/, etc., one member has absorbed another earlier phoneme, the spirant : stop opposition may well be one of the most heavily loaded in Israeli Hebrew.[61]

---

[59] It must be considered possible that the phonemes absorbed in one of the terms of the phonemicized pair have either attracted that term phonetically or else lost a non-phonemic feature by attraction: /w/ may have lost its non-fricativity in the process, likewise /b/. Loss of emphatic articulation in non-Semitic surroundings may have been facilitated by this process: /q/ absorbed in the newly formed /k/ phoneme. All the various processes combined in: /t/ : /[t]+[θ]/ : [s] > ([t]+[t]/ : /s/ (Israeli Hebrew), but > /[t]+[t]/ : : /[θ]+[s]/ (Ashkenazic, where the interdental spirancy of [θ] is lost by its absorption in /s/).

[60] In this pattern, Tiberian vocalization frequently has a "gemination" point marked in C that by traditional view is unrelated to phonetic reality ("*dågēš euphonicum*").

[61] Subtle morphological distinctions can be based on it: denominative *hitxaver* 'became friends' (*xaver* 'friend') contrasts with deverbative *hitxaber* 'joined (intrans.)'; denominative *hištavec* 'suffered a stroke' (*šavac* 'apoplexy') contrasts with deverbative *hištabec* 'became integrated' (example provided by student).

5

3.5.2 Resulting loss of quantitative distinctions

The merger of $\mathring{a}$ (in the environment —C_1C_2·V, where C_2 = /b g d p k t/ "short *qåmåṣ*", $\mathring{a}$ > Israeli Hebrew [o], in other environments $\mathring{a}$ > [a]) and *a* has had the result, in conjunction with the loss of consonantal length, of causing the development of a homophony: [—aC_1C_2V—] : [—$\mathring{a}C_1C_2$V—] > [—aC_1C_2V—], as a result of which, e.g., *ʿavda* corresponds to *ʿåbdå* 'worked (f.sg.)' as well as to *ʿabd·å* 'her servant', and *ʾašma* to *ʾåšmå* 'was guilty (f.sg.)' as well as to *ʾašmå* 'guilt'. Israeli Hebrew /a/, the successor of Biblical Hebrew [å] as well as [a], cannot any longer be said to be excluded from almost all types of open syllables, and a basic phonological rule that applied to [å] in open syllables (zeroification on removal of stress; *d·åbår* 'thing' – *d·båri·m* 'things', final syllable stressed in each case) cannot be considered applicable to Israeli Hebrew /a/, which is the successor also of Biblical Hebrew [a] (no zeroification: *ṣad·i·q* (sg.) : *ṣad·i·qi·m* (pl.) 'righteous'); all alternations (or nonalternations) of /a/ taken over from Biblical Hebrew (*davar* : *dvarim*; *cadik* : *cadikim*) must now be relegated to the morphological, or at least MORPHOPHONEMIC, level.

3.5.3 Phonemicizations and level shifting

Analogous LEVEL SHIFTING applies to the stop : spirant relation, which has become morphophonemic. In the pair *saxar* 'rented': *liskor* 'to rent', the alternation /x/ : /k/ can be described only in terms of verbal forms (*x* in the remotive tense vs. *k* in the infinitive), whilst in Biblical Hebrew it could be stated in terms of syllabic structure (ROSÉN 1958a: 188–90). Since both terms of this opposition have absorbed other Biblical Hebrew phonemes (/ḥ/ absorbed in /x/, and /q/ in /k/), there are morphological pairs of the same status, in which such alternations do not apply (/saxar/ 'traded' : /lisxor/ 'to trade', and /sakar/ 'reviewed' : /liskor/ 'to review'); as a consequence, the alternation has become stylistically unstable.[62]

---

[62] E.g. non-alternation in substandard *šapax* 'poured (m.sg.)' in view of *lišpox* (inf.) vs. standard *šafax* (BLANC 1964a: 145); *škax* 'forget', *škav* 'lie

For a given verbal stem, or for a root, it will have to be stated whether or not alternation applies: the stem of 'trade' will have to be represented as *s-x-r*, that of 'rent' as *s-k/x-r*, that of 'review' as *s-k-r*. It is to the point to recall here that these three possibilities (stable /k/, stable /x/, alternating *k/x*) correspond to different graphemes: {q}, {ḫ}, {k}, respectively. The spelling, though phonemically archaic (cf. above *3.2.1*), is morphophonemically significant and functional: the signs of the Hebrew alphabet stand, in respect to Israeli Hebrew, for morphophonemic rather than phonemic entities.

3.5.4 Emergence of morphophonemic alternations; loss of laryngal articulations; new diphthongs

Morphophonemic stem alternation applies also to roots containing an old laryngal (', ', *h*, *ḥ*). This alternation works very similarly to the stop: spirant one (Rosén 1952b: 6; 1955a: 200):

stable /x/	alternation x/ax	stable /'/	alternation '/a
grapheme {k}	grapheme {ḫ}	grapheme {'}	grapheme {'}
'pour'	'send'	'read'	'tear'

Participle

	stable /x/	alternation x/ax	stable /'/	alternation '/a
M.pl.	*šofxim*	*šolxim*	*kor'im*	*kor'im*
M.sg.	*šofex*	*šoleax*	*kore'* [kore·]	*korea*
F.sg.	*šofexèt*[63]	*šolaxàt*	*kore't* [kore·t]	*koraàt*

down', *špox* 'pour' (m.sg. imperatives) in view of *tiškax, tiškav* (2 pers.m.sg. potentialis) vs. "more desirable" *šxax, šxav, šfox* (Rosén 1955a: 216–9). Cf. Weinberg (1966: 62; objections in principle).

[63] Here it is non-alternation that is stylistically unstable (substandard -*axàt* (e.g. *šofaxàt*) for -*exèt*, but not the inverse).

5*

This table presents the most salient results of the LOSS OF
LARYNGAL ARTICULATIONS[64] in Hebrew and also shows the reason
for the peculiar position assigned to /a/ in the phoneme "block"
(3.3.1); it occupies, relative to /'/, a position comparable to that
of the spirants relative to the stops. It also makes the introduction
of DIPHTHONGS into the description of Israeli Hebrew plausible
(ROSÉN 1955b: 247; 1962a § 0.12): the groups *oa, ia, ea, ua* always
occur in final syllables and must be considered as phonologically
tautosyllabic[65] in view of the accentual mechanism: in forms that
have a finally positioned accent, prominence is borne by the vowel
preceding *a*: [šoléax], [koréa].

3.6 DELIMITATIVE FEATURES

3.6.1 Boundary signals

BOUNDARY SIGNALS (ROSÉN 1955a: 179–84) emerge essentially from
the restrictions on consonant groupings at initial and final positions; morphological "words" are consistent with absolute initial
and final positions, except, of course, that marginal lexical entities
(3.4.2) transgress the rules set for phoneme groupings. Final
CONSONANT CLUSTERS are in non-marginal lexical entities only of the

---

[64]   Laryngal "reflexes": length ([kore·t]), colouring (*koraàt, solaxàt*; the pattern
vowel is *e* as in the other forms) and syllable boundary ([kor/im]). Laryngal
reflexes that are not shown in the table: prosthetic vowel: (kotev) 'writing
(part.)' : /ktiva/ [ktiva] 'writing (abstract noun)' = /'omed/ [omed] 'standing
(part.)' : /'mida/ [(')amida] 'standing (abstr.)'; additional syllabicity: *xatam*
'signed' : *hextím* 'made sign' = *'asak* 'was busy (with)' : *heesík* 'busied (somebody) with'. The parallelism of these "reflexes" with those apparent, e.g., in
Accadian and Indo-European is important in view of the fact that Hebrew
laryngals are a historical "fact", while it is on a comparative basis that they
can be established in Accadian, and mainly by reconstruction in Indo-European.
If for Israeli Hebrew formulas of reconstructions are applied analogous to
those that are used in Indo-Europeanist laryngeal theory or that could be used
in Old Assyrian, conclusions can be reached on the existence and number of
Classical Hebrew laryngals. This is an important check for the reality of reconstructed laryngals.
[65]   But articulatorily and metrically heterosyllablic.

type -*aCt* #, that is, they exist only in one morphological type, the
2nd pers.f.sg. of the remotive tense ('*amart* 'you (f.sg.) have said').
In initial sequences of consonant phonemes (the number of which
never exceeds two, except in marginal lexemes) there is either anaptyxis (/ # rd/—[red]) or actualization in contact of the consonants
concerned (/ # dr/—[dr]); that initial [red], for instance, neutralizes
an opposition /rd/ : /red/ and can be considered a materialization
of the former, emerges from morphological patterning: /darax/
'stepped' : /drixa/ [drixa] 'stepping' ≈ /radaf/ 'ran after, perse-
cuted' : /rdifa/ [redifa] 'persecution'. By *consonant cluster* we consequently mean an immediate sequence of non-syllabic articulations
(not of consonant phonemes); it is of general significance that the
boundary signal has status on the articulatory, not on the phonemic
level: a phonemic sequence /rd/ is not a boundary signal, but may
become one if actualized [rd]. Moreover, in some cases, e.g. / # dš/
(where actualization in contact entails assimilatory neutralization:
[tš]), anaptyxis is optional. While anaptyxis ('*šwå mobile*') is
traditionally (however unfoundedly) considered the "authentic"
pronunciation ("word initial *šwå* is mobile"), no relation must be
established between Israeli Hebrew initial anaptyxis and *šwå
mobile*: whether or not initial *šwå mobile* is so continued into
Israeli Hebrew, depends on its morphemic status: the vocalic
articulation is phonemically preserved only in initial morphemes of
the pattern (Class.) *C*- (*b·*- 'in', *m*- 'participle', *l*- 'infinitive', etc.)
that have now to be phonemicized *be*-, *me*-, *le*-. In principle, all
other initial mobile *šwå*'s are phonemically zeroified, but can
secondarily undergo anaptyxis; identifying the anaptyctic vowel
with *šwå* (e.g., as implied in WEINBERG 1966: 42-7; GUMPERTZ
1938: 104-5) would deprive us of any classificatory principle for the
inventory of initial clusters.

3.6.2 Initial consonant clusters

The inventory of "admissible" initial consonant clusters (ROSÉN 1955a:
156-60; 1962a: 4)[66] is, in a general way, founded on a principle of ascending
relative sonority so that no syllable peak would intervene between the

word boundary and the first phonemic vowel (consequently, inversion
of a sequence from an ascending to a descending one converts an initially
admissible cluster into an inadmissible one; cf. /rd/ versus /dr/, above).
The features of relative sonority that may be recognized from the inventory of initially admissible clusters correspond to those in the principal Central and Eastern European languages spoken by the immigrants;
the inventory has been paralleled to Yiddish by ZAND (1965: 235–7),
earlier to Ashkenazic Hebrew vocabulary by GUMPERTZ (1938: 104–
9). However, if compulsory anaptyxis (as in /lgima/ [legima] 'sip') is
opposed to compulsory clustering (/glima/ [glima] 'gown'), disregard-
ing facultative anaptyxis (/bdika/ [bdika, bedika] 'control, check'),
the generally valid phonetic principles become obvious (as *muta cum
liquida* versus *liquida cum muta*), so that assigning the cluster inventory
to some given Jewish speech form – by way of substrate identification –
may be a trifle too forced.

3.7 SUPRASEGMENTALS

3.7.1 Prominence

Syllable PROMINENCE is pertinent: *rácu* 'ran' : *racu* [racú] 'wanted'
(both 3 pl.); *'áfu* 'flew' : *'afu* ['afú] 'baked' (3 pl.); *plagim* 'factions' :
plágim 'sparking plugs'; *dofèk* 'pulse' : *dofek* [dofék] 'knocks';
yelèd 'child' : *yeled* 'will bring forth'. Syllable prominence is materialized by expiratory stress and is liable to cause subphonemic

---

[66]   Some spectographic verification in an unpublished Paris thesis by Mme
F. BARRELL-KITE; material based on intuitive romanization (in cables) according to phonetic materialization in ROSÉN (1955a: 160–5). Cf. also the texts
published in phonetic transcription (see *3.1*). – The table in COHEN –
ZAFRANI (1968: 30–1) cannot be used; it must be misprinted. But even from the
accompanying explanations it becomes obvious that the authors have confused
initially incompatible consonants with unattested initial clusters. E.g., since
initial *w* is found in Hebrew (of all periods) almost exclusively in marginal
lexical entities (Aramaic and other loans), there are hardly any initial groups
with *v-* (all groups except *vš, vl, v'* are "non représentés" according to COHEN –
ZAFRANI; I have serious doubts about *vš-*, but count *vr-* in *vradim* 'roses'),
but this is a lexical fact and cannot be used as the basis for a statement: "*v*
comme premier élément de groupe n'est *compatible* [my italics; H. R.] qu'avec
s, š, l, r et '." (COHEN – ZAFRANI 1968: 30–1) Root incompatibilities and phonetic facts are not kept apart in this paragraph.

effects typical for stress prominence (relative length of vowel in stressed syllable, see *3.3.2.1* and cf. ENOCH — KAPLAN (1969: 212-20).

The above examples indicate that a stress opposition does not consist simply of two words differentiated only by different stress position; it would be more accurate to say that an accent opposition consists of a word with final stress ([racú]) opposed to one with non-final, i.e. penult, accent ([rácu]). Word units with antepenult or more retracted accent, see *3.7.3*, are not terms of accentual oppositions. The notation employed here, i.e. not marking any accent on a finally stressed word, indicates that we hold final position of stress to be the unmarked member of the opposition. This is in keeping with some intuitively observable facts: (1) deviations from classically transmitted accents are always in favour of non-final stress; (2) (as a result,) in case of stylistic variants, the puristically recommended form is the finally stressed one; (3) additional vocabulary items (names, loans and the like) that risk being homophonous with words of the central stock and can make use of a distinctive accent opposition, assume non-final stress, thereby leaving the final stress to the centrally located word *(plagim)*. This view is traditional: accent has always been taught as being final unless in certain specified conditions and cases.

3.7.2 The Biblical Hebrew accent system revisited

In order to assess the degree of systemic conservativism or otherwise of the Hebrew accentual system, it may be interesting to consider briefly what the Biblical Hebrew accentual system looked like phonologically. The view stated above as traditional is correct only on the phonetic level, and only if all rules are based on the contextual (sandhi) forms of the Tiberian text, irrespective of the fact that forms can by no means be considered as phonologically fundamental in Biblical Hebrew[67]. In a Biblical Hebrew phonology, based on pausal forms from which contextual forms derive by a set of hierarchically ordered juncture phenomena, the following is valid:

---

[67]   This has been set out in ROSÉN (1969b), where full details may be found.

(1) finite verb forms have "columnal" prominence on the base-final syllable: *yišmŏru, šămărti*;

(2) non-agentive suffixes are enclitic: *yilbăšúkă*, /dabaréka/ *dbărékă* (the last preenclitic syllable achieves prominence);

(3) all other forms are devoid of prominence.

By virtue of a hierarchically later rule, by which all prominenceless words (whether pausal forms with no prominence or contextual ones that have lost their prominent syllable through sandhi processes) acquire final-syllable stress, final word stress achieves the status of a boundary marker for accentually uncharacterized words. This stress is maintained even where anaptyctic vowels create a nonphonemic "post"-final syllable: /kålb/ *kåleb* [kåleb].

The best summary of Biblical Hebrew accent would be to say that functional accent is a marker of certain morphological classes, whilst the unmarked (i.e. accentless) form types develop a mechanical progressive accent of their own: the latter are, principally, nominal, the former – verbal.[68]

3.7.3 The pertinent stress features of Israeli Hebrew

This basic situation is, astonishingly enough, essentially preserved in Israeli Hebrew (which is no credit to the language revivers and purists, who could have no knowledge of these features). Stress serves as a classificatory marker of certain morphological types through the introduction, for them, of non-final stress. However, the removal of the stress from the final syllable is related to two factors that must be kept neatly apart: (1) atonic morphemes in word-final position, (2) fixed etymological stress of a presuffixal base.

These factors are conveniently represented by a double set of terms or symbols (introduced in ROSÉN 1962a § 0.41, not adopted by others):

(1) ´ to mark a PROMINENT syllable, which will be stressed irrespective of its position in the word: *studént* (sg.) : *studéntim* (pl.);

---

[68] I have worded this statement to underline the essential functional parallelism with Indo-European accent as it developed, e.g., in Greek. "Verbal" and "nominal" would, of course, have to be interchanged for Indo-European, and "progressive" would have to read "regressive" in Greek.

ruménit (ethnic, f.sg.) : *ruméniyot* (f.pl.); *pántšer* 'tyre puncture, mishap, hitch' : *pántšerim* (pl.); *'ába* 'dad', *kám* 'rose (3 pers. m. sg.)' : *káma* (f.sg.) : *kámu* (pl.c.). The prominence is an integral feature of the stem, the same suffixes added to prominenceless stems would not create penult stress situations (cf. *šamar* [šamár] 'watched (3 pers. m. sg.)' : *šamra* [šamrá] : *šamru* [šamrú], cf. below).

(2) ' to mark a SUBORDINATE syllable, i.e. a final or one of the two final syllables that is (or are) a morpheme, or part of, or contain(s) a morpheme, one of whose integral features is atony: e.g. *-tì* (1 pers. sg. c., remotive tense) is everywhere atonic, likewise *-à* (directive suffix as in *daromà* [daróma] 'southward'), *-ayìm* ('paired plural' suffix, as in *yadayìm* [yadáyim] 'hands'), *-èt* (feminine suffix in agent nouns and participles, as in *šomerèt* [šoméret] 'watchwoman'), *-šèhù* 'some-' (Lat. *ali-*) and *-šèlò* 'no matter' (Lat. *-cumque*) that occur in immediate succession of interrogative pronouns as in *mi* 'who?' : *mišèhù* [míšehu] 'somebody' : *mišèlò* [míšelo] 'no matter who' and *matay* 'when?': *mataysèhù* [matáyšehu] 'sometime': *mataysèlò* [matáyšelo] 'no matter when' or *'éyze* 'which?' : *'éyzešèhù* ['éyzešehu] 'some' : *'éyzešèlò* ['éyzešelo] 'no matter which';[69] ...*o*...*è*..., ..*e*...*è*..., ..*aà*..., ..*o(x)à*..., ...*ohà*..., ...*o*/*e*...*a(x)*, ...*o*/*e*...*ì* (discontinuous patterns of certain noun formations corresponding to Biblical Hebrew "segolates" as in *dofèk* [dófek] 'pulse', *yofì* [yófi] 'beauty', *yelèd* [yéled] 'child', *naàl* [náal] 'shoe', *nohàl* [nóhal] 'procedure'); as can be seen from these examples, stress is borne by the last syllable preceding the subordinate one, unless, of course, the word contains a prominent syllable which determines the position of stress according to (1).

If neither (1) or (2) is applicable (that is, in the absence of either a prominent or a subordinate syllable), the word is finally stressed; final stress has no morphological or lexical function.

---

[69] E.g. *Ha'ìm 'aleyhem lehaxzir ma-še-lo lakxu?* 'Do they have to return what they have not taken?'; replacing *ma-še-lo* by *mašèlò*, the sense is 'Do they have to make restitution *no matter what* they have taken?' (ROSÉN 1962a: 247). Cf. below *8.5.3*.

The 2nd person m.sg. ending *-xa* is conveniently considered indifferent
in postconsonantal position (/susxa/ [susxá] 'your horse'), but subordinate after a phonemic vowel (/susexà/ [suséxa] 'your horses', /ʾalexà/
[ʾaléxa] 'on you', /píxà/ [píxa] 'your mouth', not in /kilʾxa/ [kilʾ*ᵃ*-xá]
'your prison' with non-phonemic [*ᵃ*]). We can then state that, by an
ENCLISIS-like feature, a final morpheme following a subordinate morpheme, neutralizes, in the latter, the subordinate : indifferent opposition,
establishing accentual indifference as the representative of the archipros-
:odeme *hizhartì* 'I have warned' + *-xa* 'you' yields /hizhartixà/
t[hizharíxa] 'I have warned you'; likewise *hizhartì* + *-x* '2nd pers.sg.f.'
'or + *-v* him' result in /hizhartix/ [hizhartíx], /hizhartiv/ [hizhartív],
respectively. These object-suffixed remotive (*7.3.2*) tense forms are,
however, the only remnant of this accentual mechanism and belong to a
somewhat elevated style.
    In the light of the Biblical Hebrew features outlined here, let us stress
that what was a non-phonemic syllable (*-leb* in *kʿeleb*) emerges now as a
subordinate one (*-lèv* in *mekèv*); moreover, nonsuffixal subordinate syllables occur only in nouns, and occasionally minimal pairs are created in which
the penult-stressed noun contrasts with an otherwise identical finite verb
(*yelèd* : *yeled*; *berèx* : *berex*; *terèd* : *tered*; *dofèk* : *dofek*). Consequently,
the accent preserves its power to serve as a class marker of parts of
speech (although the situation is reversed in comparison to Biblical
Hebrew); consistently therewith, noun forms having a vowel pattern
that agrees with the original SEGOLATE type (non-phonemic last syllable
in Biblical Hebrew), acquire penult stress:

classical non-segolate form		quasi-segolate penult-stressed form in Israeli Hebrew		contrasting verb or adjective with final stress	
koˑbå̄ʿ	'headgear'	*kovà*	'hat'		
ʾemṣå̄ʿ	'middle'	*ʾemcà*		*ʾemcaʾ*	'I shall find'
ʾeṣbå̄ʿ	'finger'	*ʾecbà*		*ʾecbaʾ*	'I shall paint'
ḥĕrēš	'tacitly'	*-xerèš*	'secret-'	*xereš*	'deaf'[70]

[70] A more comprehensive list including even acronymic nouns (e.g. *cahàl*,
acronym for 'Israel Defence Forces') will be found in ROSÉN (1955a: 230–1),
where we have tacitly corrected the unfortunate shortcomings (due to haste)
of an earlier statement (ROSÉN 1955b: 243–4). BEN-ḤAYYIM (1955: 339–40),
while pointing at these misstatements, did not suggest any amended formulation
of the rules; instead, he makes the descriptive approach responsible for my
mistaken classification of observed facts. – Even before, Irene GARBELL had
attempted to furnish a purely phonetic explanation of unclassical penult accent,
relating the stress features of the types *sára* or *rívka* (female first names), the

3.7.4 Accentually subordinate morphemes

Of the subordinate morphemes, the most noteworthy are the re-motive tense personal suffixes with initial consonant: -*tì* (1 sg.c.), -*tà* (2 sg.m.), -*nù* (1 pl.c.), -*tèm* (2 pl.m.), -*tèn* (2 pl.f.). The suffixes with no initial consonant are INDIFFERENT (i.e. neither subordinate nor prominent) and bear the word stress unless the stem is promi-nent as in *káma*, *higdílu*, etc. While subordinate -*tèm*, -*tèn* constitute a deviation (created no doubt by analogical levelling[71]) from the biblically attested norm, it restores, in part at least, the fundamental Biblical Hebrew principle of columnal stem stress in the suffix tense:[72] in Israeli Hebrew, columnal accent persists where the personal suffix has an initial consonant; in all other cases, the accent is suffixal, provided, of course, the stem contains no element of prominence:

[dibár-ti]	[dibér]	[dibr-á]
[dibár-ta]		[dibr-ú]
[dibár-t]		
[dibár-nu]		
[dibár-tem]		
[dibár-ten]		

---

family names in -*i* (patterned on ethnics) as well as *'ába* 'dad', *'ima* 'mum', *'écba'* 'finger', *'émca'* 'middle', *legámre* 'entirely', and *dávka* 'though' to the "vocalic (and apparently vocalic) final" of these words (GARBELL 1930: 21). Our lists show that this criterion will have to be rejected; *legámre* and *dávka*, coupled with *'ádraba* (antepenult stress) 'by all means', tend to show that these colourful particles of talmudic discussion that are fullfledged elements of Yiddish vocabulary have come to Hebrew as Yiddish (not as unanalysable Aramaic) words preserving their stress in that language.

[71] It is not easily comprehensible what made COHEN – ZAFRANI (1968: 54) say that "chez de nombreux Israéliens" there was "une tendance à accentuer le thème devant la désinence -*u* de troisième personne plur. du passé: *gámru* 'ils ont fini'." The authors must have misunderstood some information given to them and confused the 3rd person plural with the second (which they don't mention in this context). The misunderstanding might be due to MORAG (1967: 642).

[72] Cf. ROSÉN (1969b) and BAUER — LEANDER (1922: 179).

The restitution of classically syncopated vowels (as *ă* in *šmart·em* versus *šâmắrt·ă*) is only a necessary consequence: *šamartèm, heve'-tèm* (Biblical Hebrew *hăbē'tem*).

3.7.5 The lexical pertinence of stress

Turning now to the cases in which non-final word stress is the materialization of stem prominence rather than of atony of a suffix, although the factual evidence is quite lucid, some discussion will have to be devoted to the question of what criteria can be considered classificatory in this respect. Little need be said, in this connection, about verbal morphology; correspondingly to the situation prevailing in Biblical Hebrew contextual forms, stem prominence is the distinguishing mark of the finite forms of the *hiktíl* stem type as well as of those of the ground stem *(qal)* of 'medially open' roots (ROSÉN 1962a § 45.1 [G], 4), where analytic-ally, the stress element actually takes the place of the medium radical (*kámu* derivable from a radical *k-·-m-* in the same way as *šamru* from *š-m-r-*); nor, apparently, was anything else intended by the mediaeval grammarians who represented these "hollow" roots as showing a medium *waw* or *yod*.[73]

In the nominal domain, we have to start from the basic phenomenon that whenever two otherwise equal nominal forms form a contrasting pair of final versus non-final word stress, the non-finally stressed one is situated, in various aspects, outside the system of lexical relations; it is, in comparison with its counterpart, less motivated or less motivating. I shall show what I mean by some

---

[73] However, the stress opposition could obviously not carry alone the load of a tense contrast: Classical *qắmă* and its kind, bearing final stress as a participle, has absorbed stem prominence from the otherwise identical 3rd person feminine singular remotive, a homonymy being created that calls for solutions (cf. *7.2.1*); the other aorist forms have no stem prominence. It is only the tense contrast that is obliterated, since in its use as an adjective, as BLANC (1957: 37) has pointed out, the final stress is maintained in *ba'a* 'coming, next'. This is not the case in any participial use, e.g. *ruàx habá'a mi-mizrax* 'a wind coming from the East'.

examples representing the most important classes of such contrasts:[74]

Personal name versus designation of animate	(f.)	xáya	(female first name)	xaya	'animal'
		yáfa	(same)	yafa	'beautiful' (f.sg.)
	(m.)	'árye	(male first name)	'arye	'lion'
		šálom	(same)	šalom	'peace, welfare'
		xáyim	(same)	xayim	'life'
		'ílan	(same)	'ilan	'tree'
Toponymic versus appellative		rxóvot	(name of town)	rxovot	'streets'
		ríšon	(common short designation of the town ríšon-lecíyon)	rišon	'first'
		'axúza	(quarter of the city of Haifa)	'axuza	'manor'
name of a letter of the Hebrew alphabet versus appellative		vávim	(pl. of vav)	vavim	'hooks'
		távim	(plural of tav)	tavim	'music sheet(s)'

---

[74] These classes are paralleled by Classical Greek "oppositive accent" (Γλαῦκος 'personal name (m.)': γλαυκός 'gleaning'); morphologically functional, and at the same time restricted, accent is common to Greek and Israeli Hebrew. – There is no relation between this phenomenon and what RABIN (1958: 249) terms "emphatic or oppositional accent" in Israeli Hebrew, e.g. mízraxit 'Eastern' used in the context of máaravit 'Western' (transcriptions mine; H. R.); RABIN neglects the fact that the word accent on the final syllable is present, but weaker than the "emphatic" stress on the first syllable. It appears that the "emphatic" accent is nothing more than an overstrong secondary stress on the antepenult; RABIN observes that "the emphatic accent that always falls on the first syllable is found only in words of three or more syllables" (RABIN 1958: 249).

individualized versus common noun	habíma (the national theatre)	habima 'the stage'
	mizráxi (common last name; also name of political party)	mizraxi 'oriental'
	hapó'el (Workers' Sports Association)	hapo'el 'the worker'
	tnúva (agricultural marketing organisation)	tnuva 'field produce'
specialized slang meaning versus common standard use	búlim 'collected stamps (postal or other)'	bulim 'stamps for official use (postal revenue, validation, etc.)'
	balášim 'crime stories'	balašim 'detectives'
	'íza 'pet goat'	'iza 'goat'
	maspíkim 'marks termed "sufficient"'	maspikim 'sufficient (m.pl.)'
recognized loan versus 'native' word	plágim 'sparking plugs'	plagim 'factions'
	germániy 'Teutonic'	germaniy 'German'
	pásim 'gate passes'	pasim 'stripes'
acronym versus morphologically analysable noun	mašákim (army acronym for non-commissioned officer)	mašakim 'reverberatory noises'

It would appear from the grouping of examples in our list that two layers may here be distinguished: one, in which the non-final accent is merely the result of the avoidance of stressing a Hebrew suffixal morpheme following a foreign, or otherwise extra-systemic stem (*studént-im, plág-im, 'óperot:* cf. GARBELL 1930: 26; ROSÉN 1955a: 235-6; 1962a: 334), while in the other group, in which the words are, generally, Hebrew heritage, the contrastive penult stress is operative irrespective of whether or not the noun has a suffixed morpheme. We have here consequently, two unlike phenomena: in the first-mentioned group the extra-systemic (foreign) noun is not characterized by the non-final stress; it is rather that its proper (original) stress whether final or not *(studént, 'ópera)* is maintained notwithstanding any native suffixation.[75]

It is in the first group (where penult stress was not necessarily correlated to retraction of the accent from a suffix) that the stress feature has developed into a class marker by becoming apparent in nouns where no contrast to a finally stressed one could be intended, since none was in existence. Penult stress became to be considered, by speakers and scholars alike (GOMPERTZ 1938: 101; ROSÉN 1953b: 23-4) the formal sign of a 'name'. The trouble was that names did not unexceptionally bear non-final stress and some rule was required.

[75] This phenomenon is liable to emerge in languages in which inflexional or derivational suffixes attract, on the strength of a native structural rule, the word accent; cf., e.g., for Turkish, where proper names, loans, and some other word classes are accentually treated similarly to Hebrew (LEWIS 1957: 21-2), the (however, from the Turkish point of view no longer analysable) penult stressed *efendim* 'mein Herr'. For the purpose of looking for a model of Israeli Hebrew, it would be more worthwhile to think of Russian, where suffixal accentuation and accent shift in inflexion are largely shirked by non-native nouns. – One, I think merely apparent, exception is significant. Loans with the Latin *-tor/-sor* suffix are (as in Latin) penult stressed in the singular (*dóktor, profésor, senátor*), but have penult stress on the suffix in the plural (*doktórim*, etc.). This phenomenon, which is just slightly losing ground very recently, hails from Yiddish, where, oddly enough, foreign (i.e. non-German) nouns show a predilection for the foreign (in this case Hebrew) plural suffix: *dókter: doktóyrim* (stressed *óy* is a regular pseudo-Ashkenazoid Hebrew substitute for Germ. *ó*; cf. *groys* 'big'). We may consider this formational type in Israeli Hebrew as a "back-migrant" from Yiddish, so that there would be no real deviation from the basic rules.

Some place-names are finally stressed, the majority are not. Do these groups represent "layers", and are we faced with one of the phenomena of colonization history linguistically reflected? Some suggestions were made (KUTSCHER 19 ç: 38; LARISH 1933: 84) according to which it would be conceivable₉to draw a demarcation line between the two groups according to the date of the foundation of the village or town concerned, that is at the end of the last immigrants wave from Eastern Europe, so that thereafter the influence of Yiddish with its Ashkenazi-Polish fashion of stressing Hebrew at the word penult would be excluded. But these suggestions do not account for all the facts and although we have no other proposal to make, we must dismiss them as not entirely satisfactory.

The matter is more lucid with ethnics. Here the correlation between stress retraction and the historical-cultural background is fairly obvious. While ethnic nouns and adjectives in -*i(y)* are, as a rule, penult stressed (*bélgi*), the suffix is accented where the name of the country is not the original one, but appears in a traditional Hebrew form (e.g. *carfati* from *carfat* 'France') or where the country or nation concerned must be considered culturally familiar[76] to Eastern European Jewry at about the time of the first resettlement of Palestine, e.g. *rusi, germani, 'angli* (this is linked with a particular formation of the designation of the female: *germaniya* and *carfatiya* 'Frenchwoman' versus *bélgit, šváycit,* and *yugoslávit*, more comprehensive information will be found in ROSÉN 1955a: 236; 1962a: 201–2). This is a striking example of the fact that foreignness cannot be determined by etymological considerations, nor can a noun's status as a proper noun (name) be determined extra-linguistically on the strength of realia.

3.7.6 Stylistic value of stress

While we have said above (*3.7.3*) that final word stress is devoid of any morphological or lexical function, we have to accord it some STYLISTIC VALUE, simply because the cases of presuffixal and stem prominence are campaigned against by purists. Saying [belgít] or

---

[76] Different grammatical treatment of geographical names according to whether they are 'culturally familiar' or not, is by no means limited to Israeli Hebrew. In ROSÉN (1958: 72), I brought undisputed parallels from Classical Greek (WACKERNAGEL 1926-28 2: 223), after my French parallels (*en* vs. *au* or *dans la*) had been questioned by BLANC (1956: 802); however, one of his two authorities, GREVISSE (1955: 241), was himself taken to task in this connection by GOUGENHEIM (1956: 78).

[studentím] characterizes the speaker as stilted or places him in the category of those whose professional activities (such as a being a radio announcer, an orthoepy teacher, or the like) oblige them to yield to purist demands.

4 CONTENT AND LEXICON

4.1 THE ABSORPTION OF THE INHERITED LEXICON

4.1.1 Old and new words, old and new meanings

Looking at the Israeli Hebrew lexicon, one is very easily tempted to divide the inventory of words into old and new ones. Part of the new ones are coined (and the non-professional observer often considers word coining the essence of the newness of Israeli Hebrew), part have developed from usage, the speaker very frequently being unaware of their lexical novelty. But since a lexical entity has two facets, it will be linguistically of considerable importance to bear in mind that a classically attested word can be – due to its novel content – just as new as an unattested one. Describing supposed changes of meaning would be of no use; we are, in fact, confronted with a phenomenon of superimposing inherited words on an underlying content structure. This content structure being essentially non-Hebraic, the sources of the currently existing semantic ranges have to be examined. The

transition to semantic values hailing from European languages can be noticed throughout the entire vocabulary of modern Hebrew (TUBIE-LEWICZ 1956: 345),

and we can do no more in the limits of the present exposition than to illustrate the principal processes involved by some telling case histories.

4.1.2 The Biblical layer of vocabulary and exegetical tradition

The BIBLE is still the primary point of departure for word meanings. (Exactly what part of the Hebrew Bible played an important enough role to be included in the lexicon of traditional Jewish learning alongside rabbinical literature, has not yet been thoroughly examined.)

But [...] that ancient language, contained in the small number of Hebrew[77] books within the Bible, [...] was not even all known to us, [...] For practical use the Biblical vocabulary was accepted mainly in those meanings and usages prevalent in Jewish traditional exegesis (TUR-SINAI 1952: 35).

There is no point in establishing, by way of research, the meaning of a Biblical Hebrew word and contrasting the latter to its current lexical value: not infrequently, the difference is between the scientific truth and EXEGETICAL TRADITION, and not a result of linguistic history.

4.1.3 The impact of Bible translations

However, Jewish exegesis was not the only channel through which the Biblical Hebrew lexicon had reached the Western Jew at the eve of the Revival. The use of the Biblical Hebrew ḥašmal or ḥašmalá (recalled to life in the latter form in the eighteen-seventies; now xašmal) for 'electricity' is founded on a knowledge of Christian-canonic versions: LXX ἤλεκτρον, Vulgate electrum 'amber' or 'gold and silver alloy'.[78] The Hebrew word was retrieved from the vocabulary of the versions.

It is possible that a difference of meaning between Biblical Hebrew and Israeli Hebrew (usually restriction) is not, in fact, a

[77] Part of the non-biblical inherited stock is Aramaic (from rabbinical literature); where there coexist Aramaic and Hebrew forms for approximately the same content (cf. also below, 6.5.2), the former usually holds the position of the 'learned' layer (ROSÉN 1955a: 83–8). J. KLAUSNER (1948) objects to the use of such Aramaic doublets.
[78] Three occurrences in Ezekiel; the second translation is in all likelihood the appropriate one, but only the first one furnishes an association with electricity.

6*

development of Hebrew, but one of a TRANSLATION LANGUAGE, which in the cases under examination turns out to be German. Biblical Hebrew *śimlâ* 'apparel, raiment' (*RV*, irrespective of the wearer's sex, also of soldiers) > Israeli Hebrew *simla* 'a woman's dress': Germ. *Kleid*, originally 'piece of cloth', since MHG 'piece of clothing', is Luther's standard equivalent for Biblical Hebrew *śimlâ;* the singular specialized not earlier than the end of the eighteenth century to the sense of 'a piece of woman's clothing'; the crucial process was the inversion of the lexical equation: from *simla* = *Kleid, Kleid* = *simla* was derived (ROSÉN 1969: 97). In the realm of verbs, an apparent "restriction of meaning" is the specialization of Biblical Hebrew *nâsaʿ* 'moved (intr.), migrated' to Israeli Hebrew *nasaʾ* 'moved by vehicle'; again the transition is in German: Luther's word for *nâsaʿ* is *fuhr*, which, except in metaphorical uses and in compounds, since the nineteenth century denotes only mechanical movement, not only the rider's movement by vehicle, but also the vehicle's; the same holds for Israeli Hebrew *ha-rakevèt nosaàt* 'der Zug fährt'.

4.1.4 Extra-Jewish traditions

Although Jewish translations of the Bible into German were well known in the period of "Enlightenment", the facts just shown significantly locate the cultural awareness of the European "enlightened" Jew in a particular Biblical-ecclesiastical environment. From some cases, it is quite obvious that "Biblical" notions were channelled, for the purposes of the Revival, through ecclesiastical channels. E.g., Biblical Hebrew *malʾâk* 'messenger' > Israeli Hebrew *malʾax* 'angel' (up to the twenties still 'ambassador') reflects the well-known restriction of Vulg.Lat. *angelus* to 'heavenly messenger', while other instances of LXX ἄγγελος are rendered *nuntius*. The proverbial *einsamer Rufer* (or *Prediger*) *in der Wüste* corresponds to an Israeli Hebrew idiomatic *kol koreʾ ba-midbar* 'a voice calling in the desert' or 'voice of a caller in the desert'; the faulty division of the verse *Is* 40.3 "The voice of him that crieth in the wilderness prepare ye the way of the Lord" (verse structure demands punctuation before *in the wilderness*) is not Jewish tradition, but a theological desideratum to sanction the exegetically and evangelically "necessary" misdivision in the New Testament, where (e.g. *Matth.* 3.1–3) John the Baptist is identified as the evangelic "caller in the wilderness" making explicit reference to the verse from Isaiah. This is one of the re-migrant biblicisms, whose non-Jewish physiognomy cannot be concealed.

An analogous example is that of Biblical Hebrew *p·âqad* 'visited' (*in malam et in bonam partem:* 'visit somebody',· 'visit upon somebody'), which engendered the famous Hebraism of ecclesiastical Latin, *uisitatio (in malam partem);* the fact that Israeli Hebrew has dropped the *in bonam partem* reference appears to be due to translational influence (*heimsuchen*).

4.1.5 Shift of semantic centre

The case of *p·âqad* is the more significant, since the semantic shade *heimsuchen* was, in fact, already present in Biblical Hebrew, but as a noncentral range of meaning. What was noncentral in Biblical Hebrew, is now central. This SHIFT OF THE SEMANTIC CENTRE is a phenomenon not unknown in the lexical history of languages; however, in the case of Hebrew, we are confronted not with a historical development, but with an external process. In numerous cases, what would appear by juxtaposition of Classical and Hebrew meanings to be 'semantic change' (cf. H.M. COHEN 1951: 78–9), is not a diachronic process at all.

4.1.6 Spurious semantic change

It is not very easy to distinguish in every case between GENUINE and SPURIOUS SEMANTIC CHANGE. The dictionaries make no effort whatsoever to keep them apart (ROSÉN 1955a: 100–5, with telling examples). E.g. *carevèt* Class. Heb. 'scar' > Israeli Hebrew 'heartburn' is not a "semantic change", but a reconstitution of the inherited word on the root *c-r-v* (Classical only intransitive 'be scorched'; in Israeli Hebrew, ground stem active introduced in the figurative sense of 'burning', transitive, with the passive preserving also the original sense); in this and other nouns, the formation pattern ...*a*...*e*...*èt* has undergone the semantic change from 'injury' to 'ailment (characterized by the root content)'.

4.2 WESTERNIZED SEMANTIC CIRCUMSCRIPTION

4.2.1 Hebrew-European correspondence of unit lexemes

A step preliminary to the Westernizing circumscription of semantic ranges (by calque, loan translation, or otherwise) of existing lexical entities was a tendency to create a formal one-to-one correspondence of lexemes between Hebrew and the principal substrate languages.

UNIT LEXEMES began to be preferred to multilexemic circumlocutions, in correspondence with monolexematic European expressions (AVINERY 1946: 48–54): *sefèr-milim* (*sefèr* 'book', *milim* 'words') > *milon* 'dictionary, Wörterbuch'; *beyt-ntivot* (*beyt-* 'house of', *ntivot* 'paths') > *taxana* 'station' (the former expression recently reintroduced for 'airport terminal'); *beyt-sfarim* > *sifriya* 'library'; *bate-yadayìm* (*bate-* 'houses of', *yadayìm* 'hands') > *šarvulim* 'sleeves', *kfafot* 'gloves'. One can easily see that this tendency not only contributed to an increased lexical differentiation, but also enlarged the impact of derivatory processes that had gradually come to replace the compounding ones. Increased derivation moves the question of conceptual relations into the limelight of linguistic research.

4.2.2 Calques, loan-translations

It is not always easy to distinguish CALQUES, LOAN-TRANSLATIONS, and the imprinting of inherited lexical units with European semantic ranges. While the use of the often discussed *šerut* (EYTAN 1950: 13.13; ROSÉN 1955a: 80–1; 1969: 97–8) in *šerut xaša'i* 'secret service', *šerut xitulim* 'diaper service', and *šerut mdina* 'Staatsdienst, civil service' is undoubtedly due to civilisatory loan-translation, the abundance of such uses could not fail to impart to *šerut* the compact referential range precisely of "European" *service*;

šerut = 'service' is a perfectly adequate lexical equation for Israeli Hebrew, by which the word is set off from its classical antecedent which essentially denoted 'public or holy office' (cf. *Gottes-dienst*). The question of whether Israeli Hebrew calques, irrespective of their immediate model (GARBELL (1931: 34–41) lists, under "Beein-flussung der Begriffsbedeutung", apart from "Europeanisms", Germanisms, Russicisms, and a few Yiddishisms), exceed the limits set by the European *Sprachausgleich*, has never been put: the case of *šerut* and the few others studied (such as *tnu'a* 'movement' (also in the political sense); *sviva* 'environment'; *gibor* 'hero' (also literary); *lehakdiš* 'dedicate, *widmen*'; *mo'eca* (Class.) '*consilium*', (Israeli Hebrew) '*concilium*') would tend to indicate that genuine Israeli Hebrew calques remain in the domain of the Pan-European lexicon.[79]

4.3 ISRAELI HEBREW CONTENT STRUCTURE

4.3.1 Western conceptual ranges

That the CONTENT STRUCTURE of Israeli Hebrew is essentially Western can be shown by the CONCEPTUAL RANGE of its words, and, on a higher level, by the existing conceptual relations. Those concepts denoted by word units, that were not subject to direct calque, were, over a generation at least, established without the speakers' being aware of any semantic difference between a current lexeme and its classical antecedent, by way of an illegitimate inversion of lexico-semantic equations (from *nasaa* = '*fuhr*' it follows that *fuhr* = '*nasaa*'; cf. *4.1.3*). Very frequently, the catalysing language can be readily identified, and more often than not it is, for the early layer of Israeli Hebrew at least, Russian; e.g.: *lecayen* (class.) 'mark', (Israeli Hebrew) 'point out' = замечать 'note, notice, remark, observe' (related to метка 'mark, sign'); *giša* (class.) 'act of approaching', (Israeli Hebrew) 'access, approach,

---

[79] What authors occasionally quote as striking loan-translation or calque, is very often aberrant usage or may reflect their own unintegrated idiolect (this is the case with many of the *leenvertalingen* in H.M. COHEN 1951: 97–9).

attitude' = отношение 'approach(ing), attitude'; *lvanim* (pl. of
'white') (class.) 'white clothes', (Israeli Hebrew) 'washing' = бельё
'white (pl.), washing'; *leharbic* (class.) 'lay on', (Israeli Hebrew)
'spank' = накласть 'lay on, spank' (cf. GARBELL 1930: 36;
ROSÉN 1969: 102-3). There is hardly a noun, the purport of which
conveys some degree of abstraction, for which this semantic transfer
is not observable; but the phenomenon has been in steady recession
since the thirties when, in certain avenues, Russicizing ranges came
to be replaced either by German or by "more Hebraic" ones. The
following are random samples:

For 'vote cast' early Israeli Hebrew had *de'a* 'opinion', correspondingly
to мнение 'opinion, vote'; it is now replaced by *kol* 'voice', which
corresponds to голос 'voice, vote' and Germ. *Stimme* at the same time.
– 'Recognition' in the legal sense was, at one time, *lehodot* 'admit,
confess, express thanks', which could be considered as being included
in the range of признавать 'recognize, admit, be thankful, legitimate'
(cf. Germ. *anerkennen*); the current expression is now *lehakir* with *be*-
case government, while the same verb with *'et*-government (p. *7.1.4*) is
equivalent to 'recognize' in a non-technical sense; the German relation
between *erkennen* and *anerkennen* was most likely a supporting factor
of this development. – 'Strengthen' and 'fortify' were not differentiated
(both *lehagbir*), as in крепить; they are now kept apart by the use of
lexazek for 'strengthen' and *letagber* for 'reinforce', versus *lehagbir*
'fortify, increase'. Likewise, *leyased* (earlier 'found, set up, establish',
now only 'found') appears to have covered основывать; 'set up = establish' is now covered by the classical *lehakim*, causative of *lakum*
'rise > stand'.

The recession of Slavic substrate effects is perhaps also responsible
for the semantic history, within revived Hebrew, of the curious *pitka*
'slip of paper'. Greek πιττάκιον had penetrated the cultural areas
of waning antiquity in two subdivided semantic ranges: the original
value 'tablet to write on' had specialized, in the West,[80] to 'a small piece

---

[80] Rumanian *petec, petic* has preserved both, but a reintroduction of
the Byzantine word may have taken place secondarily. WARTBURG (1956:
104–6) discusses the Romance ramifications of the word according to whether
or not the gemination of *t* is preserved. I do not understand why Romanists
have never proposed this word as an etymon for *pièce* (which would be a regular development in view of Sp. *pedazo*) or for Germ. *Fetze(n)* (cf. *Flaum* <
< *pluma*). Significantly enough this is what is said in this respect in Jacob
Grimm's *Deutsches Wörterbuch* on the origin of *Fetze(n)* which, in its earliest

of material' (neglecting the 'writing' aspect), and in the East, to 'written note, official paper, document, decree' (neglecting the 'material' aspect). The Byzantine semantic ramifications of the word are faithfully reflected in its use in Talmudic Aramaic. Up to the late forties, this was the current use of the word in Israeli Hebrew, certainly in wide circles of officialdom; ROSENBERG (1900: 89) even has it for a doctor's prescription (in current school and workers' slang, a *pitka me-rofe'* 'slip from a doctor' is a sick certificate). We would have to say that, in current Israeli Hebrew, the word had reverted to its original Greek (!) value (it denotes a piece of paper, usable for writing, but irrespective of whether or not anything is written on it), were it not for the effect of FOREIGN PHONETIC SIMILARITY that was operative, in this case and in some others, in supporting semantic ranges, and even occasionally even in creating them ("Begriffsumwandlung durch klangliche Anlehnung an Fremdwörter"; GARBELL 1930: 40–1). Taking into account the Ashkenazic (*3.2.1*) sound form of the word, *píska* (ROSENBERG 1893: 109; so in Eastern European Yiddish derivatives, while Israeli Yiddish prefers the probably Hebraizing variant *pítke*), the homophony with Russian записка is obvious: this Slavic word, derived from a compound of the verbal root (*pis-*) for 'writing', has precisely the range of 'registration (certificate), written note, (Germ.) *Schein*, slip of paper' and should be held responsible for the survival of the Talmudic range of our word in early Israeli Hebrew. The recession of Slavo-biased 'etymological' consciousness resulted in the loss of the semantic element of 'writing': since the word has no internal etymological relations in Hebrew, the 'material' aspect gained predominance, and a fairly recent verbal derivative (*pitek*) means 'extracted (data) on slips'.

4.3.2 Semantic motivation and notional structure

Semantic MOTIVATION in word formation reveals the Western NOTIONAL STRUCTURE of Israeli Hebrew. As a rule, if some content relation corresponds to a given formal relation between a motivating and a motivated Hebrew form, we can expect to find in some European language an equivalent relation on the content level

---

attestations, depreciatively stands (pl.) for 'rags', later for any piece of cloth (e.g. a flag) or of clothes: "Das it. *pezzo*, fr. *pièce*, it. *fetta* und *fettuccia* scheinen dem wort und sinne nach verwandt, enthalten jedoch nur die vorstellung des abgerissenen oder geschnittenen stücks, nicht des gewandes selbst, weshalb die heimische abkunft von *fasz*, kleid, den vorzug verdient."

between the denotatum of the motivating form and the one that is
formally motivated analogously to Hebrew ("Nachbildungen";
GARBELL 1930: 41–6):

mixbasa 'laundry': *lexabes* 'wash linen' = X 'sidewalk': *lidrox*
'tread'

yields a solution for X by association with French *trottoir* 'sidewalk': *trotter* 'tread': $X = midraxa$.

'*iton* 'newspaper': '*it-* 'time' = X 'weekly paper': *šavua* 'week'

is solved on grounds of Germ. *Zeitung* : *Zeit* in terms of $X = $
šavuᵓon.[81]

Very often, the mere fact of formal derivation, irrespective of the
normal content of the derivational morpheme, attaches the derived
word semantically to its base form according to some European
model : *maxsanit* 'magazine (of a fire-arm)' : *maxsan* 'store' (Germ.
Magazin).

4.3.3 Hebrew-European parallelism of semantic motivation

The conceptual parallelism with European languages can be fully
achieved only if a derived word is the equivalent of a derived one, a
unit lexeme of a unit lexeme, and a compound of a compound. That
there is a marked tendency in this direction has been shown above
(*2.3.2*, for the type *kapit, gumiya; 4.2.1* for the type *milon*).
In fact, there is a marked parallelism of means of lexical derivation,
which is operative in suffixation (e.g. hypocoristics: *sus-on* 'little
horse', cf. Gm. *Pferd-chen*; nomina loci: *masger-iya* 'locksmith's
shop', cf. *Schlosser-ei*; nomina qualitatis: *nox-ut*, colloquially *nox-
iy-ut*, 'comfort, ease', cf. *Bequem-lich-keit;* professional or habitual

---

[81] BEN-YEHUDA is responsible for the misinterpretation of Germ. *Zeitung*
by basing it on the 'time' concept.

agents: *sarv-an* 'object-or', cf. *Verweiger-er*, and *gan-an*[82] 'garden-er', cf. *Gärtn-er*; occupational names: *'iton-a(')i* 'journal-ist', *xašm(a)la(')i* 'electric-ian'), less in prefixation (only in "oppo-sites" : *bilti-* 'un-' (cf. *6.4.2*), *'i-* 'in-', with occasional mimicry of a Neo-Latin consonantal assimilation: *'i-reguláriy* 'ir-regular'). The complete morphemic correspondence that can be achieved between Israeli Hebrew and European intellectual language (e.g. *'i-'efšar-ut* 'im-possibil-ity, *Un-möglich-keit'*) reminds one strongly of Cicero-nian Latinizations and eighteenth century *Verdeutschungen*: the process as such is already typologically significant.

4.3.4 Adaptation of types of morphological processes to types of semantic motivation

Although none of the afformatives that make the one-to-one corre-spondence with European languages possible is in any way an in-novation in Hebrew, every one of them has come to make compet-ing non-affixal means of expression for the same derivational category obsolete. The alternative morphological processes that are hardly productive any more and are being replaced by the affixal ones consist in, or entail, vocalic pattern changes, such as the use of $C_1aC_2aC_3$ for 'professional or habitual agents' (*nahag* 'driver', *sapar* 'hairdresser'). It is obvious that these older forma-tional processes would have impaired the freedom of derivation, because they cannot be readily applied to any base form of more than three consonantal elements and would moreover, if applied, obliterate the predetermined vocalic pattern of the motivating form (cf. ROSÉN 1955a: 231). The *-ut* suffix (nomina qualitatis) has gained the upper hand over the inherited $C_1oC_2eC_3$ pattern (*kocèr*

---

[82] This is metanalysis; etymologically, *ganan* (*g·an·àn*) is a *katal* (*qat·àl*) formation ('name of profession') from *gan* 'garden', whose root final was originally long (*g·an-*). The metanalysis results, through interpretation of the final *-an* as a suffix, in the formation of a feminine *ganan-it* (regular formation for nouns that bear a suffix in the masculine form); while the feminine form that would correspond to the classical formation *qat·àl* (*katelèt*) has a differen-tiated meaning: *ganenèt* 'Kinder-gärtnerin' (BEN-ḤAYYIM 1953: 34); cf. *gan* (*-yladim*) 'kindergarten'.

'shortness': *kacar* 'short'), with some semantic differentiation involved, whereby the *-ut* formations function as nominalizations proper: from *gadol* 'big, great' – *godèl* 'size' *(uox media)* versus *gadlut* 'greatness'; from *kašer* 'qualified, fit, suitable, kosher' – *košèr* 'fitness' *(vox media)* versus *kašrut* 'quality of being kosher, ritual observance'. In some cases, the nonsuffixal derivation is relegated to the marginal lexical level *(3.7.5)*: *motèk* 'honey = darling' (but the abstract from *matok* 'sweet' is *mtikut*), *xomèd* 'darling' *(nexmad* 'nice', abstract *nexmadut)*, *šomèn* 'fatty, fat thing (affective)' (from *šamen* 'fat'). For diminutives, the inherited $C_1C_2aC_3C_2VC_3$-pattern, involving consonantal reduplication, only persists in inherited words, mainly in nursery language: x^a*taltul* 'little cat' : *xatul* 'cat'; earlier *klavlav* 'doggy' (nursery style) is replaced by *kalbon* (base form *kalb-* 'dog'). By this development, the $C_1C_2aC_3C_2VC_3$-pattern has become available for greater productivity in the qualified (quasi-diminutive) adjective class, a derivational category that is not at all deeply rooted in European languages and could not induce a compulsory affixation process in Israeli Hebrew; e.g.: *šxarxar* 'blackish', x^a*macmac* 'sourish', *karir* 'chilly'.

Once the functional identity between these suffixes and their respective foreign equivalents was established, they constituted semantic entities, which were liable to undergo all "influences" discussed above for free lexemes. In particular, they acquired new semantic ranges in accordance with European models; e.g. *-ut* added 'community' to its range: *yahadut* 'Judaism, Jewry' (cf. *Judentum* or *Judenheit*, жидейство); *nacrut* 'Christendom' *(Christentum, -heit,* христианство); *pkidut* 'civil service *(Beamtenschaft)*'; *soxnut* 'agency'; cf. ROSÉN (1955a: 242).

4.3.5 New derivational categories

The creation of NEW DERIVATIONAL CATEGORIES supports the general assimilation to Western systems. Biblical Hebrew had a form of ground stem passive nouns – *qāṭi·l* (e.g. *'āsi·r* 'prisoner', *māši·ᵃḥ* 'the anointed one') –, differentiated from passive perfect participles by vowel alternation *i/u* only (*'āsu·r* 'bound', *māšu·ᵃḥ* 'anointed').

The second form has remained productive throughout the history
of Hebrew (Israeli Hebrew $C_1aC_2uC_3$ 'pass.perf.part.'), while
qåṭi·l had to lead a precarious existence in the shadow of the inter-
fering Aramaic passive participle formation *qṭi·l* (in all suffixed
forms, the Hebrew types mentioned lose their *å*, so that in certain
derivations it cannot be told whether the basic form is Hebrew or
Aramaic in origin). The latently surviving *katil* was therefore readily
available in the thirties or forties, in order to join *katul* in a binary
derivational category as the equivalent of what was, in European or
Neo-Latin systems, much more closely associated with a passive
participle than with a nomen patientis, namely an ADMISSIVE
PARTICIPLE (cf. *6.3.4*): *šavir* 'fragile' versus *šavur* 'broken' (cf.
BLANC 1957: 406). In the first stage, 'faculty' was more noticeable
as semantic component than 'passivity': *pa'il* 'having the faculty
of acting, act-ive' (later *savil* 'passive' was added), and *gamiš* (basic
verb not in use) 'having the faculty of bending, elastic'; but soon
the ...*a*...*i*... pattern became the outright translational equivalent of *-able* (cf. *elastic* = *flexible*): *xadir* 'penetrable', *raxic*
'washable', and *'avir* 'passable', to cite some of the more recent
neologisms. The equivalence with *-able* seems to have been operative even where no passive connotation attached to the latter:
savir 'reasonable' (of animates as well as of abstracts, e.g. *mxir
savir* 'reasonable price'). While the *katil* pattern's being based on
vowel alternation does not essentially contradict Israeli Hebrew
typological features that maintained vowel alternation as a morphological process in verbs and verb-related forms, it still has a double
disadvantage: it is derivable only from the ground stem (a recent
kavil 'admissible (legally)' from the *Pi'el* (*6.4.2.2*) *le-kabel* 'receive,
admit' meets with justified objection) and, at any rate, only from
triconsonantal radicals (*6.1.2*); and, secondly, it does not answer
to the affixal nature of the *-able*-formations by a similarly affixal
process. Both shortcomings are remedied by a competing formation: *bar-*+action noun; e.g.: *bar-tikun* (*tikun* 'repair') 'reparable',
or *bar-haxlafa* 'changeable, convertible'. *Bar-* is the Aramaic equivalent of *ben* 'son', and the Hebrew forms *bat-*, *bne-*, and *bnot-* are
used in the f.sg., m.pl., and f.pl. forms, respectively, of these ad-

missive deverbatives: *bne-haxlafa*. This formation has honoured antecedents in precisely the conditions in which a *katil* form could not be derived: Hebrew *ben-mavèt* (the verbal stem of *met* 'died' is biconsonantal) 'subject to death, a person punishable by death', *ben-tmuta* (same stem) 'mortal', Aramaic (which had no *qåṭiˑl*) *bar-qyåmå* > Israeli Hebrew *bar-kayma* 'maintainable, enduring', *bar-miṣwå* 'subject to commandments'. *Bar*-formations are currently freely innovated in equivalence to the (likewise affixal) *-able*; whether the *Anklang* (*4.3.1*) with Germ. *-bar* (as in *trag-bar* 'portable') was a supporting factor, I would not venture to judge.

Another newly introduced derivational category is that of the HYPOCO-RISTICS (ALTBAUER 1949). Due to the stylistic level of these nouns, their formative suffix is still generally the original foreign one: *bubèlè* (Yiddish suffix) of *buba*, *bubà* 'doll'; *katančìk* (Slavo-Yiddish suffix) 'little one, Kleiner' of *katan* 'small'; *rútì* (German-English suffix) of *rút* 'Ruth'; *dubì* 'teddybear' of base *dub-* 'bear' (competing form with Israeli Hebrew diminutive suffix (see *4.3.4*) *dubon*); four hypocoristics of *moše* 'Moses': *mošèlè* (or genuine Yiddish *moyšèlè*), *mošíkò*, *mošon*, of which the last two have Ladino-originating suffixes.

4.4 ETYMOLOGICAL RELATIONS

4.4.1 Etymological consciousness

ETYMOLOGICAL CONSCIOUSNESS has always been an important factor in the creation of the Israeli Hebrew vocabulary, at the form as well as at the content level. Etymological consciousness means, for our purposes, awareness of the root; and roots being very much alike in Semitic languages, etymological notions could easily embrace languages other than Hebrew. This is the appropriate point to reiterate that the notion 'of foreign language' *(loaziy)* is one that does not include Aramaic, with the result that much Aramaic material was included in the inherited stock in a form that was indistinguishable from Hebrew; where some external characteristics set a form off from genuine Hebraic elements in some respect, the Aramaic-garbed word (against the inclusion on whose kin in revived Hebrew there had been some campaigning; cf. J. KLAUSNER 1948) acquired a stylistic status of "more intellectual", "more technical", "more literary" than what could be considered its Hebrew semantic or formal counterpart (ROSÉN 1955a: 84–8; 1958c: 68–9).

4.4.2 Word coining

Another effect of the inclusion of other Semitic languages in the "etymological consciousness" operative in WORD COINING and assignment of meanings is the exploitation of the Arabic lexicon in the earliest work of the then Hebrew Language Council (*Zixronot* 4 (1914): 4–66). This was the practice advocated by BEN-YEHUDA;[83] LIPSCHÜTZ, who was BEN-YEHUDA's opponent in the discussion in the Council, objected to

die unnötige Einführung arabischer Wörter, ferner die Benutzung arabischer Wurzeln mit neuen hebräischen Formen oder gar die künstliche Vornahme des spezifischen hebräischen Lautwandels an arabischen Wurzeln (LIPSCHÜTZ 1920: 38–9).

Among the takeovers from Arabic (a considerable part of which are basic stock of everyday Hebrew; cf. GARBELL 1930: 32), one finds more words in which Arabic phonemes foreign to Hebrew are replaced by Hebrew ones by way of nearest phonetic approximation (e.g. *dura, dúra* 'maize' < Arab. *ðura* '*idem*', although etymologically Arab. *ð* corresponds to Hebrew *z*) than words in which an imitation of a genealogical sound correspondence is attempted (Israeli Hebrew *rišmiy* 'official' < Arab. *rasmiy* '*idem*', supported by the pair of synonymous roots Heb. *r-š-m* and Arab. *r-s-m* 'write down, sketch').

4.4.3 Synchronic etymology

The conscious etymological relations between the items of a vocabulary, on which the notional structure of a language is of necessity based, are not scientifically discovered historical truths, but those

---

[83] For the Arabic element, particularly in early word coining (BEN-YEHUDA), see SIVAN (1961, 1966) and PIAMENTA (1961).

that constitute the SYNCHRONIC ETYMOLOGY (cf. VENDRYES 1953) of
the language concerned. While for certain words synchronic etymology is different from the historical one, it must not be confused
with what is commonly termed "popular etymology". Popular etymology results in a change of the formal aspect of the word, more
often than not giving the word an appearance quasi-etymologically
closer to its transmitted meaning (*utmost* < ME. *utemest*); synchronic etymology does not touch the expressional facet of the lexeme,
but tampers with its content, in that it contributes to fixing a semantic range or central value that fits apparent etymological relations with an existing word family ("MORPHO-SEMANTIC FIELD";
GUIRAUD 1956). While no cases of popular etymology have been
discovered in Israeli Hebrew, there is a sizable number of semantic
developments due to synchronic etymology (ROSÉN 1958a: 31–9 =
1966a: 35–44), none of which constitutes outright semantic change:
in all of these cases, the word undergoing the process hooks on to
some part of its historical area of reference[84] which appears to be
close enough to the "cognates" in the morpho-semantic fields, and
makes this subarea its central semantic value.

Usually, the word affected by the process stems from some Aramaic
root and has been absorbed into postbiblical Hebrew;[85] the Aramaic

---

[84] Semantic developments due to synchronic etymology are thus the counterpart of calques (*4.4.2*): in the latter the result of the process is an extension of
the original range.

[85] Scientifically unsound "etymology"-supported interpretations of relatively
obscure Biblical words are not a process within revived Hebrew. *Kesèt*, used
in *Ezek* 13.18, 20 to denote a sewn object to supply support for a seated body,
in Israeli Hebrew means 'featherbed', on the basis of its being linked to the
root *k-s-* 'cover'; howevei, according to LIPSCHÜTZ (1920: 36), this goes back
as far as the 12th century. The case of the often discussed *way·itrōṣṣu* (*Gen*
25.22; of what the unborn twins were doing in Rebecca's womb) is not clear
at all: while LXX ἐσκίρτων 'danced' would perfectly fit the central meaning
of IH *hitrocec* 'ran about' (based on the root *r-c*), Jewish and probably Jewish-
inspired interpretation links it to the mainly postbiblical verb *rocec* (root *r-c-c*)
'break by blows' (Vulgate: *collidebantur*). Based on the 'blowing-breaking'
root, the 'movement' component would be implied in the stem formation
(*hit-* 'by mutually alternating action). The situation in Israeli Hebrew is further
complicated by the fact that the referential value 'each other' of the *Hitpaʿel*
stem formation is linked to verbs *pluralia tantum* (cf. JESPERSEN 1911-: 2.183–4),

root is either nonexistent in Hebrew or else has, according to regular sound correspondences a phonemic shape different from its Hebrew cognate. In both cases, the integration of the word in the Israeli Hebrew lexicon is facilitated by attaching it to a "suitable" Hebraic root. Aram. *r-ʿ-ʿ* (cognate of Heb. *r-ṣ-ṣ* 'break') supplied postbiblical *rǎʿuʿaʿ* (participial formation) 'broken'; by attaching it to the root *r-ʾ* (<*r-ʿ*) 'bad', Israeli Hebrew restricts its range to 'useless, because unstable or not solid'). IH *racuc* (which is the exact historical counterpart of *raʾua*) means 'broken (in a figurative sense, as with fatigue)'; the famous *qǎne rǎṣuʿṣ* (e.g. *Is* 36.6) 'broken reed' (on which one cannot lean) would, in fact, have to be translated into Israeli Hebrew as *kane raʾua*. –The Aramaic root *ṣ-b-ʸ/ʾ* '*uelle*' yields a postbiblical Hebrew abstract *ṣibyōn* 'will, pleasure', which came to be used, in mediaeval literature, in the sense of '*forma*, external appearance, glamour, beauty' (possibly with the support of the Arabic cognate, whose semantic range radiated out of the centre 'desire, desirability'); no other representative of the Aramaic root being synchronically present in the Israeli Hebrew lexicon, *civyon* seems to have been attached to the root *c-v-ʾ* 'colour'; an adequate translation of IH *civyon* is 'shade, shading', which can be still considered as derivable from the mediaeval 'external appearance'.

Synchronic etymology is not impeded by any facts of spelling, that is, historical phonology. Biblical *nǎbǎl* (IH *naval*) 'wicked', *nablu·t* (*navlut*) 'wickedness' join Aramaic-originating Mishnaic *mnuw·ǎl* 'disfigured' to integrate the latter (IH *menuval*) in the sense of 'rascal'. Biblical Hebrew itself supplied what developed into a pair of homophonous synonyms, frequent *t·aʾǎwǎ* (root *ʾ-w-*, pattern *t·a--V-ǎ*) and rare *t·aʾǎbǎ* (root *t-ʾ-b*, no preformative), both 'desire'; IH *taava*, while spelled {t·wh}, became associated with the root *t-ʾ-v* (*ʾ-w-* is no longer prolific) to serve as the action noun of the latter (*t·ev-daàt* 'desirous of knowledge' – *taavat-daàt* 'desire of knowledge'). An abstract formation of that root, rabbinical *t·ēʾǎbon*, had occurred exclusively in syntagms with 'eating' (such as *ʾo·kēl lt·ēʾǎbon* 'eats with lust') and during the first decades of the present century, the 'eating' component was absorbed in it (>*teʾavon* 'appetite'); to express 'appetite', ROSENBERG (1900: 88–9) still uses the

---

or else necessitates a complement introduced by 'with' (cf. below 7.3.4): *hem hitxabku* 'they embraced (each other)' or *hu hitxabek ʾita* 'he embraced her (litterally: with her)'. A sentence *hu hitrocec* (sing.) can consequently be interpreted only on the basis of *r-c* ('he ran to and fro'). In cases in which that same verb occurs in the plural, Israeli Hebrew accordingly preserves some remnants of the semantic component 'conflict' (ROSÉN 1955a: 83).

derivative of the ꜣ-w- root (*taavat-ha-ꜥxila*, literally 'desire of eating').[86]
– Technical term coiners are not above employing pseudoetymological
devices founded on the exploitation of phonemic mergers: the term
introduced for 'direction indicator' (of a motor car) is *maxvan*, which is
spelled {mḥwn} (root *x-v-* 'indicate' from Aramaic, preformative *m-*,
postformative *-n*), but commonly interpreted as based on the stem
-x/k-v-n 'direct' (in that case, the final *-n* is radical).

The examples discussed are indicative of the fact that semantic
ranges developed and fixed on the strength of synchronic etymology
are only one facet of the integration of chronologically heterogeneous linguistic material in the unified language system of Contemporary Hebrew.

---

[86] For 'I like something very much' (. . . *ist mein Leckerbissen*), ROSENBERG
(1900: 74–5) gives the reader the choice of the expression written {tꜣwh npšy}
'my soul desires', but where the pronunciation of the passage is given (ROSEN-
BERG 1900: 103), this idiom is omitted.

5 PARTS OF SPEECH

5.1 CRITERIA OF CLASSIFICATION

5.1.1 Categorial dimensions

Morphologically characterized word classes (parts of speech) can be established with sufficient neatness on the basis of the categorial dimensions TENSE, CASE, GENDER-QUANTITY, and PERSON-SEX-NUMBER. We shall deal in a later chapter (cf. 7) with the nature, as concerns function and content, of these categories, and justify their labels where necessary.

By *case* we mean distinctions expressed by at least some members of the class of bound morphemes *be-*, *le-*, *'et-*, *'al-*, etc. (7.1.4). Gender and quantity (i.e. distinctions on the basis of countability or measurability) have to be united due to the inanalysability of the portmanteau morphemes concerned (e.g., the morpheme *-ot* 'f.pl.' cannot be broken up into discrete elements of gender and number, respectively). The same applies for person, sex, and number: e.g., while in a suffix like *-xen* '2 pers.pl. female' an element *-x-* common to all 2nd persons can be singled out, *-en* is not analysable into separate number and sex morphemes, and a number-sex morpheme will not be found unless amalgamated with the person element. Sex and gender are not distinguished in Israeli Hebrew any more neatly than in most other languages that possess grammatical gender, but since here the "second" persons are sex-characterized, we have a means to keep sex and gender apart: in amalgamation with person, 'm.' and 'f.' morphemes indicate sex primarily ('m.', 'f.' can be interpreted as 'male': 'female', or 'masculine': 'feminine', as the case may demand). That sex and gender are

structurally apart, is indicated by the fact that in gender, morphological marking points to the feminine (*sus* 'horse (male or sex-
uncharacterized)' : *susa* 'mare'), while in (allocutory) sex the opposite is the case ('*at* 'you (one female)' : '*ata* 'you (one male or uncharacterized individual)').[87]

5.1.2 Word classes

While the above-mentioned four dimensions are sufficient for the
basic CLASSIFICATION OF THE PARTS OF SPEECH, more refined sub-
divisions can be obtained by the use of further categories which we
will introduce later in the framework of a more comprehensive
discussion of morphological patterns. These other dimensions may,
on the syntactic level, be as meaningful and operative as the ones
just enumerated: for instance, the structure of nominal sentences
cannot be adequately described without taking into account the
movability of nouns (their being subject to a gender distinction
expressing sex) nor without classing them according to their deter-
minability (determination is not included in our present list). Further refinements will also enable us to determine the exact status of
isolated forms, such as *yeš* '*il y a un...*' and '*eyn* '*il n'y a pas de...*'
that are set off from impersonals by the same categorial dimension
as that which distinguishes their bound counterparts *yešn-*, '*eynen-*
'is (not) here' from participles.[88]

---

[87]   Whether this applies to numerals above 'two' by expansion or is original
with them, I cannot judge. The basic syntagmatic order in Hebrew is determinatum–determinans, but the above-mentioned numerals precede the governing noun (obligatorily in Israeli Hebrew, ordinarily in Biblical Hebrew). If we
wish to maintain that the preceding constituent is the determinatum, then we
must ascribe to the numeral pronominal character and status.

[88]   Cf. *yeš z'ev* 'there is a wolf, a wolf exists' versus *z'ev yešno* 'Zeev (male
first name) is here'. (Of course, such minimal pairs can be established only in
the few cases in which a proper noun is an exact homophone of an appellative.)
Amongst other restrictions of occurrence (ROSÉN 1966a: 214–5), *yeš*, '*eyn*
constitute sentences with undeterminated grammatical subjects, *yešn-*, '*eynen-*
(with person-gender-number-congruent suffixes) with determinated ones.

If it is assumed that every combination is theoretically possible, the four categorial dimensions yield sixteen word classes, of which twelve can be shown to correspond to reality:

	person-sex-number	gender-quantity	case	tense
Finite verb	person-sex-number			tense
Variants different by one dimension:				
Infinitive	person-sex-number[89]			
Impersonal, *yeš*, *'eyn*				tense
Verboid[89]	person-sex-number	gender-quantity		tense
Gerund[89]	person-sex-number		case	tense
Participle, *yešn-*, *'eynen-*		gender-quantity		tense[89]
Adjective		gender-quantity		
Adverb other than local-temporal				
Local-temporal adverb			case	
Toponymic		gender-quantity	case	
Appellative noun	person-sex-number	gender-quantity	case	
Personal pronoun, anthroponymic	person-sex-number		case	

5.1.3 The nominal-verbal dichotomy

These classes can be conveniently grouped into VERBALS (with tense dimension) and NOMINALS (no tense dimension); however, for the description of syntactic behaviour, mainly as a nucleus of endo-centric groups, it will be more useful to divide them in a conven-

---

[89] See below.

tional way and on a shifted level, into VERBS (finite, infinitives, gerunds, and participles), NOUNS (appellatives, personal pronouns, anthroponymics, toponymics), and ADVERBS, while VERBOIDS, IM-PERSONALS, and ADJECTIVES remain unattached. The last-named three parts of speech, whose syntagmatic behaviour cannot be described concurrently with their morphological characteristics, did not exist in earliest known Hebrew and owe their existence to certain historical developments.

5.2 INFINITIVE

The categorial dimension of person-sex-number (for the purposes of the verbal system: agent) has been ascribed to the INFINITIVE, because the infinitive is almost everywhere agent-determined. In a sentence like *Moše roce leexol* 'Moses wants to eat', the very use of the infinitive ascribes (since no other agent is stated) the eating to Moses. If the possibility has to be left open for a person other than the one designated by the grammatical subject of the governing finite verb to function as agent with respect to the infinitive, the construction of the entire sentence has to be changed to allow for explicit specification of that agent:

(1) *moše mevakeš*   *leexol* 'Moses desires to eat'
(2) *moše mevakeš*   *'oxèl*   'Moses asks for food'
(3) *moše mevakeš   mi-yosef* *leexol* 'Moses asks (desires)
                                      Joseph to eat'.[90]

---

[90]   *Mi-yosef* '(from) Joseph' can be deleted from *moše mevakeš mi-yosef 'oxèl* 'M. asks J. for food' without effecting the status of *'oxèl*; with an infinitive instead of the noun *'oxèl*, the situation is different. In dialogue situations, sentence (1) may be interpreted as *moše mevakeš Ø leexol*, where Ø constitutes the inexplicit designation of the interlocutor. (The semantic shade of the verb is rather 'requests' or '*läßt bitten*'; the stylistic variant is indicative of social attitudes.) This instructive example represents, however, a very restricted class of verbs with which the two infinitive constructions (1 and 3) are possible. In these cases, type (1) is stylistically somewhat elevated. Where only type (1) is found with a verb, it is perfectly ordinary style (*moše roce leexol* 'M. wants to eat').

While the infinitive in (1) can be considered to have the status of a nominal object (*'oxèl*), the infinitive in (3) is only one component of the object; the latter is a sentence content ("nexus as object", JESPERSEN 1911– 5: 9–18). However, this type of construction, contrasting an "accusative (or other object case) with the infinitive" with a "simple infinitive" in a way encountered in numerous languages, is extremely rare in Israeli Hebrew and found only with a very limited number of governing verbs. In most cases where "object case with the infinitive" goes with a verb (cf. RUBINSTEIN 1970: 137–8), the omission of the object case does not express equiagency (between the infinitive and the governing verb), but a nonexplicit agent must be considered *Ø* (*'man*; *on'*):

'ani melamed	*'otam*	*'anglit lirkod*	'I teach them	English' to dance (i.e. dancing)'
'ani melamed	*Ø*	*'anglit lirkod*	'I teach	English' dancing (to those concerned)'

It would not be unjustified to consider the *l*-morpheme of the infinitive as a personal agent-prefix of the same class as the other agent-prefixes:

ne-daber	*n-askim*	*n-itlabeš*
le-daber	*le-haskim*	*le-hitlabeš*

While the personal prefixes proper are deictic in the sense that they represent (in the first and second persons at least) individuals not necessarily mentioned before, the infinitive prefix would be an anaphoric agent-prefix ('the person or thing implied as agent in the governing form'). To interpret the *l*- element as a person morpheme is also justified by the morphophonemic structure of the infinitive: *litpos* 'to catch' and *lakum* 'to rise' are similar in structure to *nitpos*

'we shall catch' and *nakum* 'we shall rise' but different from the
gerunds *bitfos-*, *bekum-* 'at the time of . . .'s catching (rising)'; there
is no agent implied in the latter (ROSÉN 1955a: 49–52; 1964: 171).
If we are bound to consider every infinitive as person-characterized,
then anaphora referring to an agent marked Ø would again express
the '*man*-impersonal'; the "antecedent" of the anaphoric relation
needs neither physically precede the infinitive nor constitute part
of a finite verb form; e.g.:

Kaše lanù lilmod or *Lilmod kaše lanù.*	'Es ist uns schwer zu lernen.' - 'We have a hard time studying.'
Kaše lilmod, that is *kaše Ø lilmod.* or *Lilmod kaše*, that is *lilmod kaše Ø.*	'One has a hard time studying.' or: 'It is hard to study'.

Only if the infinitive is not syntactically related to a person-characterized form, is it not indicative of the agent: *Stut lehagid ʾet ze.* 'It is
silly to say this.'; *Ha-baaya hi limcoʾ ʾet-ha-kesèf.* 'The problem is to
find the money.'

5.3 GERUND

The difference between the infinitive and the GERUND (ROSÉN
1962a: 323–4; unclear in COHEN–ZAFRANI 1968: 100) arises out of
the fact that a personal suffix or a construent noun (*7.1.5*) is
obligatory with the gerund, while it is merely facultative with the
infinitive; the gerund is compulsorily construct. Consequently, in-
asmuch as what we are considering here is word classes, the gerund
with no construent element is not a word in the sense of being a
free form. This is in all likelihood related to the fact that the personal suffix (or construent noun) appended to the gerund indicates
the agent, while the personal suffix appended to the infinitive
(which can take no construent) is the designator of the patient:

Inf.: *lexabed* 'to honour' – *lexabdo* 'to honour him'
 lexabed ʾet ʾaviv 'to honour his father'
Gd.: *bexabdo ʾet ʾaviv* 'at the time (or: by means)
 of his honouring his father'

It is primarily the compulsory case prefix that makes the form deserve the name of a 'gerund'. This does not uncompromisingly apply to Biblical Hebrew, and it was a trifle more justified in Biblical Hebrew grammar than in Israeli Hebrew to include the infinitive and the gerund under the common heading of 'construct infinitives'. Syntactically they have very little in common, and their morphological relatedness, never very solid in any case, has become quite loose in Israeli Hebrew, where the gerund very frequently does not take part in the irregular behaviour of the infinitive of certain stem classes: *ladaàt* 'to know' (inf.), *ledaato* 'to know him' versus *beyod'o* 'at the time of his knowing' (gd.); cf. *yodea* 'knowing'[91].

The explicit person indication with the gerund already implies that the Israeli Hebrew gerund, like the English, but, e.g., unlike the Latin, gerund is not subject to any agent concord with the governing verb (or sentence kernel, as the case may be). Not only that *beholxo (belexto) káma* 'at his going she rose' is grammatical, but also *belexto kám* 'at his going he rose' does not oblige us to interpret equiagency to the two verbs any more than in the English translation. In case of possible ambiguity, assumption of equiagency

[91] In fact, these Israeli Hebrew gerund forms do not really continue the Biblical Hebrew "infinitive construct" forms. The "feminine" infinitives (with a *-t* afformative) found in certain stem types (*ladaàt*) were the bases for formation irrespective of the prefix used (also: *bedaàt-*). Since the distinction of infinitives from action nouns is postbiblical, all feminine infinitives with *-a-* afformative (*'ahăbà* 'to love' > *'ahava* 'love') and those with *-t-* afformative which bore a preformative other than *l-* were reclassed as action nouns; Israeli Hebrew consequently distinguishes *bedaato* 'in his cognizance, opinion, intention' from *beyod'o* 'at his knowing'. (The latter type of quite "regular" appearance is not Biblical, but an innovation.) On the other hand, Biblical Hebrew construct infinitives of "irregular" root types (in the Qal stem) were reclassified, in Israeli Hebrew, as action nouns: *-bo'-* 'arrival' (*bi'a*, since Talmudic Hebrew specialized for 'coitus', is not used as an abstract of *lavo'* 'come'), *-šuv-* or *šiva* 'return' (but see FRAENKEL 1966: 144). There are cases in which a gerund functioning as nominalization form along with a regular action noun is syntactically (and, consequently, semantically) differentiated from the latter: *prica* (regular action noun of transitive *parac* 'broke in') versus *proc* (gerund functioning as action noun of intransitive *parac* 'broke out'): *lifne pricat ha-delèt* 'before the door was broken in' versus *lifne proc ha-milxama* 'before the war broke out'; the two forms are not interchangeable.

will, however, be the preferred interpretation particularly in cases
in which the gerund is the nucleus of a more extended construction,
e.g. *bir'ota 'et-ha-sakana nirt'a* '(on her) noticing the danger she
recoiled'. Since Hebrew does not posses circumstantial participial
clauses (i.e. the type represented by the English version of the last
example, the words in parentheses not included) the Israeli Hebrew
gerund might be well disposed to embark on the course taken by
its Latin homonym, which developed into the Romance participle
in a well-defined number of syntactical uses. A development of the
last-named type to *voyant le danger, elle recula* is obviously possible
only if a time relation is implied in the very use of the gerund form
the same way a person relation is implied in that of the infinitive.
The gerund is equitemporal with respect to the governing verb (or
sentence kernel). The absence of a time morpheme from the gerund
is no indication of neutralization; in *belexto káma*, the gerund is not
time-indifferent: it cannot stand for, e.g., 'after his going she stood
up', but only for 'at his coming ... *(eo abeunte)*'. Granted, it is
the choice of the case prefix *be-* that indicates equitemporality, and
other prefixes (or prepositions) could be the expressional means of
other time relations (e.g. *'ad lexto lo káma* 'she did not get up until
his going'), but since the case marker is compulsory in Israeli
Hebrew (see above), the gerund, taken as a complete word unit,
must be credited with the dimension of (cursive) tense (cf. FRAENKEL
1966: 144).

5.4 PARTICIPLE

The PARTICIPLE is tense-characterized by the very fact that in
predicative status it is a verbal tense, the aorist that expresses a time
range which includes the speaker's present (*7.3.2*): *'ani šote kafé*
'I drink (am drinking) coffee'. It is imperative, for syntactical
reasons, to consider the sentences with a participial predicate as
verbal, and not as nominal. This relieves us of the necessity to
consider to what degree the conjunct participle has, by virtue of its
equitemporality, more time reference than certain adjectives (cf.

JESPERSEN 1911– 4: 91). It can be shown that it has, and that in other respects also the participles must be kept separate from the adjectives, which have no share either in verbality or in time. Furthermore, while adjectives are determination-marked, an attributive adjective is in determination concord with its noun, the conjunct participle is not, as is obvious from the sample sentence above, where *ha-* is no determinator, but little more than the morphological marker of the conjunct participle; whether the antecedent is *'adam* 'a person' or *ha-'adam* 'the person', the rest of the sentence stands.[92] Substantivized participles are time-indifferent and may, due to certain lexically inherent aspectual values of the verb, have 'past' or 'perfective' reference; e.g.: *yored* (*y-r-d* 'descend, emigrate from Israel') 'one who has emigrated' (differently *'ole* 'ascendant, immigrant (prior to his social absorption)'), *ha-noflim* (*n-f-l* 'fall') 'the fallen, battle casualties', *ha-ba'im* 'those who come' or 'those who have come'; *ha-'ovrim 'et-ha-gvul hoxzru* 'those who have crossed the border have been returned'.

5.5 VERBOIDS

5.5.1 Syntactic properties

To explain what we mean by VERBOID (ROSÉN 1965: 82–3; 1966a: 214–5), we shall first discuss the morphological and syntactical properties of some instructive sample sentences:

(1) *Yosef (lo) haya lo (ha-)kesèf*	'Joseph did (not) have (the) money'
(2) *Yosef yeš / 'eyn lo (ha-) kesèf*	'Joseph does / does not have (the) money'

[92] Determination-invariability of the conjunct participle recalls the gender-quantity-invariability of the Modern French participle with the status of the centre of a verbal phrase. Not unlike the situation in French, the Israeli Hebrew conjunct participle almost invariably has a complement. If it does not, determination concord applies, and the participle would have to be reclassed as an adjective, a process that is lexically rather limited. E.g.: *'et novea* 'a fountain pen' (literally 'a flowing pen') : *ha-'et ha-novea* 'the fountain pen'.

(3) *Ha-xavera šeli šma tamar*   'My (female) friend is called
                                        Tamar'
                                        'Meine Freundin heißt
                                        Tamar'
(4) *Haškafa zo mkora be-taʾut*   'This view stems from an
                                        error'
(5) Monsieur *perušo ʾadoni*   '*Monsieur* means "Sir" '
(6) *Kartis mxiro xameš lirot*   'A ticket costs five pounds'

The immediately apparent feature common to these (by the way, puristically irreproachable) sentences is the fact that a person- or gender-indicating morpheme which is not the agent suffix of a finite verb (*haya l-o, yeš l-o, šm-a* 'her name', *mkor-a* 'its origin', *peruš-o* 'its interpretation') enters a concord relation to a grammatical subject the same way as finite verbs. It is no coincidence at all that the most straightforward translation of such an expression is a finite verb (*has, means, heißt*, etc.). It is common knowledge that this (at least translational) equivalence between the expressions of the type *haya l-, šm-*, etc. (our "verboids") and, at least extra-Hebraic, finite verbs has had, in some styles, syntactic consequences, mainly the ascribing of accusatival transitivity to *(lo) haya l-, yeš l-, ʾeyn l-*, and maybe one or two others; a stylistically "undesirable" variant of (1) (with determination) would be *Yosef (lo) haya lo ʾet-* ('accusative') *ha-kesèf*.[93]

5.5.2 Verboids and the extrapositional (casus pendens) construction

This enables us to show that the verb-like properties of the expressions that concern us here are not merely an outcome of the consideration of their translational equivalents, whether in the mind of the linguist or of the bilingual speaker, but are rooted in the con-

---

[93] Verboids can be identified on the grounds of "ungrammatical" transitivity and "false" congruence also in Biblical Hebrew; *hāyā l-* 'have' is one of them (ROSÉN 1966a: 215–6; 1965: 81–2). The revivors of Hebrew were not aware of these syntactic features of Biblical Hebrew, so that the use of the type *haya l-... ʾet-...* has nothing to do with Biblical attestations. Cf. ROSÉN (1958: 30–1) and below.

struction of the sentences in which they occur. Viewing such sentences as are quoted above in the light of classical grammar, the
constituent preceding the verboid (*yosef, ha-xavera šeli,* etc.)
would represent an EXTRAPOSITED SUBJECT (CASUS PENDENS), and the
verboid with what follows it a sentence nucleus of nominal type
(šma tamar); the pronominal element in concord with the *casus
pendens* creates the predicative nexus between the two constituents.

The notion of nominative absolute (*casus pendens*) is nothing more in
Hebrew syntax than the outcome of a (European-inspired?) difference
in attitudes toward verbal and nonverbal concord in the broader realm
of Biblical Hebrew concord sentences, in which the concord-motivating
constituent (subject) precedes the concord-motivated one (ROSÉN 1955a:
81–4). A Biblical Hebrew sentence

> (a) *waʾani zōʾt b·ri·ti ʾotẩm* '... I have this covenant with them'
> (literally 'I – this is my covenant ...')

or

> (b) *wkol-hab·ʾērōt sit·mu·m p·lišt·i·m* '... all the wells did the Phi-
> listines stop' (litterally '...
> stopped them')

would be considered as containing a *casus pendens*, while

> (c) *umlẩki·m mim·kẩ yẹṣẹ·u* '... kings will issue of thee' (literally
> '... of thee will they issue')

would not; this is unjustified, because the concord in fact unites the
introducing constituent with a nuclear sentence, and the second constituent in (c) is a complete sentence nucleus as much as the ones in
(a) and (b). The notion of *casus pendens* is, as can be seen, a combination of two concepts: that of word order and that of the distinction of
verbs from nonverbs.

5.5.3 The extrapositional transformation and its stylistic status

Our sample sentences (1)–(6) do fulfil the criterion of constant order
(their initial consituents may not be removed to any other position, as
may, e.g., the initial nonverbal parts of Israeli Hebrew verbal sentences),
but it is precisely the aspect of nonverbality (in concord, at least) that
has to be examined.

Traditionally, and long before transformational theory, the *casus pendens* construction was taught to be the result of a SYNTACTIC TRANSFORMATION (e.g. ORNAN 1968a[94]), but this view shows the deficiencies typical of the applications of transformational statements for descriptional purposes: it neglects the preliminary considerations (i) whether the alleged transforms have kernels, (ii) under what conditions the transformation is excluded, (iii) what the range of attestation is. (Cf. ROSÉN 1966a: 293–4; 1965: 83.)

A genuine transformation of the type

ma rcon 'avíxa? → 'avíxa *ma rcono*? 'What is the wish of
         your father? Your father, what does he desire?'

is STYLISTICALLY MARKED. It can be assumed only in written literary style that both terms of the transformational relation are in actual use. On the other hand, samples (1)–(3) are colloquial, (4)–(6) stylistically indifferent. Furthermore, an assumption that there are differently constructed, but semantically analogous sentences ("kernels") leads to difficulties. For example, a theoretical pre-transformational kernel of (3) would be *Šem ha-xavera šeli tamar*, and it is, in conformity with what has just been said, this form that is stylistically marked as elevated (familiar colloquial has only the form (3) or *Ha-šem* (or *šma*) *šel-ha-xavera šeli tamar*, a form that precludes extrapositional transformation). In other cases, as (5), we run into the problem of the intrinsic semantic difference of the sentence that could otherwise serve as a pretransformational model: *Peruš mila zo baaya* 'the interpretation of this word is a problem' versus *Mila zo peruša baaya* 'This word means "problem" '.[95] A sentence *Ha-yarden mkoro ba-xermon* would likewise

---

[94] Inadequate discussion, whose main shortcoming is a lack of statements of constraints, the most important of which, at least, have been enumerated in ROSÉN 1966a: 239–40.

[95] This tallies with the case of *the late Churchill*, since in the second sentence (= sample 5) *peruša* belongs to the predicate portion of the sentence as does *late* in *Churchill is late*, while in the first sentence it is not predicative with respect to *mila* (neither is *late* in *the late Churchill*).

have the nonsense interpretation 'The river Jordan originates from the Hermon', while 'The source of the Jordan is in the Hermon' would have to be *Mkor ha-yarden ba-xermon*. What must be stressed is that in certain conditions (e.g. sentence-part questions; *Ma šem ha-xavera šelxa*? 'What is the name of your girl-friend?') the compulsory noninitial position of the otherwise concord-motivating subject excludes the "transformed" construction, but then we are faced with a clear case of complementary distribution of patterns, and not with genuine transformation.

Pretransformational analogues that are in fact used have syntactical properties which preclude the sample types from being considered as their transforms, the foremost of which properties is the free modifiability of the nominal or prepositional element to which the concord-motivated suffix is attached (in the extrapositional construction). E.g., in a nonextrapositional counterpart of (3), *Šma šel-ha-xavera šeli tamar*, the constituent *šma* '–'s name', would be modifiable not only by inflexional categories (*Šmotéha šel-ha-xavera šeli tamar ve-teréza* 'The names ... are ...', *i.e.* she has a pseudonym, an alias, or a non-Hebrew first name), but also by expansion *Šma ha-noxxiy šel-ha-xavera šeli tamar* 'The present name of ...'; such features could not be made to pass into the allegedly transformational pattern (3), where only *šma* with no extensions is admissible as long as we do not wish to present a stylistically marked sentence. Considering *Le-yosef haya kesèf* (nonextrapositional analogue of (1)), the 'possession'-indicating *le-* may freely undergo substitution by other semantically suitable prepositions (*'ecèl-yosef haya kesèf* 'There was money at Joseph's'), but then such modified form, extrapositionally transformed *(Yosef haya 'eclo kesèf)*, would be either awkward ("ungrammatical") or, at least, distinctly stylistically marked.

Consequently, while not excluding extrapositional transformation (creation of a *casus pendens* construction) from the syntactic features of Israeli Hebrew, we cannot consider the expressions exemplified under (1)–(6) as the result of such transformation and must accord them another status, which will have to account for their morphological properties along with their syntactical ones.

While, in a nonextrapositional shape of (1) or (2), *le-yosef* is freely movable relative to *haya (haya kesèf le-yosef, kesèf le-yosef haya)*, its pronominal representative *lo* is not and must be placed in immediate succession to *haya*. This is a feature of pronominal enclisis that is by no means characteristic only of the expressions that concern us here, but that regulates the position of governed personal pronouns in a way similar to that in which pronouns are positioned in other languages (*7.1.4*); but the consequence of this rule for pronouns, obligatory in the extrapositional construction, is that it acquires the status of a person morpheme suffixed to the bound form in immediate succession to which it must be placed:

haya-li	'I had'	*šmi*	'*je m'appelle*'
haya-lxa	'you had (m.sg.)'	*šimxa*	'*tu t'appelles* (m.)'
haya-lo	'he had'	*šmo*	'*il s'appelle*'
. . .		. . .	

The unit word thus created is sentence-constitutive in the first and second person (*Haya lxa kesèf. Šmi yosef.*), but subject to gender-number concord in the third (*Yosef yeš lo kesèf. Tamar haya la kesèf.*). These features taken together and coupled with the tense dimension of the sentences under study, in effect mean verbality, strengthened by the stylistically optional transitivity of some of the verboids. Verbality is the second and final contradiction of the notion of *casus pendens* (*5.5.2*), but since the expressions we deal with after all show no signs of verbal morphological behaviour, we have to label them separately.

Those verboids in which transitivity is emerging due to the fact that, viewed as *casus pendens* forms, they would have a grammatical subject of their own (which is developing into a direct object), are not only person-characterized (or concord-bound in the third person to the initial subject), but also concord-bound to what historically was their grammatical subject:

Yosef haya	*lo*	*sus*	'J. had a horse'	*Tamar haya*	*la*	*sus*
	-u	*-o*	*-im* ' horses'		*-u*	*-a*	*-im*

This is why we ascribe to verboids a sort of double inflection, involving person-sex-number as well as gender-quantity. Developing transitivity, of course, tends to obliterate this peculiar feature: the last quoted sentence has a substandard variant[96] *Tamar haya la susim*, in which no longer concord-motivating pl. *susim* has acquired the status of a direct object, whence likewise substandard *Tamar haya la 'et-ha-susim* (with determinated 'object' and, consequently, accusative particle *'et-*; cf. *7.1. 2*) 'T. had the horses' versus more acceptable synonymous *Tamar hayu la ha-susim*; in certain slang-bound expressions, the concordless type is obligatory, e.g. *Hayom haya* (m. sg.) *lanù história* (f.sg.) 'We had history today'.

5.6 IMPERSONALS

5.6.1 Syntactic status

Most IMPERSONALS occur only in one syntactic position, namely as the predicative constituent of a sentence nucleus whose other constituent is, or centres around, an infinitive (*'efšar lištot yayìn* 'It is possible to drink wine', 'Drinking wine is possible') or, as its substitute, a *še*-introduced clause[97] (*'efšar še-nište yayìn* 'It is possible that we drink wine', 'It is possible for us to drink wine'). While semantically suitable adjectives can take their place in this position (*Tov lištot yayìn. Tov še-nište yayìn* 'It is good ...'), the impersonals cannot replace predicative adjectives in other types of occurrence. I earlier preferred to attach to them a label on grounds of their syntactic behaviour, naming them SENTENCE CONSTITUENTS (ROSÉN 1962a § 3.5), but later switched to the morphologically better founded, and admittedly Indo-European inspired, term "impersonal s" (ROSÉN 1966a: 218–22). The parallelism with impersonal translational equivalents points to a marked German-Yiddish dependence:

---

[96] For a similar development in Biblical Hebrew see note 93.
[97] In some cases (examples below) also a quasi-conditional clause introduced by *'im* 'if'.

Keday lištot	'Es lohnt sich zu trinken', 'It is worth while to drink'
Mutav lištot *Mutav še-nište* *Mutav 'im nište*	'Es ist besser zu trinken', '... daß (wenn) wir trinken'. But: 'We had better drink.[98]
'ixpat laazov	'Es macht (einem) etwas aus wegzugehen'. But: 'One minds leaving'
'ixpat še-naazov *'ixpat 'im naazov*	'Es macht uns etwas aus wegzugehen'. But: 'We mind leaving'

Personal reference can be added to the infinitive governed by an impersonal by the mediation of *le-* 'to, for', which, however, does not create morphological word unity with the impersonal:

'efšar be-'ofèn kaze la-'orxim lištot 'In such a manner, it is possible for the guests to drink'
'efšar lanù lištot or: *lanù 'efšar lištot* 'It is possible for us to drink'

Likewise *'efšar lanù še-nište*, etc., Absence of explicit person reference may be interpreted as zero-person ('man'): *'efšar lištot* 'One can drink'. In one significant case, the introduction relative to the infinitive of personal reference necessitates a switch from the impersonal to an analogous personal morphological paradigm (participle):[99]

Carix lištot (impers.) 'One must drink'. *Est bidendum.* Должно пить. (impers.)
Carix še-nište. 'anaxnù crixim lištot (pers.) 'We must drink.' *Nobis est bibendum.* Мы должны пить. (pers.)[100]

---

[98] Equally for the adjectives that can be substituted for the impersonals: *Noax li* (*laševèt*) 'Es ist mir bequem (zu sitzen)'; but: 'I am comfortable (sitting)'' *Kar li lace't* 'Es ist mir kalt hinauszugehen', *Kar li* 'Mir ist kalt'; but: 'I am cold'. (Elliptic omission of the infinitive is possible with all impersonals: *Keday* (*li*) 'It is worthwhile (for me)', 'Es lohnt sich (mir)'). The contrast of these constructions with the Western-European type *il fait froid, j'ai froid* has already been discussed by EPSTEIN (1915: 16).

[99] Gender-quantity-inflected *carix* is the participle in a suppletive tense paradigm (remote tense: *hictarex*; potential tense: *yictarex*) 'must'. Impersonal (gender-quantity-invariable) *carix* is not paradigmatically related to these forms, but forms its tenses synthetically with the auxiliary *haya, yihye* like the other impersonals (see below).

[100] In classical (postbiblical) Hebrew, *ṣdri·k* is not the only impersonal that shows this particular syntactic ambivalence; but it is the only one in Israeli Hebrew.

5.6.2 Tense value

The tense-markedness of the impersonals consists in their being indicative of the aorist tense; other tenses can be formed from them by the auxiliary *haya* 'was' and *yihye* 'will be': *'efšar haya lištot* 'It was possible to drink', 'One could drink'; *Lo 'ixpat yihye lanù laazov* 'We shall not mind leaving'. Since the impersonals occur only in one (the predicative) syntactic position, they are barred from being used, as e.g., local adverbs can, without the unequivocal time characterization. The tense-markedness of *yeš* and *'eyn*, which can be classed under the same part of speech heading as the impersonals, likewise consists in their expressing the time content of the aorist, but here the other tenses are formed not by addition of the auxiliary *haya* and *yihye*, but by substitution by these same forms in the status of *verba existentiae*: *Yeš makom : Haya makom : Yihye makom* 'There is (: was : will be) room'. With the infinitive, *yeš* and *'eyn* approach the impersonals also semantically by absorbing the modal shape typical of the impersonal + infinitive constructions:

Yeš lilmod 'Est discendum'   *'eyn lilmod*   'Non est discendum'
　　　'One must learn'[101]   'One must not learn'
(Lo) haya : yihye lilmod 'One had : will have (did not have : will not have) to learn'[102]

These same constructions, with personal reference added, create syntactic ambiguity:

Yeš li + mašèhù lilmod (lištot) 'I have something to learn (to drink)'
Yeš + li mašèhù lilmod (lištot) 'I have to learn (to drink) something'

---

[101]   Classically (postbiblical): 'one can learn'.
[102]   Schoolchildren's style.

8*

5.7 ADJECTIVES

5.7.1 Emergence of the adjective class

ADJECTIVES as a part of speech in Hebrew probably date back to Mishnaic language. The two groups that make up the inventory of Israeli Hebrew adjectives, primary and derived ones (6.4.2.1), did not constitute an autonomous part of speech in Biblical Hebrew; the latter were part of the class of nouns, the former were participles of a morphologically and semantically characterized class of qualitative verbs (ROSÉN 1962b: 829–30; 1962a § 52.5; 1969: 105–6). BH zåqēn will be labelled, merely on the basis of its syntactical status, as either a 3rd person masculine singular perfect ('is old') or as a participle ('being old', i.e. 'old')[103]; 'I am old' is zåqånt·i (perfect, that is person-suffixed nominal), and past time cannot be expressed in these verbs unless in a time-characterized narrative chain (way·izqån 'and he was old'). The old participle zaken < zåqēn has lost all relation to the verbal paradigm and is only found in syntagms of nominal character; 'ani zaken 'I am old' : hayitì zaken 'I was old' (if zaken were considered a participle in Israeli Hebrew, this syntagm would carry an iterative on unreal meaning; cf. below 7.2.1). The old zakantì which is preserved in somewhat elevated language, must be reinterpreted as a time-indicating form (BH perfect > IH remotive, i.e. past tense), preserving its general reference ('I am old') the verb stem is reinterpreted as inchoative ('I have become old' = 'I am old'), and it needs no further explanation why this verb, like most others of the same type, has no participle in Israeli Hebrew. (Curiously enough, this formal feature has been reinstated, while the content feature has undergone the radical change from stative to inchoative.) Only very few of these verbs have a participle: gadel 'becoming big, growing'; the reason is that the corresponding Biblical Hebrew verb had one, and an irregular one at that, g·ådōl 'being big', which became available to serve as an

---

[103] They should be deemed to be one form; originally, at least, qualitative verbs had only one nominal form ('stative'), and not two (perfect, participle).

Israeli Hebrew adjective without impairing the inchoative verb's ('grow') capacity of having a complete tense system (*gadaltì* 'I grew', etc.).

5.7.2 Syntactic status of adjectives

To be sure, we do not know when all these processes that, taken as a whole, constitute the emergence of the adjective in Hebrew, took place. They are, in all likelihood, already early postbiblical. But what is more important is that the entire process exactly parallels an analogous development in Western European languages and makes it possible for the Israeli Hebrew adjective to stand in a one-to-one relation to European adjectives, if content units are taken as the basis of comparison.[104]

The typology-anchored equipollence between the Israeli Hebrew and the European adjective is underlined by the emergence, in Israeli Hebrew, of fullfledged pronominal adjectives such as *kaze* (m.sg.), *kazot* (f.sg.), *ka'éle* (c.pl.) 'such'; *ze, zot, 'éle* 'this';[105] preposited *'éyze* (uninflected)

---

[104] The process that has taken place within the limits of the European *Sprachbund* can be exemplified by colour concepts, such as 'green': time-related greenness is expressed in Latin by verbal means: *uiret* 'is green', which is a "proper" present. These expressions constitute (proverbial nominal sentences excluded) the only category in which Latin distinguishes the *hic-et-nunc* tense from generally valid statements ('is green' with no time location is *est uiridis*, likewise *ualet : est ualidus* 'is strong', and *calet : est calidus* 'is warm', etc.). Where greenness is the content of an otherwise uncharacterized verbal form in modern European languages, its concomitant semantic feature is inchoativity (or, occasionally, factitivity), e.g. *grünt* 'becomes green' or *schwärzt* 'blackens'. The Romance analogy, as *est vert* 'is green', shows that this is a result of the superimposition of Latin on probably typologically the same stratum as of classical Hebrew.

[105] This pronoun is a fullfledged Israeli Hebrew adjective due to its being perfectly capable of determination characterization (*ze : ha-ze* etc.) and, consequently, maintaining determination concord with the nouns it modifies: *sefèr ze : ha-sefèr ha-ze*. This situation is neither Biblical nor Mishnaic. In Biblical Hebrew, the distribution of *ze* and *haz·e* is primarily syntactic; the former is predicative, while due to the attributive status of *haz·e* determination concord is maintained by the modified substantive appearing in its article-determinated form (*hay·o·m haz·e* 'this day'); with other forms of determination (with personal suffix) *ze* (without "article") is used (*'ăbădé·kă 'él·e* 'those servants of yours'). This construction is maintained in Israeli Hebrew (*7.1.2*): *'avadéxa 'éle*. In Mishnaic Hebrew, probably through etymological equation of Hebrew forms with corresponding Aramaic ones and due to the absence of a prepositive and, at later stages, of any kind of article in Aramaic, only *ze* appears: *sefèr ze*. By the amalgamation of systems, typical of the exploitation of language material hailing from different layers, Israeli Hebrew has developed the full determina-

or (in higher style) *'éyze* (m.sg.), *'éyzo* (f.sg./c.pl.), *'éylu* (c.pl.) 'which, some';[106] *'oto-* (m.sg.), *'ota-* (f.sg.), *'otam-* (m.pl.), *'otan-* (f.pl.) 'that (same)'[107]. None of these words has comparable adjectival status in classical Hebrew.[108]

The "revivor" generation must have been highly conscious of the functional equivalence between the Hebrew adjectives, by then an established form and function class, and their European, for that matter Slavonic, counterparts. An adjunct denominative adjective in *-iy* (denominative suffix) was considered void of any content beyond that of the basic noun, so that a syntagm consisting of a noun with such an adjective as attribute could be regarded, semantically, as the most unspecific form of liaison between two nouns: *kitor meymiy* 'water steam' (literally 'watery steam'; *meym-iy* from *mayim* 'water'). These very obviously Slavic-inspired forms (водяной пар) have subsisted to the present time only in a number of fixed, quasiterminological expressions[109] such as *mišpat 'ezraxiy* 'civil law' (*'ezrax* 'citizen, Bürger', *'ezrax-iy* 'bürger-lich') with all the wellknown syntactical complications and implications (*civil lawyer, criminal lawyer*) involved. The expressions

---

tion-oppositive system shown above, but has had to ascribe some semantic contrast to the opposing forms: *sefèr ze* is anaphoric ('the mentioned book, that book'), *ha-sefèr ha-ze* (as unmarked member of the binary opposition) is either anaphoric or *hic-* deictic ('this book, the book visible').

[106] These forms are attested in part in Biblical Hebrew, and completely in postbiblical Hebrew, but their distribution is not as grammaticalized as in Israeli Hebrew.

[107] With determination opposition (cf. note *105* on *ze*) in Israeli Hebrew: *'oto-ha-sefèr* 'the same book' : *'oto-sefèr* (unmarked member) *'idem'*/'that (mentioned) book'. In postbiblical Hebrew both form types are attested apparently with no semantic opposition, but only a syntactic difference: in *'o·t-à 'i·r* 'that certain town', determination of the noun seems to be effected by the proleptic personal suffix (*-à*), which tends to show that in *'o·tà hà-'i·r* the article is pleonastic.

[108] For the case of *kaze* see ROSÉN (1958a: 46–8 - 1966a: 51–3). The gender-number category of *kaze* in Israeli Hebrew concords with the noun described or modified, as Germ. *ein solcher, eine solche*, Fr. *tel, telle*; in Biblical Hebrew *k·àze* functions according to its etymological analysability (*k·à-* 'as' + *ze* 'this one') and gender and number are determined by the noun designating the object compared. (One cannot ascertain from dictionaries, when the change of status took place.) – The arguments of ORNAN (1968b) contribute nothing nor are they to the point.

[109] Cf. ROSÉN (1957: 344), MASSON (1968: 158). These forms were recognized as Slavisms very early and disavowed (cf., e.g., J. KLAUSNER 1949: 73), and their substitution by "genuinely Hebrew" *status constructus* syntagms (*kitor mayim*) was successfully recommended.

in which the noun-denominative adjective construction has become obsolete are replaced by direct noun-syntagms: *kitor mayim* 'water steam', with full possibilities of establishing semantic contrasts between the two syntagms: *mosadot tarbutiyim* which in the twenties and early thirties could still stand for 'cultural institutions' (*tarbut* 'culture, civilization'), would now mean only 'cultured *or* civilized institutions' and, in its aforementioned sense, be replaced by *mosdot-tarbut*. In this case, as in all other analogous ones, the adjective has gone beyond being a mere syntagmatic means of expression and carries a descriptive class meaning of its own.[110]

---

[110] Further examples in ROSÉN (1957: 341–4; 1958a: 174–8 = 1966a: 188–92).

6 WORD FORMATION AND COMPOUNDING

The morpheme types of Israeli Hebrew may be characterized according to whether they are:

(1) continuous or discontinuous,
(2) subject or not to internal consonantal alternation,
(3) affixal or not,
(4) derivationally productive or not.

6.1.1 Root

The ROOT, which is discontinuous and subject to consonantal alternation (*šavar* 'broke' : *šavur* 'broken' : *mašber* 'crisis, Zusammenbruch'*) is no longer derivationally productive. In inherited pairs, the derivationally motivating and the motivated term may have a common root and differ only by a vowel pattern (*kacar* 'short' : *kocèr* 'shortness'), but living formations of the same semantic type have a common stem (*melumad* 'learned, scholar' : *melumadut* 'scholarliness') or a common radical (see below); cf. above *1.5.3*.

6.1.2 Radical

The RADICAL, which is discontinuous, but not subject to internal consonant alternation, has stepped into the place of the root in all living derivational processes. As the root, the radical (ROSÉN 1962a: 262–3) is tripartite; it may consist of up to five nonsyllabics, provided the first and last positions are filled by single consonants only. The consonant cluster of up to three components that can occupy the medial position can have the maximum number of elements only if it is of the type liquid (or sibilant) + stop + liquid: *tilgref* 'telegraphed'.[111]

Radicals with three nonsyllabics are of the following types:

(a) all consonants are part of the root: *l-m-d* in *limed* 'taught'; *limud* 'study' in view of *lamad* 'learned';

(b) one of the consonants is additional to a biconsonantal root: radical *m-k-m* 'place' in *makom* 'place', *mikem* 'placed, located' in view of the root *k-m* 'is positioned' as in *kám* 'got into a position, rose' and *hekim* 'set up'; radical *x-c-n* 'external' in *xicon* 'outer', *xiconiy* 'external', and *xicen* 'externalized' (root *x-c* 'outside').

(c) in rare cases, the radical represents the consonantal skeleton of an inherited proper noun or word of extra-Hebraic origin: radical *y-v-n* 'Greek' in *meyuvan* 'Hellenized' in view of *yavan* 'Greece' and *yvani* 'Greek', and *z-v-g* 'pair' in *zivug* 'pairing, combination' in view of *zug* (more authentically Talmudic *záweg* 'pair' from Gk. ζεῦγος, hellenistic [zévγos] 'pair'); postformatives are omitted: *n-c-r* 'Christian' in *hitnacer* 'embraced the Christian faith' and *nocri* 'Christian, Nazarene' from *nálsrat* 'Nazareth'.

Inherited types of radicals of four nonsyllabics:

(a) so-called quadriliteral "roots": *x-šm-l* 'electricity' in *xišmel* 'electrified'; *p-rn-s* 'provide for' in *pirnes* 'provided for', *parnasa* 'livelihood';

(b) reduplicated biconsonantal roots: radical *d-fd-f* in *difdef* 'leafed through' and *dafdefét* 'atlas' in view of *daf* 'sheet';

(c) one of the consonants is additional to a triliteral root: *t-zm-r* in *tizmer* 'orchestrated' in view of *tizmorèt* 'orchestra' and the root *z-m-r*

---

[111] Isolated exceptions are marginal (stylistically marked; 3.4.4): radical *sm-rt-t* 'rag' in *smartut* 'rag': *mesmurtat* 'having the nature or appearance of a rag (or rags)'. – The model for the "periphrastic denominatives" was probably Yiddish (cf. BLANC 1965: 191–2), where Hebrew words are frequently verbalized in this way (Yidd. *kále maxn* 'annihilate' from Heb. *kale* 'nonexistent'), but the Turkish parallels (*organize etmek* 'organize' on the basis of Fr. *organisé*) may have made some contribution (the Israeli Hebrew pattern was already in use at the end of the Turkish rule in Palestine). However, unlike the Yiddish and Turkish parallels, the Israeli Hebrew paraphrases are not fully absorbed in the verbal system in that they do not admit the direct-object government: *'irgen 'et-ha-misrad* ('organized the office' versus *'asa re'organizacyà ba-misrad* 'reorganized the office').

ʿsing, make music'; *x-šb-n* 'calculate' in *xišben* 'figured out' in view of *xešbon* 'account' and the root *x-š-v/b* 'consider, reckon'; radical *m-šm-a* in *memušmaàt* 'well-disciplined' in view of *mišmaàt* (postformative omitted) 'discipline' and the root *š-m-ʾ/a* 'hear, obey'; radicals with preformative *š-* or *h-* in derived verbal stems (*6.4.2.2*), such as *š-xt-v* 'rewrite' (*šixtev* 'rewrote') and (*h-*)*xt-v* 'dictate' (*hixtiv* 'dictated', *yaxtiv* 'will dictate) considering the root *k/x-t-v* 'write' (*katav* 'wrote', *yixtov* 'will write').

Other radicals of four, and all radicals of five nonsyllabics represent the consonantal skeleton of a name or a loanword: radical *p/f-st-r* in *pistur* 'pasteurization' and *mefustar* 'pasteurized (part.)'; *t-lf-n* in *tilfen* 'made a phone call' in view of *télefon*; *ʾ-kl-m* 'climate' in *hitʾaklem* 'became acclimatized' in view of *ʾaklim* 'climate'.

As can be seen from these examples, one of the principal functions of the radical is to serve as the basis of denominative derivation of verbs, including many of foreign origin. The phonological limits set to the radical (see above) do not permit such derivation from foreign expressions the number of whose consonants exceeds five, or whose consonantal skeleton is unsuitably structured: while 'organize' can yield a radical (*ʾ-rg-n* in *ʾirgen* 'organized', *ʾirgun* 'organization'), 'reorganize' cannot (*r-ʾrg-n* is not structured according to the constraints stated above); in cases as the latter, the foreign abstract is used in conjunction with a suitable auxiliary verb (*laasot* 'do' or *latet* 'give') to replace the denominative verb that cannot be formed: *ʾasa reʾorganizacyà* 'reorganized', *natan ʾilustracyà* 'illustrated'.

The consonant alternations to which the discontinuous morphemes (roots, radicals) are subject are the outcome of the phonologization of Biblical Hebrew allophonic relations (*3.5.3*): *p/f*, *k/x*, *b/v*, *ʾ/a*. Of these, only the first is predictable. Once it is stated that a root or a radical contains an alternating element in its initial position (*k/x-t-b/v* 'write', in contrast to *k-t-b* 'pole' or *x-t-v* 'cut (trees)'), the alternation in that position can be stated in simple morphophonemic rules (e.g. exclusion of the stop alternant in immediate succession to a preformative: *mixtav* 'letter'); no morphophonemic rule, however, applies to medial and final alternations. The avoidance of [p] and [b] in word final position is no morphophonemic alternation, but the result of phonological neutralization (*kotèv* 'pole' : *kotbiy* 'polar'; cf. *3.5.1*); otherwise, final alternation has much receded (standard *rtuvim* 'wet (m.pl.)', classicizing *rtubim* : *ratuv* (m.sg.), classicizing *ratov*), as a consequence of which forms showing it may be classified as irregular (e.g. *braxa* 'greeting' : *bir-kat-* 'greeting of').

Alternation in the medial position is not generally morphophonemically statable. It is characteristic of roots, and several radicals that have a common root may reveal different medical alternants (*x-b/v-š* 'dress (a wound)' : *xoveš* 'first aid (male) nurse' and *taxbošèt* 'bandage'); but the medial element of a radical is not an alternating consonant: while *hitxaber* 'joined (intr.)' selects the stop alternant from the alternating verbal root *x-b/v-r* 'join', in *hitxaver* 'became friends with' (*7.3.4*) which is derived from the nominal radical *x-v-r* in *xaver* 'friend', there is no feature of alternant selection; likewise *mesufam* 'mustached' from the radical *s-f-m* in *safam* 'mustache', the root of which is *s-f-* 'lip' (ROSÉN 1955a: 239; 1956b: 144–5).[112]

The radical has come to replace the root in all of the formational processes in Israeli Hebrew. Patterns that from the point of view of classical Hebrew had to be regarded as part of a verbal paradigm, i.e. root-based, have now to be considered as radical-motivated. A case in point are the numerous forms of the types $hitC_1aC_2eC_3$, $meC_1uC_2aC_3$ (cf. the examples above) that have, in current formation, nominal ramifications, but very frequently no paradigmatic relations to the verb system. Considering such forms as root-motivated would entail making the medial element subject to consonantal alternation; it is precisely in this respect that a clash is created between classical morphology and living morphological structure: classical morphology excludes the selection of the non-occlusive alternant in the medial position of the types $meC_1uC_2aC_3$, $hitC_1aC_2eC_3$, and of some others. The radical can take the place previously occupied by the root in practically any formational type; this becomes particularly significant in cases in which the radical is triliteral and consists of an afformative added to a biconsonantal

---

[112] Naive attempt at justifying this type by considering it as a stem type different from that of *hitxaber*: CHOMSKY (1958: 184–5).

root (cf. above), e.g. *m-s-d* 'institution' (root *y-s-d* 'institute, establish')
in *mosad* 'institution', *mised* 'institutionalized', and *mimsad* 'the
Establishment'. It is surprising that in spite of these possibilities
disturbing radical homophonies can be avoided; while there is, for
example, a radical *m-n-'/a* 'motor' (*manoa* 'motor', *memunaa*
'motorized') cognate with the root *n-'/a* 'move', a form *mimnaa* or
minua that could be brought into relation with the root *m-n-'/a*
'impede' would be utterly unthinkable. It can be seen that the Israeli
Hebrew radical functions correspondingly to the stem of European
languages.

6.1.3 Base

The BASE is derivationally productive; it is the continuous portion
of a word that contains the radical. It is obvious that the base is
normally bimorphematic, since it includes a discontinuous morpheme in addition to the radical, namely the BASE PATTERN, which
fills the empty spaces of the radical: *haxtavat-* 'dictating of' consists
of the radical *h-xt-v* 'dictate' and the base pattern *-a-a-at-* 'action
of', or rather '-ing' (which shows that the base patterns quite
frequently play the role of formational suffixes of European languages). However, some bases are not analysable into radical and
pattern morphemes (e.g. *yam* 'sea', *tapuax* 'apple', *ša'a* 'hour') and
must then be considered monomorphematic. While preformatives
that are part of a base are also part of its radical, any postformatives
are part of the pattern: *tizmorèt* 'orchestra', root *z-m-r* (*6.1.2*),
radical *t-zm-r* (as in *tizmur* 'orchestration'), base pattern (*R* for
radical element) *RiRoRèt* (as in *bikorèt* 'criticism' of the radical
b-k-r 'criticize'), base *tizmorèt*; *misgerèt* 'frame', root *s-g-r* '(en)-
close', radical *m-sg-r* (as in *misgur* 'framing', also in *masger* 'locksmith'), base pattern *RiReRèt*) as in *'ivelèt* 'foolishness' in view
of *'evil* 'fool'). The base pattern is subject to vowel alternation
(*tizmorto* 'his orchestra', *tizmorot* 'orchestras'; *misgarto* 'his frame',
misgarot 'frames'). These vowel alternations are the essence of
Israeli Hebrew inflexional morphology.

6.2 STEMS

6.2.1 Suffixes and prefixes

The morphological segment consisting of the base and all derivational SUFFIXES can suitably be termed STEM. The stem and the base may be identical (all examples of bases quoted hitherto are stems at the same time). In *'akšanuti* 'my obstinacy', the base *'akš-* 'obstinate' is enlarged by the derivational suffixes *-an* 'ordinarily characterized by (being)' and *-ut* 'quality' to form the stem *'akšanut*; the ending *-i* '1 pers.sg.' is not part of the stem. There is only one derivational PREFIX, the negator *'i-*, which can occur if the stem is characterized (by suffix or base pattern) as abstract, and will then be considered part of the stem: *'i-bhiruto* 'its unclearness' (the stem *'i-bhirut* contains the abstract suffix *-ut*), *'i-rišum* 'non-registration' (the base contains the pattern *RiRuR*, which characterizes it as the base of an action noun). Privative *bilti-* is an alternant of *'i-* (cf. below *6.4.2.1*).

6.2.2 Nominal, verbal, and compound nominal stems

The type of the stem determines the nature of the word in terms of the part of speech it represents: a stem containing derivational suffixes is nominal, a stem without them may be either nominal or verbal. It follows that in the fundamental opposition verb versus nomen, the nominal type is the marked term. This emerges from still another fact: verbal stems are always simple, nominal ones may contain two bases, and will then be considered COMPOUND STEMS (e.g. *rav-lšoniy* 'multilingual: bases *rav* 'much, many' and *lšon-* 'language', derivational suffix *-iy*). Compound stems have suffixes only after their second base. There are bases that exclusively occur as initial base of a compound stem, such as *xad-* 'one' in *xad-lšoniy* 'monolingual', or *tat-* 'sub-' in *tat-hakara* 'the subconscious, *Unterbewußtsein*'. These bases are of Aramaic origin (ROSÉN 1962a: 345–6; 1966b: 133–4). The features of compounding will be discussed below in section *6.5*.

6.2.3 Word openings, word endings

Since syntactically pertinent morphemes can precede the stem or
follow it, we should speak, in Israeli Hebrew, of WORD ENDINGS as well as
of WORD OPENINGS; both are continuous. The categorial contents of
'case' or positional-logical relation (*5.1.1*, *7.1.4*) are expressed by
openings, those of gender-number and sex-person by endings after
nominal stems, by openings as well as by endings after verbal ones
(*7.2.2*). The hierarchy with nominal forms is such that the personal
follow the gender-number endings: *dod-at-i* ('uncle' +' f.sg.'+' 1 pers.sg.')
'my aunt'. (It should be noted that there is no hierarchy for formational
suffixes: *-ut* 'abstract' and *-iy* [denominative adjective morpheme] may
follow each other in whatever order: *mahut* 'essence' [from *ma* 'what']:
mahutiy 'essential', and *xofšiy* 'free' [from *xofèš* 'freedom']: *xofšiyut*
'free behaviour'; there may even be repetition: *mciʾut* 'reality' [from
macuy 'existing'] : *mciʾutiy* 'real[istic]' : *mciʾutiyut* 'realism'.) Two successive positional-relational openings can occur in front of the noun stem;
in this case, the hierarchy is such that the first expresses a directional,
the second a positional content: *mi-taxàt-ha-šulxan* 'from under the
table' (*me-ha-šulxan* 'from the table', *taxàt-ha-šulxan* 'under the table')
and *ʾad-ʾaxare-šabat* 'until after Sabbath' (*ʾad-šabat* 'until Sabbath',
ʾaxare-šabat 'after Sabbath'); no such feature applies to other than
"local" prepositions (such as "logical" ones, as *bišvil* 'for'); cf. ROSÉN
(1955a: 207). A personal ending can occur, in formal or elevated style,
at the end of every verb, irrespective of whether the sex-person category
is already expressed by an opening or another ending: *ʾavakešxa* ('a-
'1 pers.sg.'+ -*xa* '2 pers.m.sg.'); in that case, the additional, non-obligatory
personal morpheme denotes the object: 'I would request you'. Two
successive personal morphemes are, consequently, admissible at the
end of verbs (comparable to the admissibility of two successive 'local'
prepositions at the beginning of the noun): *hizhartì-xa* ([-tíxa]; cf.
3.7.3) (-*tì* '1 pers.sg.') 'I warned you'.

6.3 DERIVATION

6.3.1 Morphological means

While the derivation of verb stems still rests exclusively on the base
pattern (*6.1.3*), affixal derivation is reserved for the formation of
nominal forms (this concerns nouns only, as we shall presently

show). It is typologically instructive to examine how formation types are related to semantic classes; since it has already been stated what categorial relations are expressed by the inflexional endings and "openings" (*6.2.3*), we shall now turn to the derivational suffixes.

6.3.2 Transformational suffixes

Two of the derivational suffixes are semantically void, and have transformational value only: -*ut* which is a 'name of a sentence content' and accords the stem to which it is attached the status of a noun (*b(a)ri'*(-) 'healthy' : *bri'ut* 'the state of being healthy, health'; *l-himace'* 'be found, *se trouver*, exist' : *himac'-ut* 'existence'); -*iy* accords the substantival stem to which it is attached attributive status (*5.7.2*): *yam* 'sea', *yamiy* 'marine, sea-'.

6.3.3 Contents of productive derivational suffixes

The contents expressed by the productive derivational suffixes are the same as in the European type of languages, so that Israeli Hebrew derivational suffixes can be considered the translational equivalents of European ones (cf. *4.3.3-5*). Needless to say that the equivalence is much greater for suffixes than for stems or radicals.

Following MASSON (1968), we can classify the productive derivational suffixes semantically as follows:

(1) Designations of females: -*a* (*sus* 'horse'; *susa* 'mare'; *xazir* 'pig': *xazira* abusive designation for a woman) is primary in the sense that the stem to which it is attached is in itself not morphologically characterized as an animate (see below); if the stem is so characterized, sex characterization is expressed (ROSÉN 1962a: 187-8)[113] by the suffix -*it* in case the ʿanimate' characterization is suffixal (*kamcanit* 'niggard (f.)': *kamcan* (m.) from the verbal base *kam(e)c-* 'be avaricious'; *'itona'it* 'journalist (f.).': *'itona'i* (m.) from *'iton* 'newspaperʿ) or by -*èt* with base pattern alternation if the 'animate' characterization is by base pattern (*mšorerèt* 'poetess', base pattern *me-o-e* 'participle'; *cayerèt* 'painter (f.).': *cayar* (m.) with base pattern -*a-a-* 'occupational noun', radical *c-y-r* 'depict') or by suffix other than 'animate' (*yaldonèt* 'girlie': *yaldon*

---

[113] Cf. COHEN – ZAFRANI (1968: 169-71).

diminutive from *yelèd*, *yald-* 'child'). The suffix *-it* is the "unconditioned" alternant in that it expands also over unanalysable stems (*'ezraxit* 'citizen (f.)' : *'ezrax* (m.)) or marginally situated (*3.4.2*) lexical entities (*studéntit* : *studént*; *mašákit* : *mašák*, army acronym for 'non-commissioned officer').

(2) Designations of animates: by character, occupation or the like: *-an*(*harpatkan* 'adventurer': *harpatka* 'adventure'; *mizraxan* 'Orientalist': *mizrax* 'Orient'); by occupation only: *-a'i*[114] (*'itona'i* 'journalist'; *xašm(a)la'i* 'electrician' : *xašmal* 'electricity'.

(3) Diminutives-hypocoristics: with countables: *-on* (*sifron* 'booklet': *sefèr*, *sifr-* 'book'), hypocoristic (ALTBAUER 1949) with animates (*tipšon* 'dear little fool': *tipeš* 'fool'; *xaziron* 'piggy, little boy behaving like a pig': *xazir* 'pig, swine'; *suson* 'Pferdchen' and *suson-yam* 'hippocampus' : *sus* 'horse'); diminutive only: *-it* (*mapit* 'napkin': *mapa* 'tablecloth') (cf. *7.1.1*). Hypocoristic interpretation of the *-it* suffix is excluded, since it has, in 'animate' surroundings, another function ('female', see under (1)), so that in this case, as in all others, apparent polysemy is merely complementary distribution of semantic ranges.

(4) Designations of objects: with non-countables (cf. under (3)) *-on* (*karxon* 'iceberg': *keràx*, *karx-* 'ice'; *šalgon* 'icecream stick': *šelèg*, *šalg-* 'snow'; *'iton* 'journal' : *'et*, *'it-* 'time'; cf. *4.3.2*); *'aviron* 'aeroplane': *'avir* 'air', and *sfaton* 'lipstick' : *sfatayìm* 'lips' show the trend for more specific usage as *nomina instrumenti*.

(5) Designation of localities: *-iya* (*tikiya* 'file cabinet' : *tik* 'file'; *nagariya* 'carpenter's workshop' : *nagar* 'carpenter').[115]

(6) Designation of groups: with motivating stem in the 'numerical' field: *-iya* (*šlišiya* 'trio' : *šlišiy* 'third'; *'asiriya* 'decade, a ten-pound note' : *'asiriy* 'tenth').

6.3.4 Relations between suffixal and nonsuffixal derivation

A concluding remark must be made concerning the mutual relations between the various derivational means of expression, that is base patterns and suffixes on the one hand, and compounding,

---

[114] The current shape of the suffix differs from the puristically required one (*-ay*, same spelling {-'y}) only in the endingless m.sg. M.pl.: *-a'im* in both styles.

[115] For localities with reference to designations of "functionaries", the abstract *-ut* is used by extension calqued on European models: *soxnut* 'agency' from *soxen* 'agent'; *gizbarut* 'cashier's office' from *gizbar* 'cashier'; *mazkirut* 'secretariate' from *mazkir* 'secretary'.

which we shall have to treat in a later section,[116] on the other. There is some competition still between the base pattern and the derivational suffix, in cases in which, in inherited words, a pattern expresses a content, normally denoted by a suffix, and no replacement or semantic shift (such as that in the case of *godèl*; *4.3.4*) has taken place; e.g. *xošèx* 'darkness' : *xašux* 'dark'. As a rule, such words are semantically much more flexible than the suffixal formations, which generally stay within the limits of a *nomen qualitatis*: e.g. *'omèk* 'depth, deep water' versus *'amkut* 'depth, profoundness'; as in this case, there is frequently semantic differentiation between the suffix-bearing and the suffixless abstract: *'onì* 'poverty of means' versus *'aniyut* 'poverty of certain qualities'; *košì* 'difficulty' and *kašut* 'hardness', both from *kaše* 'hard (*hart*), difficult', cf. *cold* (noun) versus *coldness*. The suffixless abstracts tend to serve as *voces mediae* (*4.3.4*): *xom* 'heat, temperature' (its opposite, *kor* 'cold', is not a *vox media*).

A base pattern that expresses a content which is not a term of a derivational relation in the ordinary lexicon of European languages does not risk being ousted by a suffixal formation. For instance, the 'ailment' pattern (*4.1.6*) *-a-e-èt* has no suffixal competitor (*cahevèt* 'jaundice' : radical *c-h-b/v* 'yellow', adj. *cahov*); a "translation" of this pattern would be *-osy* (Graeco-Latin *-osis*), which cannot be regarded as a centrally located vocabulary item in European languages. Such pattern is inserted in radicals irrespective of whether they are identical with roots or not: *gar'enèt* 'trachoma' (radical *g-r'-n* : *gar'in* 'kernel, nucleus, granulum').

The interplay discussed above (*4.3.5*) between the pattern *-a-i-* and the compositional formation with initial member *bar-* (followed by action noun), both corresponding to '-able' and complementarily distributed according to radical structure (the pattern formation admissible only with triliteral radicals) remains an isolated case. Otherwise, there can be no functional relation between compositional formations and patterns, the reason being that in an endo-

---

[116] The section in COHEN – ZAFRANI (1968: 144–51) is inadequate (non-distinction of affixation and compounding, of reference and meaning, of syntactic function and derivational properties, as well as of stylistic levels).

centric compound, the initial member is the determinatum, and in derivational formations, the determinatum is a suffix (unless a base pattern). It follows from these fundamental order properties that anything even remotely resembling agglutinatory processes is inconceivable in the development of Hebrew.

6.4 STRONG AND WEAK MORPHOLOGICAL TYPES

6.4.1 Definition and criteria of classification

No description of morphological, and even some syntactic, types of Israeli Hebrew can be adequate without a division into STRONG and WEAK form classes; two factors are mainly responsible for the emergence of this necessity:

(a) the synchronic coexistence of form types that, by chronology and evolution, succeeded each other in classical Hebrew,

(b) the prevailing tendency of assimilation to European-type processes of derivation and inflexion.

The scope of the strong and, respectively, weak classes appears to be analogous to the correspondingly named morphological classes in Indo-European, Germanic in particular:

(a) inflexional and derivational relations within the weak class show no alternations of stem or base elements (which, in the case of Israeli Hebrew, implies consonantal as well as vocalic alternation);

(b) the alternations, on the other hand, that are apparent in the strong types are generally synchronically unpredictable, while diachronically in part interpretable (conversion of allophonic relations into morphophonemic ones);

(c) in certain types, categorial distinctions expressed by vocalic, and maybe consonantal, alternation in strong forms, are expressed by affixation in weak types;

(d) word stems that underlie "strong" formational processes are neither derived nor secondary, but have to be considered radical or primary;

(e) a general tendency constantly and consistently shifts currently used lexical items from the strong to the weak class;

(f) wherever an older and a recent layer of form types can be distinguished, the ancient stock is of the strong type; the weak types alone are formationally productive and increasingly represent regularity in morphological processes.

While the weak versus strong distinction has been clearly and not inexhaustively set out in most of its implications for verbs (ROSÉN 1962a: 31-2, 106, 125-6, 134-5, 140-2), nouns (ROSÉN 1962a: 54-5, 58, 100-1, 162, 172, 181), and adjectives (ROSÉN 1962a: 30, 198-9, 215, 241-2, 263-4) (admittedly, terminology was inspired by the Indo-European parallels), this useful and necessary classification has not been followed up by other grammarians: we may ascribe this to a general reluctance to re-classify morphological material, nurtured by the assumption that the tabulation of Hebrew word forms was *chose acquise* and adequately covered by classical-based paradigm tables. We shall, therefore, have to present here some of the most salient facts and features that entail the necessity of the strong : weak classification for purposes of morphological as well as syntactic description.

6.4.2 The distinction of strong and weak types

6.4.2.1 Adjective morphology

The discussion of the adjectives proves more illustrative than that of other morphological classes for which the strong versus weak distinction has been established. Let us consider the following set of forms:

nakiy[117]	'clean (m.sg.)'	*yamiy*[117]	'marine (m.sg.)'
nkiyim	(m.pl.)	*yamiyim*	(m.pl.)
nkiyot	(f.pl.)	*yamiyot*	(f.pl.)
nkiya	(f.sg.)	*yamit*	(f.sg.)

[117] The final *-y* has morphophonemic status only and corresponds to no phonetic reality.

9*

The two paradigms represent the two adjective classes: the one to be termed "strong" in the left column, weak adjectives in the right one. The two columns exhibit two concomitant differences: suffix fem.sg. -*a* (strong) versus -*t* (weak); loss of the open -*a*-vowel in the suffixed forms (strong) versus maintenance of the stem vocalization (weak). The strong class represented by *nakiy* consists of the old stock of qualitative radical verbal nominals (ROSÉN 1962b: 829–31) that has ceased to be productive, apart from radical passive participles (types *CaCuC*, *CaCiC*) that are freely formed. The weak class comprises all other participles and, mainly, all derived adjectives (-*iy* in *yamiy* is the common derivative adjective suffix) the motivating stem may be either of a noun, as *yam*- 'sea', or of an inflexionless form, e.g. *'efšar* 'it is possible' → *'efšariy* 'possible'; and even composite phrases are found as the base of derivation : e.g. *xad* 'one' (aram.) + *paàm* 'instance, *Mal'* → *xad-paamiy* 'occurring once, not repeated, *einmalig*', cf. *6.5.2.2*). This abundantly productive class continues a no less copious stock of post-biblical derived adjectives, the -*t* ending in the feminine singular significantly testifying to the absorption of Aramaic morphology; the strong class, in contrast, is made up of Biblical words (the Biblical Hebrew feminine singular ending being -*à*, with -*t* being optional in voice-characterized participles only). The Israeli Hebrew vowel alternation in the strong class goes back to the allophonic variation of Biblical Hebrew *à* that disappears due to accent removal (*3.5.2*) and is the characteristic vowel in the first syllable of voice-uncharacterized (stative-qualitative) verbal nominals; Biblical Hebrew nouns unrelated to verbal paradigms (e.g. *ṣad·i·q*) may have *a* (not *à*) in a closed pretonic syllable, and if such nouns are, in Israeli Hebrew, reclassed as adjectives, their non-alternating *a* (*cadik* 'righteous') may constitute an exception that necessitates individual listing (*cadika, cadikim*); such exceptions are, however, few, although some post-biblical adjectives tend to be thus inflected in current spoken style (*vatik* 'old-timer, of old standing', *vatika, vatikim*).[118]

[118] The answer to the question whether this adjective was classically strong or weak still rests with *variae lectiones*, although *à* in the initial syllable of the suffixless form is unanimously attested. The fact that our two base examples,

Now, the question is whether what has been said up to here is merely a descriptive statement or whether the distinction of strong and weak adjectives is of any classificatory value in a way that further descriptive statements can be reached making use of the one already made. The latter is clearly the case:

(1) The formation of adjective constructs (*6.5.2.3*) can be attested only for first members that are either strong adjectives (morphologically in construct state: *ktan-koma* 'of small stature') or participles (*megudal-zakan* 'with a beard grown', or *štul-lev* 'with a planted heart, heart-transplantee'); derived adjectives have no construct forms (ROSÉN 1962a § 40.1).

(2) The privative prefix *bilti*- joins weak adjectives only: *bilti-'efšariy* 'impossible'[119], or *bilti-menumas* 'uncourteous'; the generally used adjective negator is *lo* 'not', which is not restricted to any one class of adjectives, and can also be used in litotic construction with *bilti*- (e.g. *lo-bilti-menumas* 'not uncourteous'); this shows that *lo* and *bilti*- are categorially different: *bilti*- does not negate, but rather converts; its semantic effect can be reached, with weak adjectives, only by selection of another lexical entity of "opposite" sense: *lo-katan* 'not small' is litotically analogous to *gadol* 'big'; cf. *lo-ra'* 'not bad'.

(3) The most significant use can be made of the adjective classification according to the strong and weak classes for the purpose of describing as well as teaching formal relations between otherwise semantically equivalent adverbs and adjectives ('free' : 'freely'). This feature has to

---

nakiy and *yamiy*, although rhyming, are of different structure, and would have to be vocalized, in Tiberian vowel signs, the latter *-am·-*, the former *-âq-*, is not pertinent for our purposes, since it is not the classically doubly closed vowel *a* of *yamiy* (which, besides, is not really attested in its vocalized form) that is responsible for the weakness of its inflexion; the traditionally accepted forms of postbiblical derived adjectives allows of no replacement of *â* by Ø, although quite some infringement on basic vocalization rules results; cf. *dât* 'religion' and *dâti·* /datiy/ 'religious' : *dâtiy·i·m* /datiyim/.

[119] Justification for the term *privative*: (1) *bilti*- is not negative (see below), so another term is needed; (2) it appears that *bilti*- does not negate the derived adjective which it precedes, but the adjective's base word; *bilti*- replaces *'i*- in derivation: *'efšar* 'it is possible', *'efšariy* 'possible', *'i-'efšar* 'it is impossible', *bilti-'efšariy* 'impossible'; *sedèr* 'order', *mesudar* 'well-ordered, orderly', *'i-sedèr* 'disorder', *bilti-mesudar* 'disorderly', so that *bilti*- is suitably paraphrased by 'not inherently possessing or having what is expressed by the base noun'; (3) to invoke the analogy of IE *Xn: (Gk. ά privativum, Skr. *a(n)*-, Lat. *in*-, Germanic *un*-) that have all developed into "negatives" from "privatives" through the mediation of derived adjectives.

be viewed in its various aspects that also include puristic treatments, in which environmental limitations were misinterpreted as "trends". The facts are best exhibited by four sets of constructions:

	1 (nominal construction)	2 (verbal construction)
A	*ktiva yafa* 'beautiful writing'	*katav yafe* 'wrote beautifully'
B	*ktiva kcara* 'brief writing'	*katav kacar* 'wrote briefly'
C	*ktiva brura* 'clear writing'	*katav barur* or:
		katav be-ʾofèn barur 'wrote clearly'
D	*ktiva xofšit* 'free writing'	*katav be-ʾofèn xofšiy* 'wrote freely'

The verbal construction in B represents a type declared "incorrect" by purists, and is admittedly familiar style. It contains as an adverbial complement a masculine singular adjective form (*kacar*), a use that has been compared to German or Yiddish (*er schreibt kurz*, although *kurz* is properly neither masculine singular nor adjectival[120], but simply devoid of suffix), but more exactly fits Russian, where the adverbial form corresponds to the gender-uncharacterized ("neuter") nominative-accusative singular of the adjective. The adverb *yafe* (A) is also a masculine singular form, but not campaigned against by purists, since precisely this form, although of an entirely different morphological and syntactic status, is biblically used as a "circumstantial" complement.[121] However, describing the occurrence of masculine singular adjective forms as adverbial complements as either a "common mistake" or a "characteristic tendency" of "spoken Hebrew" is inadequate in that respect that this usage is excluded in any style from the great majority of Israeli Hebrew adjectives: the weak ones that are not of participial pattern (example D). Consequently, the productive class of adjectives assigns, in keeping with Western typology, a regularly used morpheme (*be-* + *ʾofèn* 'in a ... fashion, in a ... way') to creating a morphologically marked class of adverbs.[122] But this formation, inversely, is excluded

---

[120] In *Er ist kurz* the form *kurz* must be properly considered an adverb; there is no other type of occurrence for *kurz*. This fact as well as the parallelism between *Die Zeit ist kurz* : *die kurze Zeit*, and *Der Vortrag war gestern* : *der gestrige Vortrag* are not irrelevant to the question of *the late Churchill*, not to speak of *the second Chomsky*.

[121] Cf. AVINERY (1933: 34), ROSÉN (1962b: 831–2). That adverbial BH *yάpe* can be < *yapiya, as I have there posited in accordance with other grammarians, is now corroborated by *-*iya* > -*e* in verb forms.

[122] I do not know when exactly *be-ʾofèn* began to function as described; at any rate, this seems to have occurred within revived Hebrew. The similarity with, e.g., -*mente* is functional only, in no way lexical, and takeover must be excluded. There are also some stylistic variants, e.g. *be-cura* 'in ... fashion' (with feminine singular adjective form), or *be-ʾoràx* 'in ... way', that are, however, of restricted use.

from strong adjectives: *be-ɔofèn raɔ 'in a bad fashion' would be about as impossible[123] as *mauvaisement, and *be-ɔofèn tov 'in a good fashion' as inadmissible as goodly in adverb status; only type C (weak adjectives of participial pattern) admits both formations. In what way adverbial tov or raɔ can be replaced by stylistically more desirable forms, need not concern us here;[124] in this context, we had only to show the indispensability of classifying the adjectives into strong and weak in order to describe adverb formation adequately.

6.4.2.2 Verb morphology

The introduction of a strong : weak distinction for verbal morphology is not really a necessity that arises out of any development that has taken place in or before Israeli Hebrew; it is only a very useful and lucid way to state facts and relations that have always been is existence in Hebrew (let us be reminded here of the fact that verbal inflexion is probably the most conservative part of Hebrew morphology), and it is eminently fitted to serve as the basis for a well-planned course of teaching. It might even be well applicable, mutatis mutandis, to Semitic in general.

A Hebrew verb form is traditionally always assigned to one of the STEM PATTERNS (binyanim) that contain the root and the pattern formatives, but in one of which the pattern formative is nil, so that

---

[123] A sort of morphological zeugma may, however, occur in cases in which two or more adjectives, one of which (usually not the first) go with adverb-forming be-ɔofèn, e.g. be-ɔofèn lakuy ve-raɔ 'deficiently and badly'; also negated strong adjectives admit be-ɔofèn more freely: be-ɔofèn lo raɔ 'not badly'.

[124] See also note 122. It is not true that "les nuances exprimées par les adverbes de manière [unless French adverbs are meant] peuvent l'être analytiquement au moyen de constructions comme bɔofen, bɔura, bɔmida qui signifient 'de manière, de façon' etc." (COHEN – ZAFRANI 1968: 236). There is no non-analytical synonym given of, e.g., be-ɔofèn barur; the vast sample list of "modal adverbs" (COHEN – ZAFRANI 1968: 235–6) is almost entirely made up of nouns prefixed by a preposition and univerbated (as beracon 'gladly') or of forms that, although their initial segment is be-, are no longer analysable (as beserugin 'intermittently'); almost none of these forms are replaceable by be-ɔofèn-phrases. Unfortunately the entire chapter (COHEN – ZAFRANI 1968: 231–9) is questionable, mainly because no neat distinction is drawn between adverbs and words functioning as adverbial complements or between adverbs and modifiers of various kinds.

The weak verb system

		Active	Passive
NON-NARRATIVE BASE	Infinitive	I lesader 'arrange' II lehagdil 'enlarge' III lešaxzer 'reconstruct' IV lehitlabeš 'get dressed'	— — —
	Aorist ('Present' or 'Participle') Stem	I mesader- II magdil- III mešaxzer- IV mitlabeš-	I mesudar- II mugdal- III mešuxzar-
	Imperative-Potential ('Future') Stem	I -sader- II -(h)agdil- III -šaxzer- IV -(h)itlabeš-	I -sudar- II -(h)ugdal- III -šuxzar-
REMOTIVE ('PAST') STEM		I sider II higdil III šixzer IV hitlabeš-	I sudar- II hugdal- III šuxzar-

there the consonantal radical (*6.1.2*) of the stem would equal the root: *Grundstamm, binyan kal* (or *Qal* or *Pấ'al*); it is this radical formation that we will consider as STRONG (because underived and for other reasons to be set out immediately) although traditional terminology implies a different impression (*qal* 'light'), while all other stem formations taken together shall be termed WEAK. The justification of such a procedure will come to light in sets of forms like the one in the table on p. 136.

This table represents the well-known Hebrew verbal stems (other than the *Qal* and its passive counterpart *Nif'al*), namely:

Pattern (R = radical element)	*k-t-l* root active	Pattern word passive	Traditional active	Name passive
I *RiReR*	*kital*	*kutal*	Pi'el	Pu'al
II *hiRRiR*	*hiktil*	*huktal*	Hif'il	Hof'al
III *šiRReR*	*šiktel*	*šuktal*	Sif'el	Suf'al
IV *hitRaReR*	*hitkatel* (voice-indifferent, intrans.)			Hitpa'el

Only one minor omission is made for the sake of simplification: the formation type *hištaRReR* (Hištaf'el) which is a combination of types III and IV is not specifically mentioned. The table is therefore representative of all weak verb stems and exhaustive of all productive formations, whether deverbative or denominative. Cf. also 7.3.4.

An exhaustive description of verbal forms for all categorial distinctions would contain formation of person-number characterized forms as well as expression of voice distinctions and time-modality differences. The relation of person-number-affixed forms to the tense stem is common to all stem types, weak and strong, and need not concern us at the moment. Furthermore, the mutual relations of the stem types are derivational, lexical, or transformational (*7.3.1,4*) and therefore outside the scope of verbal inflexional morphology proper; as a result, description of verbal inflexion can and must be carried out without any reference to the root (as in other types of languages where a root : stem distinction exists, e.g. in

Types of strong verb stems

	I	II	III	IV	V	VI	VII
	Isolated verb[125]	Inchoatives and some other intransitive verbs[126]	Biblical intransitives developed into transitives[127]	Intransitives not included in previous classes and transitives[127]	Irregular type	Irregular type	Irregular type
	'be able'	'grow'	'wear (a garment)'	'guard'	'live (at a place)'	'sing'	'be seated'
Infinitive (Act.)	—	ligdol	lilboš	lišmor	lagur	lašír	lašévet
Imperative-Potential Stem (Active)	-uxal- (no imper.)	-(i)gdal-	-(i)lbaš-	-(i)šmor-	-(a)gúr-	-(a)šír-	-(e)šev-
Aorist Stem (Active)	yaxol-	gadel-	loveš-	šomer-	gar-	šar-	yošev-
Remotive Stem (Active)	haya yaxol or[128] yaxal-	gadal-[129]	lavaš-	šamar-	hay- gár- or[130] gár-	šár-	yašav-
Infinitive (Passive)			lehilaveš	lehišamer	isolated irregular forms		

			(numerous intransitive verbs without corresponding passive forms)
Imperative – Potential Stem (Pass.)			-(h)išamer-
Aorist Stem (Pass.)	nilbaš-	nišmar-	
Remotive Stem	nilbaš-	nišmar-	

[125] Only remainder of a formational type of qualitative verbs that have all been reclassed as adjectives (cf. ROSÉN 1962b: 830, especially footnote 13).

[126] Inchoativity is a secondary development (ROSÉN 1962a § 52.5; 1962b: 829–30 footnote 12; 1969: 106) and so is transitivity in class III (BH *lābēš* 'be clad'); some semantic developments and differentiations indicate that intransitive inchoativity is felt to be attached to class II (*lilmod* has two aorists: *lomed* (class III) 'learn, study' and *lamed* (class II) 'learn, become aware'); *yašen* (class II) has, in some styles (in which foreign lexical influence is strongly noticeable), the meaning 'fall asleep, go to bed' (BLANC 1964a: 148), while the standard meaning is 'sleep', for which a sub-standard aorist of class IV is in widespread use.

[127] Verbs of this class with diphthongally alternating third radical (*liftoax* 'open', *lišmoa* 'hear') have *a* in the potential stem (*yiftax* /yiftaax/, *yišmaa*) which makes them appear like class III aorists; a verb should consequently be considered as unequivocally belonging to class III only if its third radical is nondiphthongal.

[128] *Yaxal* (3 m.sg.) is sub-standard, arising out of generalization of the *a*-vowel in the final syllable of strong remotive stems. For the use of the auxiliary, see 7.2.1.

[129] The Biblical perfect was *gᵊādēl*; the characteristic sign of qualitative-stative verbs in Biblical Hebrew was the identity, for all practical purposes, of the two nominals ('participle' and 'perfect'); Biblical Hebrew verbs of the stative class should be considered as having only one form besides the prefix-tense. IH *gadal* (*gadel* obsolete for the remotive) is due to the generalization of *a* (cf. the foregoing note) that already begins in Biblical Hebrew.

[130] For the use of the auxiliary in sentences otherwise not time-characterized to avoid ambiguity due to homonymy with the aorist, see 7.2.1.

Indo-European) and base itself on stem types ("conjugations"). Now, if we take into account that conjugation by person-number is describable for all verb types in common, an exhaustive presentation can be made for the formal relations within each weak stem by means of prefixal relations and one single ablaut-type alternation $a/i/u$:

(1) Voice-characterized stems have (unless of phonologically deviant root type) a in the first syllable of their non-narrative active base, which is replaced by i in the active remotive tense and by u in the passive forms of all tenses; these passive forms have, moreover, a in the final stem syllable. No such predictable regularity is observable in the strong verbs (see below).

(2) Where several stems have the same base, their formal relation is affixal: prefixes le-, me-, $\emptyset$ for the infinitive, aorist, imperative (active only) respectively, whereby contractions arising out of the loss of a base-initial h can be conveniently accounted for.[131] In strong verbs, not only can no similarly predictable regularity be seen, but, moreover, alternation of the stem elements takes the place of, or crosses with, the prefixal relations.

The intricacy of the strong verb system, the description of which may easily result in a quasi-individual listing of verbs, can be shown by a confrontation of various typical representatives of the strong (Qal) conjugation; note that no non-narrative base common to several tense stems may here be posited (table on pp. 138-9).

While the examples of "irregular" types introduced on pp. 138-9 constitute a far from exhaustive presentation of exceptional features due to deviant root structure, still only part of the particular root types need be considered when weak stems of these roots are described as to their inflexion. Those irregularities, for example, that are due to the intermittent appearance of a certain third radical element at initial root position (traditional classes I^{ae} *yod*, as in the example 'be seated', I^{ae} *nun*) do not create any necessity for indi-

---

[131] There are comparatively very few roots with initial h, and only about a dozen *pi'el* stems with initial h are in current use, so that they form a small group of "exceptions", if we wish (as we should) not to introduce the notions of root and *binyan* into the description and teaching of verbal inflexion.

vidual description within the system of the weak stem: the base type
(-)*yašev-*/*yišev-* 'settle' (*I^{ae}* *yod*) and (-)(*h*)*asia-*/*hisía* 'let ride'
(*I^{ae}* *nun*) are subject to exactly the same inflexional rules as any
other weak verb base; root structure, however, must be taken
account of in discussing the relations between weak and strong
stems of the same root, but then, this belongs to formation and not
to inflexion. Furthermore, many of the inflexional phenomena that
are due to particular root structures (e.g. alternation of *b k p* in
alternating stems; alternating diphthongs in root final position;
finally open[132] biconsonantal roots) can be covered by rules that are
common to both the weak and the strong stem types. A considerable
amount of economy can consequently be achieved, even with
respect to "irregularities", by a strong : weak classification of verbal
morphology.

6.4.2.3 Noun morphology

While, admittedly, the weak : strong distinction has no classificatory value for noun morphology, since no further facts can be
derived from a given noun belonging to either class, it is of considerable theoretical interest and allows some insight into how the
present shape of Israeli Hebrew has grown out of certain characteristically Semitic features of morphology.

Vowel alternation may play a role in morphological distinctions
of two dimensions: number (*sefèr* 'book': pl. *sfarim*; always concomitant with affixation) and status (*7.1.5*; e.g. *ša'a* 'hour' :
construct state *š'at-* '-hour'; may be concomitant with affix alternation, but not with affixation). These two types of strongness are
essentially different, historically and comparatively as well as
descriptively, and one will be well advised to keep them neatly
apart; this has been attempted by introducing the term SEMI-WEAK
for those nouns that show no vowel alternation in the number opposition, but reveal alternation in the status contrast (ROSÉN 1962a:

---

[132] I.e. whose third radical is neither consonantal nor diphthongal, but a
simple vowel; e.g. *kaniti* : *kana* 'I : he bought' (Semitic *III^{ae}* *yod* class) (ROSÉN
1962a §§ 45.1[G], 4; cf. BAR-ADON 1959: 8).

88–9[133]); the noun *ša'a* just quoted is, in effect, semi-weak. The strong noun *sefèr* shows alternation for status (in the plural) in addition to alternation for number: *sifre-* (pl. constr.) '-books'.

Alternation for status is the result of the phonological reshuffle (rephonemicization) of the Hebrew vowels (*3.5.1–4*). All differences of vocalization observable in the Tiberian Biblical text between the construct and absolute (non-construct) form of a given noun are subphonemic in nature (ROSÉN 1953c: 36–40); a phonemic representation of both forms is identical apart from whatever affixal alternation intervenes; the juncture feature materialized by uniting the construct and the construent (governing noun) by means of "hyphenating", whereby the construct has to give up its proper stress and all its vowel phonemes are materialized as stress-remote, accounts for the appearance of such antepretonic allophones as Ø (*šwâ*) as a replacement of *â* (ROSÉN 1964: 166): BH /qâṣir/ *qâṣi·r* (abs). 'harvest' : /qâṣir-ḥiṭ·im/ *qṣi·r ḥiṭ·i·m* 'wheat-harvest'. We have explained elsewhere (*3.5.2.*) why the vowel differences that distinguish absolute from construct forms can no longer be considered subphonemic in Israeli Hebrew; an ancient allophonic variation has developed into morphophonemic alternation (/kacir/: /kcir xitim/).

The same type of originally allophonic, now morphophonemic alternation can be found in the relation of singular to plural forms of masculine nouns, where the additional suffix of the plural form attracts the accent and creates the conditions for the alternation discussed: /dâbâr/ *d·âbâr* : /dâbârim/ *d·bâri·m* > /davar/ : /dvârim/.

However, there are differences in stem structure in the singular and plural that could at no stage be considered as due to allophonic variation, and here the strong character of the noun stems concerned has been a historical fact for all periods of Hebrew: *sefèr* : *sfarim*, and *simla* 'dress': *smalot*; but this type of strongness exceeds the boundaries of Hebrew; it is, if not a Semitic feature, at least characteristically an isogloss for some of the Semitic languages for which the vocalic structure of word-stems is on record. It is this feature that has given birth to the sentiment of strongness versus non-strongness in the minds of Semitic native grammarians as well as to a picturesque term for strong morphological behaviour: BROKEN. In an Arabic noun like *malik* 'king' : *mulūk-* (pl. stem), the "broken" plural is truly of strong nature, since here the vowel

---

[133] The terms used in the book referred to are *strong, semi-strong* (nouns with vowel alternation for number, but not for status inflexion), *semiᵇweak*, *weak*. We shall here drop the distinction between strong and semi-strong nouns, since this classification has, at most, didactic value.

alternation excludes the occurrence of a plural suffix that characterizes plurals of 'unbroken' form. In Hebrew, strong plurals are overcharacterized: the otherwise corresponding BH /malk/ *melek* : /mlåkim/> IH /melèx/ : /mlaxim/ has the plural doubly marked: by vowel alternation as well as by the affix. It is only because of this that, synchronically, they can be put at the same level as the above-quoted type /davar/: /dvarim/, where there is no original strongness at all.

If we have correctly assessed the "Semitic" situation as presenting strongness, for one formational type of radical (primary) nouns, in respect of the singular : plural relation, but not for the *status absolutus* : *status constructus* relation, then we have found, at the same time, a good formula for what the "trend", at least, is in Israeli Hebrew. Like many languages that possess strong alongside weak morphological processes, Israeli Hebrew shows the characteristic signs of levelling inflexional relations in favour of the weak type. However, these "analogical" processes are hardly noticeable in cases where morphological strongness pertains to the category of number (the types of radical nouns *ReRèR* : *RRaRim*, and *RiRRa* : *RRaRot* that are precisely the Semitic strong nouns are so negligibly affected by intrusions of weakness even on the part of less educated speakers that they have to be considered outright the regular representatives of strong nouns (ROSÉN 1962a: 53–4)); on the other hand, consistent observation of strong vowel relations in the 'status' category is an eloquent sign of erudition; daily, many nouns leave the semi-weak class to become perfectly weak; analogies are mostly based on the absolute form, but in cases of highly frequent use in construct phrases, or in constantly compositional or possessive environments are occasionally also based on the original construct form; e.g. *ymin* 'right side' (mostly with construent personal suffix: *ymini* 'my right') has, in standard style, lost the particular absolute form (Biblical Hebrew) *yåmi·n*. Since strongness in status relations appears in radical as well as derived nouns, but is restricted to primary and agent nouns[134] as far as the number category is concerned, the obvious tendency not to include status

---

[134] Compare the analogously intermediate position of participles and participle-type adjectives; see *6.4.2.1.*

in those categories, expression of which can be morphologically strong, creates a new correlation between strongness and radicality in nouns, comparable to that shown for verbs and adjectives.

While even weak regular feminine singular and masculine plural nouns still differ by status due to the difference of endings (*-a* : *-at*; *-im* : *-e*; *-ayìm* : *-e*), weakness in the other half of nouns (fem.pl., m.sg.) is tantamount to morphological identity of the two forms, that is to neutralization of the status opposition, and consequently converts status, with these nouns, into a purely syntactic category (ROSÉN 1957: 341–2). If it is borne in mind that status (i.e. the fact of a noun's governing or not another noun) is not a morphological category at all in Western languages (only the fact of being or not being governed is) and, secondly, that the preservation of strong morphological behaviour in the Israeli Hebrew number category may have been supported by the perseverance of vowel change (albeit not of ablaut but rather of umlaut-character) as a means of plural formation in German and Yiddish, then Israeli Hebrew, at the cost of obliterating certain subtleties of Biblical vocalization, not only tends to reconstitute its original (Semitic) behaviour in this respect, but also clearly assimilates to European typology.

6.5 COMPOUNDING

6.5.1 Structure of compounds

COMPOUNDING as a morphological process yields only nominal forms; the maximum number of bases represented in any one compound is two. In endocentric compounds, the order is determinatum – determinans: *'eglat-yladim* (*'agala*, construct *'eglat-* 'carriage', *yladim* 'children') 'perambulator' (cf. *Kinderwagen*).

Compounding has semantic effects; in the absence of formal criteria to decide whether compounding has taken place or not, these effects may be used to reach a decision: *beyt-(ha-)mlaxa* (*bayìt*, constr. *beyt-* 'house', *mlaxa* 'craft') '(the) workshop' will be considered a compound due to the non-preservation of the semantic component 'house' with the concomitant severe restriction of the replaceability of any one of the components by members of its substitution class (such as *binyan* 'building' for *beyt-*, or *'avoda* 'work' for *mlaxa*); on the other hand, *beyt-'even* 'stone house' is not a compound (*beyt-* freely replaceable by, e.g., *binyan, gedèr-* 'fence', and the like, *'even* by the name of any building material).

Each inflexional category is only once represented in a compound.[135] The determinator appears between the two components, but semantically belongs to the compound as a whole[136]: *beyt-(ha-)-mlaxa* (above). The same is valid for personal determination: *beyt-mlaxti* 'my workshop' (1 pers.sg. -*i* does not refer to *mlaxt-* 'craft'). It is only apparently that there are two number-morphemes in a compound; in *'eglot-yladim* 'perambulators', only -*ot* represents the number category (*'eglat-yladim* sg. versus *'eglot-yladim* pl.), but the plural suffix -*im* does not represent any category, since it is not replaceable by Ø 'sg.'; the choice of an irreplaceable plural or singular morpheme at the end of a compound is very often indicated by a foreign model: *'eglot-yladim* 'Kinderwagen' (ROSÉN 1957: 327). For the gender category, the elimination of double representation in a compound has led to *ben-dod* 'cousin (m.)' (literally 'uncle's son') versus *bat-doda* (f.) (literally 'aunt's daughter') to the exclusion

---

[135]   The double adjectives of the type *datiy-ʰumiy* (*dat* 'religion', *ʰom* 'nation', double -*iy* as denominative suffix) 'religious-national', discussed by KADDARI (1965), with repeated adjectival -*iy* (only this suffix occurs in such formations) are not properly compounds. There is no syntactic relation between the terms, every one of the members of the compounds may independently of the other replace the entire compound (*miflaga datit-ʰumit* 'National-Religious Party', with double feminine ending -*t*, may be replaced by *miflaga datit* or *miflaga ʰumit*), that is, these expressions would have two centres! Accordingly, the appositional constructions of this type (*appositional* is the term appropriate for the mutual syntactic relation of the two complete adjectives) cannot even be considered dvandvas.

[136]   That double occurrence of a determinative morpheme is excluded is a fact going back to Biblical Hebrew; closer moulding together of components with double determination (BH *hă'ărōn-hab·ri·t*, literally 'the 'The-Covenant Ark''') is isolated even in Biblical Hebrew; achieving the same effect in Israeli Hebrew by different placement of the "article" (*ha-ben-'adam* 'the son-of-man') is clearly substandard. Cf. also ROSÉN (1961a: 21-5).

from standard usage of formations whose literal rendering would have been 'aunt's son', and 'uncle's daughter', respectively.

6.5.2 Degrees of compounding

6.5.2.1 Univerbated compounds

There are various DEGREES OF COMPOUNDING, ranking from complete univerbation[137] to looseness of composition. Only UNIVERBATED COMPOUNDS, that do not represent inherited formational types, have their affixal morphemes (other than personal ones, see above) at the end of the final member, and only they may serve as motivants of derivational processes by having formational suffixes appended to their final member (MASSON 1969: 117–8):[138] *madxanim* 'parking metres' (sg. *madxan*; for the formation see below); *šmartafit* or *šmartapit* (*šmar-* '-watcher', *taf, tap-* 'infant(s)', *-it* 'female'; see *6.3.3*) 'babysitter (f.)'; *kolno'iy* 'cinematographic' (*kolnoa* 'cinema', containing *kol* 'voice' and *noa* 'movement'); *kadursalan* 'basketball player' (*kadur* 'ball', *sal* 'basket'; for *-an* see *6.3.3*).

MASSON (1969) subsumes under the class of compounds nothing

---

[137] In ROSÉN (1952a: 25–9), the label "univerbation" was attached to what would constitute the most extreme case of that process, namely the forms of *'af-'exad* 'nobody', since prepositions attached to them are placed in front of the form (*le-'af-'exad* 'to nobody') and not between its historical components (*'af* 'even' and *'exad* 'one', with classically compulsory explicit negation in all cases (cf. *8.3.2*): *'af lo le-'exad* 'not even to one'). While the comparison there made with the Late Greek development οὐδὲ παρ' ἑνός > παρ' οὐδενός is undoubtedly appropriate, I now doubt whether the description as "univerbation" is the most economic one or even correct; this syntactic behaviour of *'af* applies to its construction not only with *'exad*, but with every countable noun (*8.3.2*), e.g. *le-'af sefèr* 'to no book'; we would best say that the classical "particle" *'af* 'even' has acquired the status of a (quantifying) pronoun.

[138] A not at all trivial comparison can be made with Greek univerbation: there, the initial position (of the verbal augment or perfect reduplication) is the mark of univerbation: ἐκάδιζε 'sat down' and μεμετιμένος 'released' indicate by the position of ἐ- and με-, respectively, that the morphemes κατ- and μετ- do not occupy, in relation with the subsequent ἰζ- (ʿ)ι-, a status of initial compound members. (The normal position for the augment or reduplication syllable is between the preverbial and the stem components of a verbal compound.)

but univerbated ones. They are of two principal types according to the expressional means by which the feature 'composition' is materialized:

(a) The initial member is a form of no other use; it is the root of only strong (radical) verbs with *a*-vocalization, which synchronically appears (MASSON 1969: 127–30; cf. GARBELL 1930: 49–50) as a zero-degree with anaptyctic vowel – *madxan* (root *m-d(-d)* 'measure'), *šmartaf* (root *š-m-r* 'watch')[139] – but which is, in fact, a consciously formed artificial pattern invented at the beginning of the century (earliest formations with the biconsonantal *mad-* '-metre'; SIVAN 1966: 6); the syntactic structure of these compounds is one of a "verbal dependence compound" *(Rektionskompositum)*, the final component representing the object.

(b) The number of non-syllabics in the compound is five or less, arranged in such a way as to correspond as far as possible to the structure of a radical *(6.1.2)*. The preference for biconsonantal initial members points in this direction (*kolnoa*; see above); "haplological" (MASSON 1969: 114) simplification at the composition suture (which, however, is not a phonemic process, but an artifact in coining) reduces the number of consonants: *maxazemèr* 'musical' (*maxaze* 'show' + *zemèr* 'song'), *kaduregèl* 'football' (*kadur* + *regèl*) which engendered *kadursal* (see above; *kaduraglan* 'footballer' leads to *kadursalan* 'basketball player'); initial ' of the second member does not count as non-syllabic (nor is it written): *migdalor* 'lighthouse' (*migdal* 'tower', *'or* 'light'); the clustering of consonants in *katnoa* 'motor scooter' (*katan* 'small' + *noa* 'motion, -mobile') is preferred to that of puristic *ktan(n)oa* and, in fact, fits better the consonantic structure of a radical, as does *'ofnoa* 'motorcycle' (*'ofan* 'wheel', in literary style) which is preferred to puristic *'ofan(n)oa*, the number of whose vowels would exceed that of a base pattern *(6.1.3)*.

Univerbated compounds are written as unit words.

---

[139] Note again the parallelism with ancient Indo-European compound types with final (!) member in the shape of the zero-degree of a verbal root: Gk. νεογνός (verbal root γ-ν- 'be born') 'newborn', Skr. *vedavid-* (verbal root *v-id* 'know') 'Veda-knowing, conversant with the Veda'.

10*

6.5.2.2 Compounds with composition suffix and their typological importance

Another type of compound in which close coherence of the components is morphologically achieved (by a COMPOSITION SUFFIX) is the one best exemplified by *beynl'umiy* 'international' (*beyn-* 'between, among', *l'om* 'nation'). While none of the components of these words is an ADJECTIVE, the whole is, due to the *Kompositions-suffix -iy (6.4.2.1)*, which is the only morpheme thus functioning. This class, which is of considerable typological importance, has been abundantly discussed (ROSÉN 1962a: 345–6; 1966b; 1969: 104–5). Words of this type have the constituent structure $(A+B)+$ *-iy* (quite often, there is no word B-*iy;* e.g. for *tatkarka'iy* 'subterranean' with *tat-* 'sub-' and *karka'* 'soil', no derived adjective '*karka'iy*' exists). Irrespective thereof, they are commonly hyphenated (A-B*iy*), and only where the initial member is a preposition of Hebrew origin (as in *beynl'umiy* given above, or *'altiv'iy* 'supernatural' ['*al-* 'above']) is their graphic representation as unit words accepted practice. In very isolated cases, they serve as underlying forms for derivation; e.g. *'alxuta'i* 'wireless operator' (for *-a'i* see *6.3.3*; from *'al-* 'non-', *xut* 'wire') and *bin'um* 'internationalization' (base pattern *-i-u-* '-ization', the stem *l'um-* replaced by the phonetically similar synonymous *'um-* (cf. *'uma* 'nation') to keep the total number of non-syllabics in the compound at five).

The TYPOLOGICAL IMPORTANCE of the existence of this uninherited word class lies in the fact that, stylistically as well as formationally, it exactly reflects the pan-European Neo-Latin compounds of the educated (intellectual) level of style.

It is appropriate here to recapitulate briefly the limits within which Republican Latin adjective compounding moves, except, of course, for Graecisizing poetical calques (cf. ROSÉN 1968: 367–9). We have type (A) hypostatic *subterraneus* (preposition with noun, united by a composition suffix), (B) bahuvrihi *trimestris, multiformis* (numerical expression with noun, united by a composition suffix), (C) bahuvrihi *inermis* (privative component, composition suffix). (D) *Rektionskompositum armiger, magnificus*. Types (A)–(C) are continued in abundant productivity, escaping listing in dictionaries in European languages as well as in Israeli Hebrew (see below); type (D) persists in "European" verbal formations (*magni-fy, electri-fy*) and corresponds to the IH *madxan* type (above, *6.5.2.1*), concerning which it must be noted that phonetic convenience for composition is assured by monosyllabicity of the initial member in Hebrew, as it is by the restriction of the choice of verbal roots as final components in Latin, where only biconsonantal bases that somehow resemble suffixes (*-ger, -fer, -fic-, -dic-*) are admitted in that position.

The identity of the first component in the European successors of this class is stylistically significant: as a rule, non-native lexemes are preferred in languages that have not inherited that formational process (Romance, English): *pre-* (and not: *before-*) *historic*, but *vorgeschichtlich*. The initial component is taken from the Latin or Greek lexicon, but where there is etymological identity between a Latin and a Romance prefix, the Romance one may stand for the Latin one: It. *sotto-stazione* opposite *sub-agente* (DEVOTO 1957: 82-5), Fr. *sous-terrain* opposite *sub-alpin*. Correspondingly, while the Graeco-Latin component is reflected in Israeli Hebrew by Aramaic (that is, learned; *4.4.1*) lexemes (*xad-* 'mono'-, *tat-* 'sub-', etc.), where there is etymological identity between a Hebrew and an Aramaic term, the former is not avoided (*beyn-* 'inter'). In type (C) (privative compounds), European languages have reserved a specific Latin-inspired morpheme *(non-)* for this purpose; Israeli Hebrew likewise does not use here the ordinary negatives, but employs *'al-* (which otherwise serves as a pre-verbal prohibitive): *'alxutiy* 'wireless (adj.)'.

Israeli Hebrew examples:

Type (A): initial components *tat-* 'sub-' (*tathakaratiy* 'subconscious', *hakarat-* 'consciousness'), *btar-* 'post-' (Aram.) (*btarmikra'i* 'postbiblical', *mikra'* 'Bible'), *me'eyn* 'quasi-' (*me'eynciburiy* 'quasipublic (adj.)', *cibur* 'public (noun)'), also *'anti-, pro-* (*prosovyétiy, 'antišémiy* 'antisemitic').

Type (B): initial components *xad-* (Aram.) 'mono-', *du-* (Greek loan in Talmudic Aramaic) 'bi-', *tlat-* (Aram.) 'tri-', and *rav-* 'multi-' with *šana, šnat-* 'year': *xadšnatiy, dušnatiy, tlatšnatiy, ravšnatiy*).

Type (C): *'almotiy* 'immortal' (also earlier *'almavèt* - from *mavèt, mot-* 'death' – 'immortality').

Outside the limits of these Latin-originating types there are only direct calques, mainly of geographical terms, in which German, and occasionally English, likewise exceed the limits set by Latin composition: *mizraxtixoniy* 'Middle-Eastern' (base: *mizrax tixon* 'Middle East', which is a noun-plus-adjective syntagm), *merkaz'eyrópiy* '*mitteleuropäisch*' (*merkaz* 'centre'), and *cfon'afriká'iy* (base: a noun-dependence syntagm (construct) with *cfon-* 'north of') '*nordafrikanisch*'.

To underline the typological status of these formations, it is worthwhile to add that Contemporary Arabic has no corresponding compound formations and is incapable of replicating types such as *anti-Semitism*, *peninsula* (DROZDÍK 1967: 19–20).

6.5.2.3 Loose compounds

LOOSE COMPOUNDS may be an apposite term for expressions suitably exemplified by *beyt-sefèr* (*beyt-* 'house', *sefèr* 'book') 'school' (even where no books are implied, such as driving schools) or *'ᵃruxat-bokèr* (*'ᵃruxa* 'meal', *bokèr* 'morning') 'breakfast'. The term *loose* appears appropriate since there are endocentric[140] constructions that exactly match these compounds (with the first member morphologically marked as construct; cf. *6.4.2.3*) that are not segmentally distinguishable from them. To distinguish non-compositional from compositional nominal constructs, we shall have to apply criteria similar to those that help us to keep apart *party(-)line* from *party line* (political), *party interests* (JESPERSEN 1911-: 6.140; 1937: 30). This is the more important since the morphological features of direct noun connection (construct state forms; cf. *6.4.2.3*) are by no means an automatic result of the direct nexus of nouns, and construct type syntagms are in opposition to those in which the first member appears in its non-construct form (*mana basar* 'a portion of meat', *m(a)nat-basar* 'a meat dish') (cf. ROSÉN 1957: 340–1).

First of all there are, of course, semantic considerations, about whose merits see JESPERSEN (1911- : 6.134–8). The semantic "isolation" of the terms in the compound "displaces" their content: the value of *sefèr* 'book' is not present in *beyt-sefèr* 'school'; cf. *begèd-yam* (*begèd* 'raiment', *yam* 'sea') 'swimsuit', *tapuax-zahav* (*tapuax* 'apple', *zahav* 'gold') 'orange', and *beyt-knesèt* (*knesèt* '(national) assembly') 'synagogue'. (*Binyan-ha-knesèt* (*binyan* 'building') 'Parliament Building' is not a compound.) (Cf. ROSÉN 1966a: 177–87.)

---

[140]   There are exocentric constructions whose first component is a strong adjective (*6.4.2.1*) and which have the designation of an inalienably appurtenant object as second member: *kxol-'eynayèm* (*k(a)xol(-)* 'blue', *'eynayèm* 'eyes') 'blue-eyed'. They have no composition suffix, but while they cannot be classed as compounds, they are typologically important by virtue of their complete parallelism with Indo-European bahuvrīhis (ROSÉN 1962a: 242–3; 1966b).

Substitutability of a term in composition by what would normally be a member of its substitution class is extremely limited, or else yields surprising results. As in *beyt-ha-knesèt* versus *binyan-ha-knesèt*, substitution of a term by a synonym yields a new expression which is by no means synonymous; cf. *'eglat-yladim* 'perambulator' (*6.5.1*) versus *kirkrat-yladim* 'children's cart' (*'agala* 'carriage' and *kirkara* 'carriage, cart' are, unless in composition, near synonyms); *'azut-panim* (*'azut*, abstract from *'az* 'strong, valiant', *panim* 'face') 'impertinence' – replacing the initial term by another abstract formation of the same adjective would yield the nonsense expression *'*oz-panim*. It need not be demonstrated that the same would apply to the replacement of a compositional term by its antonym.

Restrictions of substitutability are, of course, only another facet of the semantic "isolation" undergone by a term of the compound. The most decisive of these restrictions applies to the replacement of a member of the compound by an anaphoric pronoun; were it possible for any one of the terms to be thus replaced, the anaphoric would necessarily refer to that term as used as an autonomous word rather than as a term in that specific compound, that is, were *party* in *party-line* replaced by *it* (to form *its line*), or *bird* in *blackbird* by *one* (to form *a black one*), the content of such a pronoun would by necessity be identical with the content of the previously occurring noun (*party*, *bird*) referred to by the anaphoric and would not be affected by the semantic "displacement" incurred by it in composition, or would not affect the other term correspondingly: that is to say, with *its* referring to an antecedent *party* in *party line*, the syntagm could only stand for the content of *party line*, not for that of *party-line*, likewise *the black one* (with *one* = *bird*) only for *the black bird*, not for *the blackbird*. Only the complete compound is pronominally substitutable: *a big one* = *a big blackbird*. The same applies to Israeli Hebrew compounds, even where no obviously specified or displaced meaning is observable in either one of the members: *bokèr* in *'*a*ruxat-bokèr* 'breakfast', while obviously meaning nothing else than 'morning', can still not be replaced by *-o* 'it' while preserving the meaning (*'*a*ruxato* 'his meal'). The case becomes even more critical when an attempt is made to carry out such replacement for the initial member of the compound: pronouns have no construct form and cannot, consequently, enter a direct adjunct relation with a subsequent noun; the adjunction is compulsorily being effected by mediation of a suitable preposition, such as *šel-* 'of' (*zo šel-ha-bokèr*, with f.sg. *zo* replacing *'ᵃruxa*). Insertion of a preposition between the two terms, however, destroys the nature of the expression as a compound, morphologically as well as semantically (cf. *2.6.3*): the expression just formed with *zo* would mean 'the one of the morning', just as inserting *šel-* into the compound discussed, to form *ha-'ᵃruxa šel-ha-bokèr*, would create meanings such as 'this morning's meal, the meal of this morning'. It is needless to stress that wherever the semantic properties of the term in composition are comparatively very remote from those of the same term in independent use, pronominal substitution has much more dramatic effects; *beyto* (with *-o* replacing *sefèr* in *beyt-sefèr*) would not designate anything remotely resembling a school, but only 'his home', *ze šel-sefèr* (*ze* for *beyt-*) a 'previously mentioned object (animate or inanimate) related to, or possessed by, a book'. These severe restrictions of substitutability are, of course, related to the otherwise trivial fact that a host of Israeli Hebrew compounds have unit-words translations in other languages, and it is very often the existence of such unit word in a foreign model that has encouraged the speakers of Israeli Hebrew to create if not an Israeli Hebrew unit word (cf. *4.2.1*), then at least a two-stem expression endowed with the characteristics of a compound.

6.5.2.4 Compounds and syntagms

There is no way further to discuss Israeli Hebrew compounds, other than by their lexical listing. For the identification of the legion of compounds, the substitution test, and in particular the pronominal one, is of paramount importance. Any sequence of directly connected nouns morphologically characterized by the construct state of the first one that admits pronominal substitution of any single participant term, is not a compound, but a SYNTAGM and, consequently, situated outside the scope of morphology.

7. INFLEXIONAL CATEGORIES

7.1 NOMINAL CATEGORIES

7.1.1 Gender

In the bipartite category of grammatical GENDER, the feminine is marked by one of two suffixes, -a or -t, the latter also in a complex suffix -it (developed out of -i(y) + -t). This is the result of prehistoric phonetic processes by which postvocalic final t was lost (*malkat > Biblical Hebrew malk·å > Israeli Hebrew malka 'queen'), while t in Ct* was preserved (with anaptyxis, e.g., in /gbirt/ > gverèt 'lady'; differently for C = y: *š'ēriyt > Biblical Hebrew š'ēri·t > Israeli Hebrew š'erit 'remainder'). The suffixes -a, -èt, and -it have consequently entered an allomorphic relation to each other in the formation of designations of females derived from those of males (6.3.3): sus 'horse' : susa 'mare'; xayal 'soldier' : xayelèt 'girl soldier'; melcar 'waiter' : melcarit 'waitress'. Only where there is a functional binary opposition (as in the examples just quoted or, e.g., in sak 'bag' : sakit 'little bag'; see below) is the plural suffix -ot (susot, xayalot, melcariyot, sakiyot) a marker of feminine gender; otherwise, nouns with gender-unmarked singular may be treated, for the purpose of gender concord, as masculines irrespective of whether their plurals end in -ot[141] or in characteristically

---

[141] In Biblical Hebrew, pl. -o·t is a gender marker, in "broken" plurals, of afformativeless radical nouns (base patterns: /qaṭl/, /qiṭl/, /quṭl/, and phonologically conditioned alternants): šemeš (pl. šmåšo·t) 'sun', qeren (qråno·t) 'corner, horn', ru·ᵃḥ (ru·ḥo·t) 'wind, spirit', k·ap (k·ap·o·t) 'hand, sole', no·gah (ngo·ho·t) 'brilliance', nepeš (npåšo·t) 'soul, person', 'ereṣ ('åråṣo·t) 'country', ḥereb (ḥåråbo·t) 'sword', 'ayin ('åyåno·t) 'well', b·ēr (b·ēro·t) 'well' (note that "breaking" of the plural base is neutralized in certain phonemic conditions)

masculine *-im* (*makom* masc. 'place', pl. *mkomot*), and on the other hand, pl. *-im* does not impair the gender-marking effect of sg. *-a* (*mila* 'word', pl. *milim*, but construct normally *milot*, all feminine).

All these "irregularities" are survivors from Biblical Hebrew and, in part, postbiblical classical language. Where nouns with gender-unmarked singular, but pl. *-ot*, have classically feminine concord (such as *kos* : *kosot* 'cup'; *gader* : *gderot* 'fence'), this feature is preserved (deviations, that is "Sprachfehler" under "fremdsprachlicher Einwirkung", that were still observable in the late twenties (cf. GARBELL 1930: 46–7) have by now disappeared); where classical usage offered an option of apparently regular masculine or apparently irregular feminine gender (*derèx* : *draxim* 'path, way'; *sakin* : *sakinim* 'knife'), the latter maintained the upper hand obviously as some sort of "*locutio difficilior*", and the masculine is stylistically marked (but also preserved in specialized usage, such as *sakin-giluax* 'razorblade' (m.)).

The $\emptyset$: *-it* opposition becomes available with 'inanimate' nouns for the expression of 'diminutive' (not hypocoristic; *6.3.3*) relations as in *kos* : *kosit* 'Gläschen', but very often with semantic detachment from the motivating base word: *mapa* 'tablecloth' : *mapit* 'napkin'; *maxsan* 'store' : *maxsanit* 'magazine (of a fire-arm)' (cf. *4.3.2*). The relation of the diminutive suffix and the feminine gender marker is not fortuitous: Talmudic diminutives in *-iˑθ* (e.g. *ˀl(o)nṭiˑθ* 'linen cloth', *maṭˑliθ* 'tablecloth') rest on Greek base forms, and *-iˑθ* reflects the basically diminutive Greek *-ιον* (*linteum*, λίντιον;

– are all of feminine gender; this applies also where the gender is already determined by affixal formation of the singular (*dˑelet* (*dˑlåtoˑt*) 'door', *qešet* (*qšåtoˑt*) 'bow' with probably nonradical *-t*) and indicates that the synchronically valid marker-status of *-oˑt* is the result of a diachronic process. In Akkadian, where cognate *-aˑt-* has a morphemic status analogous to that of BH *-oˑt*, gender marking occurs in sg. *erṣetu* (pl. *erṣête*) 'country', sg. pl. *napištu* (pl. *napšâti*) 'life'; here the plural is not "broken". With unbroken radical plural formations (names of plants), Biblical Hebrew has gender marking in the singular, and pl. *-iˑm* which is the unmarked term of the pair of plural suffixes: *šiṭå* (*šiṭˑiˑm*) 'acacia', *tˑēnå* (*tˑēniˑm*) 'fig(tree)', *šiqmiˑm* (postbiblical *šiqmå*, sg.) 'sycamores' is feminine, *sˑōrå* (*sˑōriˑm*) 'barley', *ḥiṭˑå* (*ḥiṭˑiˑm*) 'wheat'. In all these cases, the singulars are either unitatives ('a fig') or mass singulars ('wheat'), the plurals are mass plurals; it may appear that, basically, brokenness is the expression of countable plurality.

*μαντίλιον < *mantile*) by way of retrograde singularization (Gk. -ια = -iyōθ yields the singular in -i·θ). The Israeli Hebrew diminutives in -*it* may be derived from masculine as well as from feminine base words (MASSON 1968: 116, D.41): cf. *kos* : *kosit* (see above); *k'ara* 'dish' : *k'arit*; *sak* : *sakit* (see above); *pax* 'jerrycan' : *paxit* 'small (tin) container'. The competing diminutive suffix -*on* (m.), however (*6.3.3*), goes with 'masculine animate' motivants exclusively (*dov* 'bear' : *dubon* 'teddybear'). In view of this obvious connection between the grammatical gender of the base noun and that of the diminutive, it must be recalled that Russian has an analogous feature.

7.1.2 Determination

The difficulties we encounter in the description of the category of DETERMINATION are a result of the fact that, in Israeli Hebrew, it applies not only to paradigmatic, but also to syntagmatic relations.

Determination is a binary inflexional category, since one of its members is the syntactically operative bound morpheme *ha-*, the "DEFINITE ARTICLE", which forms a binary[142] opposition with Ø (*tipeš* 'foolish, a fool' : *ha-tipeš* 'the fool(ish one)'). Other members of the same category are portmanteau morphemes that express the content of *ha-* (and occur in all of the environments in which *ha-* is required to the exclusion of Ø) concomitantly with contents included in the non-binary person-sex-number category: -*i* in *beyti* 'my home', -*o* in *beyto* 'his home', and -*enù* in *beytenù* 'our home'; the conjunction of determination and personal markings yields appur-

---

[142] There is no indefinite article *'exad* 'one' in Israeli Hebrew, *pace* ORNAN (1965: 18). While, in some environments, *'iš 'exad* and *a man* may be adequate mutual translational equivalents, *'exad* and *ha-* cannot be considered to belong to the same category due to their compatibility: *ha-'iš ha-'exad* 'the one man'. (Of course, there are other possible translations of *a man*, primarily *'iš*, and also e.g. *'eyzè 'iš*.) To stress our point, let us add that, in French, the categorial situation is different: *un* (in article status) cannot be determinated by *le* (it can in *l'un des hommes*); Germ. *ein* (in *ein Mann*) and *eine* (in *der eine Mann*) belong to different morphological classes. Engl. *a* is not a member of the category 'numerals': *a full twenty dollars*.

tenantive contents.[143] Non-inflexional morphemes (preadjunctive modifiers) that preclude the article (as we shall henceforth say briefly for "definite article") are invariably of non-delimitative character (*'éyze(?)* in *'éyze 'iš(?)* 'some man, what man?'; *šum* in *šum 'iš* 'no man, nobody';[144] etc.) and have consequently to be deemed as representing portmanteau morphemes containing the zero member of the determination category.

Determinable (i.e. occurring in the same syntactic function either with or without the article) are nominals (*5.1.3*) that have the gender-quantity dimension. Participles are not nominals: they do not occur without the article in attributive position (see below) nor with it in predicative function. Toponymics are, in fact, determinable (see below). Non-determinable nouns include the interrogative *mi* 'who', *ma* 'what', anthroponymics, and the personal pronouns (more details ROSÉN 1966a: 231); they occur in the syntactic environments of determinated determinables, as do also the anthroponymics and toponymics:

ha-'iša ha-yafa	'the beautiful woman'
'at ha-yafa	'you (f.sg.) the beautiful, beautiful you'
yrušalayìm ha-yafa	'beautiful Jerusalem'
yosef ha-katan	'little Joseph'
'aleksánder ha-gadol	'Alexander the Great'
hénri ha-šminiy	'Henry VIII'

Deindividualization (undetermination) of noun-phrases with non-determinable nuclei can, consequently, be effected only when that nucleus is modified by a *ha*-characterized satellite, such as an attributive adjective; the minus-*ha*-morpheme characterizing the noun-phrase as a whole is here, as in other cases (cf. p. 162) equivalent to an indefinite article of other languages: *yrušalayìm yafa* 'a beautiful Jerusalem' as in *ha-'aguda lmaàn yrušalayìm yafa* 'the Federation for a Beautiful Jeru-

---

[143] Separate and independent expression of person-sex-number and determinative contents in *ha-bayìt šel-o* 'his house', literally 'the house of his', versus *bayìt šel-o* 'a house of his'. Cf. *2.6.3* and note.

[144] Cf. ROSÉN (1958c: 75; 1962a: 210–3).

salem', *'anaxnù rocim bi-yrušalayìm nkiya* 'we want a clean Jerusalem'. (The same minus-*ha*-morpheme also deindividualizes hydronymics characterized by *ha-* (below, p. 161): *širi holex kmo yarden* 'my song goes like a Jordan' (hit song) versus *ha-yarden* 'the Jordan (river)'. The minus-*ha*-morpheme thus "creates" a "class" of Jordans, or Jerusalems, respectively, of which the one referred to is taken as a representative; pluralization of these proper nouns is, however, not found.

While, in classical language, determination also has the effect of a 'vocative' purport (residues: *ha-more!* 'teacher!', *Yosef ha-yakar!* 'Dear Joseph!', as in opening a letter, *ha-gverèt!* 'Madam, Miss!' *ha-mfaked! 'Mon Commandant!'*, etc.), it is, in particular with non-determinable nuclei, undetermination which serves, in current language, as the 'vocative' morpheme: *Yosef yakar!* (about as frequent as the just quoted *Yosef ha-yakar!*) may be Yiddish-induced (cf. Germ. *lieber Josef* : *der liebe Josef*), likewise *gverèt!* 'Madam, Miss!', *yarden!* 'oh Jordan!' (in a hit song: *hal'à, yarden, hal'à zrom!* 'On, oh Jordan, on do roll!'), *nahag!* 'driver!', where the specific driver in question is addressed, not as in *sabal (,bevakaša)! '*porter (,please)*!'*, where just any available porter is called; one of the earliest cases seems to be *kinerèt šeli!* 'oh my Lake of Galilee' (*ha-kinerèt* 'the Lake of Galilee'; see p. 161).

Very broadly speaking (for details see ROSÉN 1966a: 233–55), in a bipartite equational (classificatory) sentence (that is, nominal + nominal), both of whose constituents are determinable, determinateness is the mark of non-predicativity:

Ha-menahel 'ašem	'The director is guilty'
ha-'ašem menahel	is a sentence in which the subject-predicate relation is inverted ('He who is guilty, is director')

(Inversion of order in both sentences would have merely stylistic effects or cause a shift of emphasis.) In every such sentence, there is consequently at least one constituent in respect to which the opposition determinate : indeterminate is neutralized:

menahel 'ašem	is a non-sentence[145]; in fact it is a sentence-part ('a director who is guilty')
ha-menahel ha-'ašem	is also a non-sentence ('the director who is guilty')

---

[145] It may be a sentence in cases in which the noun has a very broad class reference, e.g. *'adam 'ašem* (strong stress on the first word) 'it is a human being that is responsible'; cf. below.

> *Ha-'ašem ha-menahel*   'Who is guilty, is the director =
> It is the director, who is guilty,
> *Schuld ist der Direktor'*

In view of such neutralizations, it is not in such sentences that the semantic purport of determination can be established:

> *Ha-'adam 'axzariy*   'Man is cruel' (*'adam 'axzariy* 'a cruel
> person')

Here *ha-'adam* refers to any one, or all, of the representatives of the class 'man'; it would be inadequate to speak of "generic determination". Even though *'adam 'ašem (ve-lo mxona)* 'Man is guilty, ([and] not a machine)' is possible, it is synonymous with *Ha-'adam 'ašem (ve-lo ha-mxona)*. (Cf. note *145*.)

The considerable functional load in terms of syntactic distinctions that rests upon the determination correlation may be taken off its shoulders through a change of any one of the fundamental conditions in which it so functions (bipartite equational nominal sentence with two determinable constituents). A third constituent, for example, lifts the restriction of determinateness for the constituents:

> *Be-mikre ze menahel 'ašem* 'In this case, a director is
> guilty'

The immediate effect is the functional pertinence of determination:

> *Be-mikre ze ha-menahel 'ašem* 'In this case, the director
> is guilty'

The inclusion of the copula pronoun *hu* (m.sg.), *hi* (f.sg.), *hem* (m.pl.), and *hen* (f.pl.) to form an identificatory (*8.1.4*(XI)), or of the invariable copula *ze* to form a commentational sentence (*8.1.4*(XII)) yields analogous results:

	Ha-menahel	*hu ha-'ašem*	'The director is the guilty one'
versus	*Menahel*	*hu 'ašem*	'A director is guilty'
and	*Menahel*	*hu ha-'ašem*	'A director is the guilty person'
	Ha-'ašem	*ze ha-menahel*	'He who is guilty – that's the director. –· *Le coupable c'est le directeur*'

	Ha-tipeš	*ze ha-kone*	'The fool is the customer. – *L'idiot c'est le client*'
versus	*Tipeš*	*ze kone*	'A fool – that is a customer. *Un idiot – cela veut dire un client*'
and	*Tipeš*	*ze ha-kone*	'A fool is the customer. *C'est le client qui est idiot*'

Also if the predicative constituent is non-determinable:

	Yosef 'ašem or *'ašem Yosef* 'Joseph is guilty'	
versus	*Yosef ha-'ašem. Ha-'ašem Yosef* 'J. is the guilty (one)'	
	Mi 'ašem?	'Who is guilty?'
versus	*Mi ha-'ašem?*	'Who is the guilty person?'
	'Ani rišon	'I am first' (but not second, *or*: but not you)
versus	*'Ani ha-rišon*	'I am first (but not you). *C'est moi le premier*'
	'Ata xaxam	'You are clever'
versus	*'Ata ha-xaxam*	'You are the clever one'
	Hu šomer 'al-ha-xok	'He abides by the the law'
versus	*Hu ha-šomer 'al-ha-xok*	'He is the one who abides by the law'

It is in these patterns that the "determinating" nature of *ha-* (and its allomorphs which we shall discuss below) emerges.

A noun can be determinated separately from its adjunct only if the adjunction is effected by a preposition (*ha-'iš 'al-ha-gag* 'the man on the roof' versus *'iš 'al-ha-gag* 'a man on the roof'); otherwise the determination feature is valid for the entire syntagm constituted by the noun (or adjective) and its adjuncts: *'ᵃruxat-ha-bokèr* 'the breakfast' versus *'ᵃruxat-bokèr* 'breakfast'.

As in this example, it is always the adjunct that is marked for determination, but where the adjunct is determinable, it exercizes concord effects on the centre of the syntagm:

(1) A noun whose adjunct is a determinated adjective is itself determinated (adjectives are determinable: *gadol* 'big': *ha-gadol* 'the big (one)'): *sefèr gadol* 'a big book'; *ha-sefèr ha-gadol* 'the big book'; *sifri ha-gadol* (cf. p. 160) 'my big book'. The article marks determination, and the determination concord marks the attributive relation; gender-number concord, of course, also applies, but is not a marker of attributive relation, since it also applies in predicative nexus (*8.1.4(X)*).

(2) No concord applies with adjuncts that are nouns (*'aruxat-ha-bokèr*, see p. 159).

(3) There is likewise no concord with adjuncts that are participles that are not determinable (see above) and have a fixed article as class marker:

> *ha-'iš ha-yoce' min-ha-bayit* 'the man going out from the house'
> *'iš ha-yoce' min-ha-bayit* 'a man going out from the house'.

(4) The adjunct *ze* (m.sg.), *zot* (f.sg.), *'éle* (pl.) 'this, that' excludes an articulated noun centre: *sefèr ze* 'this book', *sifri ze* 'this book of mine'; this pronominal adjective is determinable, and in case it is articulated it motivates accordingly: *ha-sefèr ha-ze* 'this book', but *ha-ze* is not admissible as an adjunct of *sifri* unless through mediation of a determinated adjective (*sifri ha-gadol ha-ze* 'this big book of mine'). This complicated situation can be analytically solved only by an assumption that the article covers two categorial contents (say, determination and deixis; cf. *ha-yom* 'today' versus *yom* 'day'), the personal suffix three (determination, deixis, anaphora), [146] and *ze* anaphora alone (in fact, *sefer ze* is anaphoric,[147] *ha-sefèr ha-ze* anaphoric or *hic*-deictic), and that anaphora concord overrides determination concord (non-anaphoric *ha-sefèr* is incompatible with anaphoric *ze*, and anaphoric *sifri* is in anaphora concord with likewise anaphoric *ze*). Finally, the pronominal adjective *kaze/kazot/ka'éle* 'such' (ROSÉN 1962a: 60) is, for the purpose of adjunct-motivated concord, non-anaphoric as well as undeterminated: *sefèr kaze* 'such (a) book' (cf. fn. 147). This categorial solution is corroborated by the behaviour of preadjunctive *'oto* (m.sg.), *'ota* (f.sg.), etc. 'that' which is compatible with *ha-* (*'oto ha-* 'the same'), but not with the

---

[146] Due to the categorial affinity between *ha-* and the personal suffixes, the former can enter the paradigm of the latter to express the '*man*'-'*on*'-person, but only where the third categorial component of the personal suffixes, that is, the one that carries the load of 'possessive' content, is redundant; this is the case for names of appurtenant ("inalienable") objects: *kše-ro'im 'et-ze ha-lev nišbar* 'When one sees this, one's (*ha-*) heart breaks' versus *kše-'ani ro'e et-ze, lib-i nišbar* 'When I see this, my (-*i*) heart breaks'. (Cf. ROSÉN 1961a: 25–6.)

[147] The "accusative" particle *'et-*, which is, in ordinary style, compulsory with a determinated nominal (*kibalti 'et-ha-sefèr (ha-gadol)* 'I received the (big) book'), is optional with *sifri ze*, inadmissible with *sefèr ze-*. as well as with *sefèr kaze* 'such book' (see below). Substantival *ze* 'this, *ceci*' is deictic and determinated (*kibalti 'et-ze* 'I received that'. *'et-ze kibalti* 'This – I have received') and requires *'et-* as shown.

personal suffixes; anaphoric content must be ascribed to it (ROSÉN 1955a: 206–9; 1962a: 264–5; 1966a: 273–5).[148]

The categorial-environmental prerequisites once clarified, the deictic-determinative purport of the article comes to light wherever neat contrastive pairs can be established. To start from the last-mentioned case, *'oto-ha-sefèr* 'the same book' versus *'oto sefèr* 'that book' shows the restriction of reference brought about by *ha-*. The same principle can even be applied to some odd cases, such as the obligatory determination of oronymics (*ha-xermon* 'Mount Hermon', *ha-karmel*) and hydronymics (*ha-yarkon*) in view of the obligatory non-determination of toponymics (*yisra'el, yrušalayìm*); where contrastive pairs exist, the localities so designated are topographically adjacent and the hydronymic (or oronymic) may be considered as of more specific reference: *yarden* 'Jordan' (state): *ha-yarden* 'Jordan' (river); *kinerèt* (name of a village situated on the Lake of Galilee): *ha-kinerèt* 'the Lake of Galilee'; *ha-tavor* 'Mount Tabor': *(kfar-)tavor* (name of a village situated on its slopes). (For 'vocative' *yarden!, kinerèt!* 'oh Jordan (river)!', etc. see above).

The individualizing effect of articulation becomes obvious in pairs of nouns in which the undeterminated form is appellative, the determinated one a proper noun: *histadrut* 'organization' versus *ha-histadrut* 'Labour Federation' (ROSÉN 1961a: 22–3); *soxnut* 'agency': *ha-soxnut* 'the Jewish Agency'. For cases such as *ha-šemèš* 'the sun' and *ha-yareax* 'the moon', ORNAN (1965: 29) has proposed the term "noun with unique referend"; they appear, however, to be included in the class of "proper nouns by determination"; cf. *'erèc* 'country' : *ha-'arèc* ("noun with unique referend") 'Palestine, Israel'. Very often, it is particularly in nominal constructs (that is, syntagms of a noun with directly adjunct noun) that the individualizing[149] force

---

[148] *'et-* (see foregoing note) is optional with a noun modified by *'oto*. Cf. also ROSÉN (1961a: 221), where a not fully adequate solution is proposed.

[149] Note that this is the same kind of individualizing effect that can also be created by retraction of stress (*3.7.5*). Whenever the preindividualized form of the noun has an article (*ha-po'el* 'the worker'), stress retraction is the only means of expression for individualization (*hapó'el*, name of a sports association affiliated to the Israel Labour Federation). It may be noted *en passant* that the comparatively large number of "proper nouns" derived (by stress retraction or determination) from appellatives hails from a period (up to about 1940) in which Hebrew did not yet enjoy a hundred percent "vernacular" status. Brand names, for instance, that were frequently formed, in the said period, by prefixing the

11

of the article is employed: from *xag* 'feast' and *molad* 'birth', *xag-ha-molad* 'Christmas' is formed (ROSÉN 1961a: 23). In such cases, a complication is created by the fact that the article has determinative force (with respect to the syntagm; p. 159) and individualizing force at the same time; undetermining such an expression would cause the risk of losing the individualized reference, but this difficulty is overcome by interpreting *xag-molad* as *xag-ha-molad* 'Christmas' + (minus *ha-*) 'a' = 'a Christmas' (as in *šir xag-molad* 'a Christmas song'); likewise: *kitme-šemèš* = *kitme-* 'spots of' + *ha-šemès* 'the sun' + (minus *ha-*) 'indetermination' = 'sun-spots'; *leyl-yareax* 'moonlit night, *Mondnacht*'; *rexèv-yareax* 'a lunar vehicle'.

This class of noun phrases has led to the discovery of allomorphs of the *ha-* : *Ø* pair: *Ø* for the determinated content, (minus *ha-*) for the undetermined one. In very similar conditions, the determinating *Ø*-allomorph contrasts with indeterminating *mi-*; since this is, basically, the preposition 'from' and the conditioning environment is the plural of certain construct syntagms, we have termed *mi-* the Israeli Hebrew "*article partitif*" (ROSÉN 1961a: 23–4; 1962a: 340; 1966a: 183); the construct syntagms concerned are similar to those of the *xag-ha-molad* type, except that there is no *ha-* present in the construent proper noun: *mi-ycirot-šerif* 'works by Sherif (an Israeli composer), *des œuvres de S.*'.[150] It would appear that proper

---

article to the noun designating the product, would in Europe be based on a Latin stem, or, at least, not on a word in the language of the country in which the producer was domiciled.

[150] That *article partitif mi-* is not identical with the preposition *mi-*, from which it has, of course, emerged (for Biblical forerunners, see ROSÉN 1961a: 25, note 12), may be proved by the same method by which the nonidentity of Fr. *de* (*article partitif*) and *de* 'from' can be demonstrated. FREI (1960: 318–9; 1968: 54–5) does this by showing the different substitutional properties of the two *de*'s: substitution of *de* in *Elle a sorti de la paille* by *une* or *cette* to form *Elle a sorti une/cette paille* identifies *de* as partitive article, while substitution of *là/ce sac* for *de* identifies the latter as preposition in *Elle est sortie de là/ce sac*. Same procedure for Israeli Hebrew: *Kol-yisra'el šider mi-ycirot-šerif* 'The Voice of Israel (broadcasting service) broadcast works by Sherif' versus *Kol-yisra'el šider 'et-ha-'ópera 'a'ida* '... broadcast Aida' identifies *mi-* as partitive article, while *Kol-yisra'el šider mi-tel'aviv* identifies it as preposition ('from Tel-Aviv'). A much more effective test would be mutual compatibility:

nouns (and constructs formed with them) are already determina-
tion-deixis characterized (*ycirot-šerif* admits anaphoric '*éle*, but not
anaphoric-determinative-deictic *ha-'éle* as adjunct), so that in fact
the absence of *ha-* in conjunction with them is unmarkedness, and
the marked term in such oppositions must be considered to be the
undeterminated one.

Cf. also the following expression (noted by a student from his own
speech) which reflects the 'superlative' construction of a construct adjective with a determinated construent noun (*tove-ha-'ᵃnašim* (literally
'the good ones from amongst the men') 'the best men' : *Li-yxida zo
ba'im 'im lo tove-ha-'ᵃnašim, 'az mi-tove-ha-'ᵃnašim lefaxot*. 'To this
unit come, if not the best men, [then] (some) of the best men at least.'

The type of expressions represented by *ba-zman* 'in time', *le-veyt-
ha-sefèr* 'to school', *ba-mita* 'in bed', and *be-veyt-ha-xolim* 'in
hospital' (the prepositions *be-* 'in', *le-* 'to', and *ke-* 'as' contract with
the article through elision of /h/, so that *ba-* is a preposition followed by the definite article) call for a further statement on the determinative force of the article. The correspondence with English
zero-article syntagms is not in itself surprising in view of the juxtaposition of a tripartite determination category (*the, a, Ø*) with a bipartite one, but the conformity with the English construction ("zero
in prepositional phrases"; JESPERSEN 1911- 7: 459–63) invites comment. (German and French would have obligatory determination
just as Hebrew: *in die Schule, à l'école*.) It would appear that we
are again confronted with an individualizing function of the Israeli
Hebrew article: *ba-'ir = in town* would, in each given case, refer
to a specific town whose identity is determined by some agent involved, and not by its being previously mentioned; *ha-yelèd kvar
holex le-veyt-ha-sefèr = The little boy already goes to school* implies

---

Elle sort de la paille de ce sac, and even *Elle sort de la paille de la paille*(!) 'She
takes (a) straw out of the heap of straw'; for Israeli Hebrew: *Kol-yisra'el šider
mi-ycirot šerif mi-tel'aviv* 'Kol-Israel broadcast works by Sherif from Tel-Aviv',
'*az kiblu mi-bne-mišpaxto mi-bne-mišpaxta 'et-kol-ha-rxuš* 'Then members of
his family (*mi-* art.part.) got from the (*mi-* preposition) members of her family
the entire property'.

reference to a given, but not necessarily known school. This, as we would say, relative identification, can be illustrated by the following fact: in the two sentences *John goes to school* and *John goes to the school*, either different schools or different Johns are referred to, that is, not the same kind of intimate (quasi-inalienable) connection exists in the second sentence between John and the school as in the first. The same applies to the relation between the two Hebrew sentences *Moše holex le-veyt-ha-sefèr* and *Moše holex le-veyt-ha-sefèr šelo* '. . . to his school' (where normally 'his' would not refer back to *Moše*, or else the school would not be the same school as in the first sentence, or another *Moše* would be meant, say the principal of the school). Consider also, what modifying adjuncts would, or would not, impair the construction: *John goes to high-school*, or *to nursery school*, but with *driving school*, the article *a* would be required, if *goes* would at all be considered appropriate. Likewise in Hebrew, we can have *holex le-veyt-ha-sefèr ha-tixon* '. . . intermediate school', that is, 'high school' (or . . . *la-gan* 'to kindergarten'), but . . . *le-veyt-sefèr le(-)nhiga* ('. . . for driving') without article. This is the illustration we can give for this peculiar category.

7.1.3 Quantity (nominal number)

NUMBER is, with certain exceptions to be dealt with immediately, a binary category: *sus* 'horse' : *susim* 'horses'. Since not all singular : plural oppositions reflect singularity versus plurality, this category may have to be more appropriately termed QUANTITY (see 5.1.1) to include the contents of non-countable mass-plurals (below, p. 166). Morphologically, number is inseparable from gender, since all number morphemes are, in fact, number-gender portmanteaus (7.1.1); on the other hand, number alone can be syntactically operative (for concord), as is the case concerning the person-sex-number morphemes, some of which undergo sex neutralization (e.g. *halxu* 'went [3 pers.pl., irrespective of sex])'.

A dual form (in *-ayìm*) occurs in nouns that designate frequently counted units (*xodèš* 'month' : *xodšayìm* 'two months' : *xodašim*

'months'; cf. ROSÉN 1962: 208); a common stylistic variant for the
dual form is a syntagm composed ot the numeral 'two' and the
plural form *(šne xodašim)*. In these forms, the dual suffix is not
determinative of gender (the dual has the same gender concord as
the singular).

In all other cases, the suffix *-ayìm* is not a dual, but a plural
morpheme, since normally nouns showing it have no third number
form and the forms in *-ayìm* functions as plural referring to any
number of objects above one: *šen* 'tooth' : *šinayìm* 'teeth' (number
not implied) : *šaloš sinayìm* 'three teeth'; *regèl* 'foot, leg' : *('arba')*
raglayìm '(four) legs'. These plural forms, all of which stand for
objects that basically occur in pairs, unless singly, can also be
dualia tantum (objects that consist of a pair of components, such as
miškafayìm 'eyeglasses', *'of(a)nayìm* 'bicycle'). "Paired object"
plurals are marked as of feminine gender, *dualia tantum* have, in
Israeli Hebrew, unstable grammatical gender; likewise designations
of paired objects, not usually considered singly (*šadayìm* 'breasts').
Some nouns have a "paired" as well as a "pluralic" plural, with
appropriate semantic differentiation; e.g. *yad* : *yadayim* 'hands' :
yadot 'handles' (and other transferred significations). Since neither
adjectives nor verbs have more than two number forms, all nouns
in *-ayìm* command plural concord, so that the number category
remains basically binary.

As has been stated above *(7.1.2)*, nominals that have the gender-
number dimension are determinable; this establishes a complex
categorial purport 'gender + number + determination'. With some
nouns, however, the determined member of the *ha-* : *Ø* opposition
will not occur unless syntactically conditioned (e.g., by expansion
by a restrictive relative clause: *ha-gešèm še-yarad 'etmol* 'the rain
that fell yesterday') or else with no noticeable semantic contrast
between the determinated and the undeterminated form (*gešèm* and
ha-gešèm 'rain' have equal reference).[151] One must therefore distinguish nouns with unconditioned occurrence of the articulated
form (and, consequently, with different ranges of reference for the

---

[151]   This type of nouns includes those of "unique reference" *(7.1.2)*.

determinated and the undeterminated form) from those for which the opposite is true. The first mentioned make full use of the possibilities offered by the gender+number+determination complex (which may suitably be interpreted as 'countability').

It will prove useful to distinguish a class of COUNTABLE from one of NONCOUNTABLE nouns.

The distinction of "countables" from "noncountables" has made the plural forms of names of "noncountables" capable of expressing semantic relations comparable to those prevailing between Engl. *rains* and *rain;* e.g. *gšamim* (singular form *gešèm* 'rain'), *ksafim* 'monies, funds' : *kesèf* 'money'; *xolot* 'dunes' : *xol* 'sand'; *šlagim* 'heavy snow' : *šelèg* 'snow' (as can be seen, the quantitative shade of the 'plural' form constantly persists). It may be less tangible in cases where content relations are clearly taken over from a European model, as in *nyarot* 'papers, documents' (sg. *nyar* 'paper', never 'a paper' as in 'examination paper'), a Classical attestation of which has the word as a "countable" ('pieces of writing paper, sheets', a use also maintained in contemporary familiar style). As in the last mentioned example, a double relation of quantity is not unlikely to emerge, particularly in nouns that, in the singular, denote measurable materials or, as countables, objects made thereof:

ʾec 'tree'	ʾec (ʾexad) '(one) piece of wood'	ʾec 'wood', i.e. 'Holz'
	(ʾéyze) ʾec '(what sort of) wood'	
ʾecim 'trees'	'pieces of wood', 'sorts of wood, woods', i.e. 'Hölzer'	

Such double-track distinctions will be found to resemble closely some of the examples given by JESPERSEN (1911-: 2.85–90) under the somewhat noncommittal heading "The Differentiated Plural" (as *waters* 'a number of tumblers of water'/'kinds of (mineral) water' : 'water area'). While the "differentiation" obviously exists in Israeli Hebrew, the two semantic ranges of the plural (as well as of the singular) form are kept apart by certain syntagmatic restrictions:

possessive suffixes, for instance, will not normally be found with "noncountable" plural bases (unless "unseparable" appurtenance is clearly present, as in *nyarot-av* 'his papers, his personal documents'), so that the occurrence of such suffixes marks the noun concerned as countable; the same effect is, of course, yielded by any numeric modifier (*šne nyarot* 'two sheets') or by a totalizer like *kol* 'all, every'; 'countability' seems therefore to be the marked member of a contrast in plurality as well as in singularity.

The nature of the European model may be responsible for the occasional impossibility of positing a reasonably suitable "noncountable" singular for a "noncountable" plural, as in

ši'ur	'ratio, quota, teaching period, lesson (given or taught)'	—	—
ši'urim	'lessons given, teaching periods'	'instalment' (часть 'portion', по частям 'by instalments')	'homework (уроки 'homework' versus урок 'lesson')

Dictionaries of current usage should (but do not) point out these cases; artifical singularization (like *nyar* 'document') should not be resorted to. Until more adequate sources are available, students will be well advised to check with their informants the existence and usability of corresponding singular forms, whenever a noncountable plural is encountered.

Some of the "noncountable" plurals are inherited (cf. e.g., Bibl. *g·šåmi·m* 'constant rain'); the wide use of this morphosemantic class may have been fostered by a likewise inherited, but no longer productive, class of essentially abstract pluralia tantum (Biblical as well as postbiblical), as *n'urim* 'youth' and *nisu'im* 'marriage'[152]; the fertility

---

[152] It is only in the *pluralia tantum* that the Aramaic plural ending *-i·n* (taken over to rabbinical Hebrew) survives in Israeli Hebrew stylistic variants: *nisu'in*, *gerušin* 'divorce', *'erusin* 'betrothal', *piturin* 'dismissal'; synchronically, *-in* is not a plural suffix (cf. COHEN – ZAFRANI 1968: 178). The learned or terminological status of these survivors is obvious; cf. also *dine-'onšin* 'penal law' and *dine-nzikin* 'law of torts'. They tend not to require plural concord; in syntactic situations in which concord is required, the Hebrew-shaped variant in *-im* (where available) is preferred (*nisu'im me'ušarim* 'a happy marriage'), while in other cases, such as with artificially innovated pseudo-Aramaic *modi'in* 'intelligence (service)' (opp. sg. *modia* 'informer') singular concord applies: *ha-modi'in ha-cva'iy* '(the) military intelligence'.

and application range, however, of the plural formation of nouns denoting uncountable objects, unmistakably bear the imprint of European notional models. The same may probably be said of the "polarity" phenomenon of assigning concrete collective meanings to plurals of abstract singulars: *'omèk* 'depth' : *'omakim* 'depths'; *govàh* 'height': *gvahim* 'heights' (both plural forms, while attested in mediaeval texts, are not yet concretized at that period).

7.1.4 Case

The discovery of the fact that Israeli Hebrew prepositions function in two discrete ways (ROSÉN 1958a: 83–112 = 1966a: 95–124) has led to the establishment of the nominal inflexional category of CASE (also 1962a: 62–5). It is worthwhile justifying here why the different syntactical behaviour of the prepositions seemed to call for the term of *case* in one part of the uses.

Free, that is only extralinguistically restricted, substitutability exists for the occurrences, e.g., of the preposition *lifne-*[153] 'before';

---

[153] Etymologically, *lifne-* consists of the preposition *le-* and the construct form of a noun which, in its absolute form denotes the 'front' or 'visible side' of an object or, with reference to the human body, its 'face' (whether with Biblical Hebrew nouns such as this one, or *p·e* 'opening, mouth', *yàd* 'hand, side', *ro'š* 'head, top', the anatomical reference is cardinal, and the locational one transferred, or *vice versa*, may be open to discussion). The original stock of Hebrew prepositions is composed functionally only of those that came functionally to replace the case-endings (*b·-*, *l-*, *'et-*, which may be governed, in the sense to be defined below, in Biblical Hebrew); the class of Biblical Hebrew prepositions is then found broadened by nominal forms in adverbial status, governing other nouns as their adjuncts (*neged* 'opposite side', *neged hàhàr* 'against the mountain'); these latter "nouns turned prepositions" are, in that function, not common Semitic, nor has the process remained productive beyond Biblical Hebrew. The formational process that extends over the entire history of Hebrew and is operative in constantly adding new members to the class of prepositions is the creation of "compound prepositions" (ROSÉN 1955a: 115–8) from a preposition of the first Semitic stock and a semantically appropriate construct noun (*li-fne-*, *'al-yad* 'at the side of', *le-fi* 'accordingly' already Biblical, others later or current formations: *bi-fkudat* 'by order of', *mi-sibat* 'by reason of'); this living and very productive process is nowadays a reflex of a typologically occidental feature (*be-cause of, in charge of, à raison de, à côté de*). For the distinction between these compounds and otherwise similar syntagms (*bešem* 'in the name of, representing' versus *be-šem* 'in a name of, by the name of, called') see ROSÉN (1955a: 115–8; 1958a: 171–2; 1966a: 184–7; 1957: 331–5).

in *'avo' lifne-ša'a ševà* 'I shall come before seven o'clock', *lifne-* is replaceable by any one semantically compatible preposition, such as *'axare-* 'after', *'ad-* 'by', or *sviv-* 'about'; it is this paradigmatic replaceability that lends *lifne-* its content of 'before'.

No substitutability whatsoever exists for the preposition *'et-* (with its allomorph $\emptyset$ with nondeterminated nouns, *7.1.2*): in *ra'itì 'et-ha-hacaga* 'I saw the show', replacement of *'et-* by another preposition would render the sentence ungrammatical; its omission would only be conceivable by omitting the article *ha-* at the same time (*ra'itì hacaga* 'I saw a show').[154] The irreplaceability of *'et-* immediately points to the fact that *'et-* can have no lexical, but only grammatical, that is syntagmatic, function: it marks the verb *ra'itì* and the noun *ha-hacaga* as belonging to, and constituting, one verbal syntagm (verb + object); this is underlined by the fact that *'et-* and $\emptyset$ are allomorphs. The syntagmatic type constituted by a verb and a noun linked by $\emptyset/'et-$ is the one with the most "direct" connection of a verb and a "governed" noun: *'et-* has been, traditionally and rightly, considered as the morpheme of the accusative case.

The question now arises whether there are cases apart from the "nominative" ($\emptyset$-case) and the "accusative" ($\emptyset/'et-$case). There is a number of prepositions for which replaceability prevails in some environments, while in others no substitution of the preposition concerned is grammatically possible. This is true for approximately half a dozen prepositions and it can be seen easily that irreplaceability and, of course, inomissibility, of the preposition is concomitant with the occurrence of certain verbs, and vice versa, e.g.:

*le-*case: *N mecape le-N*	'N expects N'
*be-*case: *N metapel be-davar*	'N treats something'
*'al-*case: *N mevater 'al-davar*	'N gives something up'

There are more of these "types of transitivity", the preposition constitutes the government properties of the verb, and the sugges-

---

[154] Omission of compulsory *'et-* is, however, a marker of certain personal styles.

tion (ROSÉN 1958a: 96–107 = 1966a: 108–20) to consider the governed preposition as forming one constituent with the verb (*vater 'al-* as lexical unit) has been largely met with approval.

The crucial point is that these same prepositions can also occur as members of substitution classes, and, at that, fairly frequently in a verbal group whose centre is the same verb that governs the preposition concerned:

'ani metapel be-'inyanxa	*be-*	*yom rvi'i*
	'ad-	
	lifne-	
	'axare-	

'I am going to deal with your case on		Wednesday'
	by	
	before	
	after	

It is the irreplaceability of the first *be-* that defines the noun prefixed by it as a GOVERNED OBJECT, while the noun (*yom rvi'i* 'Wednesday') preceded by substitutable *be-* (which in this case has lexical function and is translatable: 'on') has the status of a (noncompulsory) adverbial complement (ROSÉN 1958a: 90–9 = 1966a: 102–11).

It appears expedient to point out here some of the respects in which the distinction between governed and ungoverned prepositions (that is between objects and adverbials) is structurally operative:

(1) Paradigmatically: pronominal substitutes (interrogative, anaphoric, or other) of a governed object compulsorily contain the governed prepositional element (e.g., for *be*-case objects *bame* 'what', *bo* 'it'), while adverbials may be replaced, according to the semantic class to which they belong, by pronominal adverbs that stand for the syntagm formed by the ungoverned preposition and the noun (or noun group) (e.g., for *be*-introduced complements: *'éyfo* 'where', *šam* 'there', *'eyx* 'how', *kax* 'thus', *matay* 'when', *'az* 'then').

(2) Morphologically: in one case, at least, that of the preposition *le-*, personal inflexion differs in the "governed" occurrences from that in the ungoverned ones, e.g. for the 2nd person masculine singular: *lxa* (governed) and *'eléxa* 'to you' (ungoverned). In fact, the suffixless (person-uncharacterized) form of the latter may be *le-* just as well as *'el-*.

(1) *Šalaxtì lxa'et-ha-kesèf*	'I sent you the money' (i.e. to be yours, for you to keep)
(2) *Šalaxtì'et-ha-kesèf 'eléxa*[156]	'I sent the money to you' (i.e. to your address)
(3) *Šalaxtì'et-ha-kesèf le-yosef*	'... to Joseph' (i.e. either to be his, for him to keep, or to his address)
(4) *Šalaxtì'et-ha-kesèf 'el-yosef* and also[156]:	'... to Joseph' (i.e. to his address)
(5) *Šalaxtì lxa'et-ha-kesèf 'el-* (or *le-*)*yosef*	'I sent you the money to Joseph' (i.e. to be yours ... to Joseph's address)

One can, of course, contend that the opposition *le-*: *'el-* is neutralized unless in immediate precedence to a personal suffix; the suffixal forms of *le-* would then enter the ranks of those case-forms that are employed only in governed use.

Furthermore, the prepositions that can function as governed (case) prefixes are subject to a certain rule of sentence-part order, irrespective, however, of whether they thus function or are employed to introduce adverbials; the other prepositions (of the class of *lifne-*) are not. The rule concerned is the compulsory postverbal[157] enclisis of the suffix-bearing forms of such prepositions, cf. the word order in sentences (1)–(5) above; while *'eléxa* (sentence 2) could take the place of *lxa* (1), the inverse is impossible.[158]

[155] For the order of the sentence parts see below.
[156] See above, 7.1.2 and note 150, on *Elle sort de la paille de la paille.*
[157] Also post-verboid (5.5.3) and post-impersonal (5.6.1); see ROSÉN (1962a: 22; 1966a: 280).
[158] Except in very special circumstances (not duly accounted for in ROSÉN 1966a: 280), that is if the sentence is continued by alternative negative predication (cf. ROSÉN 1966a: 227) (*šalaxtì 'et-ha-kesèf lxa ve-lo le-yosef* '... to you and not to Joseph') or if a negative sentence is continued by alternative positive predication (*šalaxtì 'et-ha-kesèf lo lxa 'éla le-yosef* '... not to you, but to Joseph'). Since this rule does not depend on the place of the verb in the sentence (i.e. the suffix-bearing preposition is not sentence-enclitic), the Israeli Hebrew phenomenon is typologically related not to French (as I have rashly assumed in ROSÉN 1966a: 280), but rather to German: *Ich habe dir das Geld geschickt* versus *Ich habe an dich das Geld geschickt, Ich habe das Geld an dich geschickt; Ich habe das Geld an Josef geschickt* or *Ich habe an Josef das Geld geschickt,* while *Ich habe das Geld dir geschickt* would also be restricted to conditions of alternative negative (or positive after negative sentence) predication (*... und nicht ihm; ... nicht dir geschickt, sondern ihm.*)

If, as shown, the sentence part linked to the governing verb by a governed preposition constitutes what was termed, in German structural grammar, on the basis of the same considerations, a "prepositional object" (MOTSCH 1970: 92[159]), we have still to justify why the term *case* has been considered appropriate and need not be abandoned even after the discovery that, in German, case and prepositional constructions have like status as elements governed by transitive verbs.

German is a representative of a type of language in which cases are, inter alia, governed by prepositions. In a *Präpositionalobjekt*, the case is governed by the transitive verb, in addition to the preposition; but these are not two discrete governments, since in every occurrence of a preposition, the case ending is part of a discontinuous morpheme made up of itself and the preposition. In languages with no inflexional marking of case distinctions, or where a single (pronominal) case form is governed by all prepositions, as, for example, in Romance (*à lui*) or English (*to him*), the object-marking function carried in Latin-type systems exclusively by the case morphemes must be considered to be executed by (that is, historically, devolved upon) the prepositions, to be exact, those prepositions that are not replaceable in all of their occurrences (p. 169f.), such as *à/de* in French. Traditional French school grammar was very wise in assigning precisely to these two prepositions a status of case markers and in considering the process of their prefixation to the noun one of inflexion.

Since the greater part of the case prefixes can also be used as introducers of adverbial complements, the question arises, in Israeli Hebrew as in other languages in which this is the case, whether a natural or "logical" connection exists between what bears the time-honoured name of "local" or "adverbial" use of the cases and their "grammatical" one. It would seem that no link can be discovered between the content type of verbs governing a certain case and the

---

[159] *An* in *man erinnert sich an Erlebnisse* introduces a *Präpositionalobjekt*, while in *wir trafen uns am Abend*, it introduces an adverbial complement. "Der Begriff des Präpositionalobjekts muß zunächst noch als ein sehr vager Begriff betrachtet werden. [Why? H. R.] Eine genauere Begriffsbestimmung auf der Basis einer Transformationsgrammatik wurde von R. Schädlich (*Zur Syntax des deutschen Adverbs* [Diss. Berlin, 1965]) vorgeschlagen. Danach unterscheiden sich Präpositionalobjekte von gewöhnlichen Präpositionalphrasen dadurch, daß mit dem Verb auch die Präposition determiniert ist. [Cf. above, 169; H. R.] Bei adverbial verwendeten Präpositionalphrasen dagegen hängt die Wahl der Präposition von der syntaktischen Funktion des Adverbials ab." (MOTSCH 1970: 92)

meaning of that same preposition in lexical status; in other words, a *lokale Kasustheorie* would find scanty support through Israeli Hebrew (or for that matter, simply Hebrew) facts. There seems to be, however, a shade of a difference in this respect between the two prefixes *be-* and *le-* that were, so to speak, "born" to be case markers (fn. *153*) and those prepositions like *'al-* and *mi-* that only secondarily joined the ranks of the case prefixes. While, of course, in governed uses of *'al* ('on, upon') or *mi-* ('from') hardly a shade of local relations is observable, it is still noteworthy that case government in other languages might occasionally be found to be lexically analogous: *laamod* 'stand' versus *laamod 'al-* 'insist *on; insister* sur, *bestehen* auf'; *ledaber* 'talk' versus *ledaber 'al-* '*sprechen* über'. These two examples are inherited; as to the first, it would seem that the similarity of rection in the languages compared is rather a similarity of metaphors in the verb concerned (*laamod* 'stand' versus 'in-*sist*'). Only a complete inventory of Israeli Hebrew verbs with their case governments will help us to throw light on these questions.

If the notion of case has been established on the basis of the structural concept of conditioning, then it is not only lexical conditioning (that is, the identity of a given verb) that has to be taken into account for our purposes. There might also be conditioning by the identity of a syntagmatic pattern or by a morphemic class, in other words, transformational conditioning. On the basis of such considerations we would immediately have to include in the list of case prefixes the preposition *'alyde-*[160] which is the marker of the agent in a passive construction (for details and alternants such as *le-*[161] see ROSÉN 1962a: 126–7).

---

[160]   For its formation (*'al-yde-*) see note *153*.

[161]   Possessive *le-* expresses the "agent" status with perfect participles of verbs of "intellectual activity": *zaxur li* 'I remember' (literally 'it is remembered to me/by me'), *muval li* 'I understand' (*muvan* 'understood'); cf. ROSÉN (1962a: 127). I am not sure whether there are classical antecedents of this phenomenon, but cannot propose any dating for its emergence. I would venture to suggest that the verb 'to know' might have served as catalyst: all passive forms of this verb (and not only the perfect participle *yadua li* 'known to me') are so construed (already in Biblical Hebrew), and this matches European syntax (*mir bekannt*). The restriction of quasi-possessive expression of the agent with the perfect passive of "*verba intelligendi*" is interesting in the respect that – according to

A complex feature of conditioning, composed of transformational and morphological factors at the same time, can be discovered for *be-*. It concerns the nominalization of sentence contents in which the subject is an appurtenant ("inalienable") object and their exocentrical placement in descriptive relation to the "appurtenee"; in other words, an exocentric "possessive" nominal syntagm (of bahuvrīhi character) is created:

> *ha-yalda +ˀeynayìm kxulot → ha-yalda kxulat-ha-ˀeynayìm*
> 'the girl' +'eyes' (are) 'blue'   'the blue-eyed girl'

These are the cases in which adjectives are used as constructs *(6.5.2.3)*, but there is a constraint on these uses in that only radical (and not derived) adjectives can so occur *(6.4.2)*. The case prefix *be-* functions as an alternant of the construct state if this condition is not fulfilled, that is if the adjective is "weak" (derived):

ha-ˀiš   +haškafot xofšiyot → ha-ˀiš ha-xofšiy be- haškafotav
'the man' +'views' (are) 'free'   'the man' 'free'   'his views'
                    i.e. 'the man of free views'.

yelèd   +tfisa mhira → yelèd   mahir be- tfisato
'a child' +'comprehension' 'a child' 'quick'   'his comprehension'
      (is)'quick'
                    i.e. 'a child quick of apprehension'

(Note the automatic occurrence of the preposition *of* in the English versions.)

In the second example (where the adjective is not "weak") a bahuvrīhi compound is not excluded: *yelèd mhir-tfisa* 'a child of quick apprehension'; in predicative status however, the *be-* transform would be preferred: *ha-yelèd mahir be-tfisato* 'the child is of

---

what is stressed in BENVENISTE's teaching – the late Latin type *habeo compertum, est mihi compertum* is, in the earliest layers of its occurrence, precisely so restricted in use. Extension of the *est mihi compertum* type in Israeli Hebrew is substandard and extremely rare; as a sure case one could only mention *katuv li* literally '*(hoc) scriptum mihi est*', '*(hoc) scriptum habeo*', where the agent is not necessarily '*ego*'; but here, transitivization (as with verboids; *5.5.3*) already takes place: *katuv li ˀet-ze ba-maxberèt* 'I have this written (*or*: written this) in my notebook'.

(*or:* has) quick apprehension'. In fact quite a few bahuvrīhi compounds occur only in attributive status, and in these cases again, the *be*-construction serves as syntactically conditioned alternant in predicative status.

A transformational operation, identical to the one apparent in the foregoing examples, and with identical results, takes place also in other cases in which the predicative element of the included sentence (say, *xofšiy* in the first example) cannot be made undergo morphological conversion into a construct state, notably if that element is verbal:

basar + *ha-xmir* 'ala → *basar* 'ala *ba-mxir.*
'meat' + 'the price has risen' 'The meat(-price) has
gone up.'
Yosef + *ha-miškal* *yarad* → *Yosef yarad ba-miškal.*
'Joseph' + 'the weight has 'Joseph has lost weight.'
gone down'

(Note that the appurtenantive personal suffix (*-o*, etc.) obligatory in the adjectival examples, is absent here.)

There are even some isolated usages, in which nouns, that for some reason, semantic incompatibility or otherwise, cannot serve as predicates relative to the governing noun, undergo the same transformational process:

Yosef + *mikco'o* *nahag* → *Yosef nahag be-mikco'o.*
'Joseph' + 'his profession' 'Joseph is driver by profession.'
(is) 'driver'

Also *le-* may be found syntagmatically governed. Most notably, it is an alternant of the construct state of a noun, if the noun whose placing in construct position would be required is itself a compound; if we compare the two expressions

beyt-xarošèt *le-gafrurim* 'match factory'
'factory' 'matches'

and

taaṣiyat-   *-gafrurim*   'match industry'
'industry'
(construct state;
the absolute state is
taasiya)

or

cva'-(ha-)hagana   *le-yisrae'el*   'Israel Defence Forces'
'(the) defence army'   'Israel'

and

mišterèt-   *-yisra'el*   'Israel police'
'police'
(construct state; the
absolute state is
mištara)

we find that in the first term of each pair a compound noun followed by *le-* takes the position of a construct simplex in the second term. Compounds cannot be made subject to the absolute : construct distinction of state (*7.1.5*).

The same goes for compositionally determined noun-adjective phrases, for which there is no morphological possibility of converting them to the construct state, and again *le-* fulfils the function of the construct; compare

kerèn kayemèt   *le-yisra'el*   'Israel Permanent Fund'
'fund' 'permanent' 'Israel'

with

keren-ha-ysod   'Foundation Fund'
   'the foundation',

or

šana rišona la-limudim   'first year of studies'
'year' 'first'   'the studies'

with

šnat-   *limudim*   'academic year, *Studienjahr*'
'year'
(construct)

7.1.5 Nominal status; nominal transitivity

The binary category of NOMINAL STATUS, consisting of the terms
ABSOLUTE STATE (*davar* 'thing', *dvarim* 'things, words'; *sus* 'horse',
susim 'horses'; *mora* 'lady teacher', *morot* 'lady teachers'; *šana*
'year', *šanim* 'years') and CONSTRUCT STATE (*dvar-*, *divre-*; *sus-*,
suse-; *morat-*, *morot-*; *šnat-*, *šnot-*) whose inflexional characterization may be either by suffix, by stem alternation, by both, or else
neutralized (cf. examples given) has been dealth with in its morphological aspects (*7.1.4*), its nexal function (*6.4.2.3*), and semantic
purport (*6.5.2.3*). We have only to give a general appraisal here of
the overall effect of "constructing" in the nominal sphere.

The marked term of the opposition is the construct state; its
occurrence is restricted to nouns (or certain adjectives; *6.4.2.1*)
immediately preceding a noun; these two nominals may be termed
construct and *construent*, respectively (Rosén 1962a: 87–9). The
construent is always the determinans of the construct; this is not
necessarily the case where two nouns in immediate sequence constitute a noun phrase: *bakbuk* (absolute state; pl. *bakbukim*) 'bottle'
in *bakbuk yayìn* 'a bottle of wine' (Rosén 1957: 340–1) will be rightly
considered the quantitative determinant of *yayìn* 'wine' which follows it. Where two nouns in immediate succession are mutually
determinative, the respective status of each one of these nouns as
either determinans or determinatum is unmarked unless the first
member of the pair of nouns is morphologically construct and thereby characterized as determinatum.

We wish to propose here, for the specific type of purport con-
veyed by the characterized construct forms, the term NOMINAL
TRANSITIVITY. (Morphological marking of transitive syntactic behaviour, in verbs at least, is nothing unheard of.) What would be
primarily implied by this term is that the identity of the syntactically
dependent member of the construction is a necessary prerequisite
for the assignment of *Sinn* to the regens (*smoke* in *smoke fish*, *smoke
cigarettes*, *smoke a weed*, or *smoke a room*) and occasionally even
the identity of the regens is necessary for the assignment of sense
to the dependent term (*weed* in *pluck a weed* or *smoke a weed*); in

other words, the semantic effect of transitivity may be seen in the creation of referential compatibility of the two terms linked by the syntactic relation. What would tend to emphasize the appropriateness of the proposed term is the fact that the marking of the direct ($\emptyset$/'et-) object transitivity with action-nouns is precisely the construct state (*ktivat-sefèr* 'the writing of a book'; cf. *ktiva* 'writing', *katav 'et-ha-sefèr* 'wrote the book'; ROSÉN 1957: 335–40; 1958a: 148–61 = 1966a: 160–73), while with other governed object-cases (*7.1.4*) the case-prefix is taken over into nominalization, and the action noun has absolute status.

For the relation between nominal and verbal transitivity cf., e.g., *moray* 'my teachers (i.e. those who teach or taught me)' versus *ha-morim šeli* 'my teachers (same as foregoing *or* my teaching staff)', which again tends to indicate that the marked term of the opposition is the construct state.

While dealing with "loose compounds" (*6.5.2.3*), we have already given some examples of how the content of the construct and the construent are mutually determined.[162] We shall recall here that very frequently the "isolation" (*6.5.2.3*) of the content of a construct goes as far as to require specific translational equivalents according to whether the noun is in construct or in absolute state, or, if in construct state, according to the nature of the construent (ROSÉN 1957: 325–8; 1958a: 141 = 1966a: 153; 1962a: 97, 102). This must, of course, be expected for languages that do not possess a "status" category and can match the syntagmatic means of expression available in Israeli Hebrew only by lexical mechanisms; this phenomenon again tallies with verbal transitivity in that in translational situations we very often find it necessary to assign two or more translational equivalents to one and the same verb according to whether it is used transitively or intransitively (in "absolute" use).

The noun *davar* (*6.4.2.3*) signifies 'word, saying' in construct state, if the construent is semantically compatible (*dvar-ha-melèx* 'royal order'); such signification is never attributable to it in singular absolute state.

---

[162]   This is particularly true for the exocentric adjective constructions (*6.5.2.3*).

The absolute state appears to be the *terme marqué*, but some interference is noticeable from the number category (*dvarim* 'things, objects, words, sayings, speech'); likewise *ben* (construct) 'son' and (absolute) 'son, young male, boy', pl. *bne-* (construct) 'sons, children' (as in *bne-yisra'el*) and *banim* (absolute) 'sons, boys'; as a biblical survivor,[163] pl. (abs.) *b'alim* coincides in the meaning of 'owner' (or 'owners') with the construct forms *baàl-/baalat-* (f.sg.), *baale-* (m.pl.), and *baalot-* (f.pl.) 'having, possessing, owning' (ROSÉN 1962a: 230), while absolute state *baàl* and *b'alim* are restricted to the signification of 'husband'. Number and status enter a remarkable relation of categorial crossing in the nominal domain, a phenomenon, however, a study of which has yet to be undertaken.

7.2 CATEGORIES INDIFFERENT TO PART OF SPEECH

7.2.1 Aspect

Israeli Hebrew ASPECT is a marginal case of an inflexional category; while inflexional means of expression participate in the marking of one of the two members of the aspect category (e.g. *nV-* in inchoative *neemad* 'came to a halt, placed himself in a standing position'), an aspect opposition is never solely expressed by two contrasting inflexional morphemes. Furthermore, the aspect category is on the borderline of verbal and nominal morphology: it can be stated with almost general validity that of a contrastive pair of aspectually distinguished terms, the one which is more on the "stative-constative" side has more nominal, the one which is more "fientive-cursive"-characterized (RUNDGREN 1963: 56) – more verbal features. E.g.:

Ha-tikun naase 'The repair-work is being done' (The "aorist" [7.3.2] *naase* is part of a tense paradigm, e.g. versus *naasa* 'was done'.)

---

[163] In Biblical Hebrew, person-suffixed sg. *b·a'al* is 'husband', while person-suffixed pl. *b··ál- (b··álá-w, b··áleyhá)* is 'owner, possessor'; while the singular reference of the latter forms seems to be clear, they never occur in syntactic concord situations that could indicate their grammatical numerical status.

Ha-tikun 'asuy 'The repair work is done' (The participle *'asuy*
forms part of a nominal sentence, into which tense distinctions
can be introduced by added verbality: *ha-tikun haya 'asuy* 'The
repair-work was done'.)

While it is in itself remarkable enough that the Israeli Hebrew
aspect category preserves, in terms of content, the typically Semitic
inherited shades of fientive : stative, it is still more noteworthy that
its "renewal" (to use RUNDGREN's [1962] words) in fact takes up the
most archaic means of expression that led to the integration of the
verbal system: the Biblical Hebrew "perfect" (suffix-tense) *šåmå'ti*
'I have heard' and *yådå'ti* 'I have learned, I know' are of nominal
origin ('I am the hearer'), so that for an *état de langue* immediately
preceding Biblical Hebrew, the nominal[164] : verbal distinction
(suffix tense : prefix tense) was correlated to the aspectual category:
"perfect" : (narrative or non-narrative) "cursive"; the adoption, in
postbiblical Hebrew, of the suffix-bearing form as the (only)
narrative tense made it necessary, for the purpose of "renewing"
aspectual relations and of making them again realizable (cf. RUND-
GREN 1962), to devolve the expression of the latter to new formal
entities, which had in the part-of-speech system the very status of
their functional predecessors: (verbal) nominals.

The morphological means employed to express aspectual content
relations have other functions besides; one must therefore describe
the limits in which these formal features serve as carriers of aspectual relations and those in which other tasks are vested in them.
There is no ambiguity: the environmental limits are neat and allow
of no overlapping. For example, the base pattern *(6.4.2.2)* *niRRaR*
(nif'al stem) functions, in contrast with the *RaRaR* pattern, as
passive morpheme with transitive radicals (*šamar* 'watched' : *nišmar*
'was watched'), while it is available as a marker of inchoativity
with intransitive ones (*šaxav* 'was lying' : *niškav* 'lay down'). Likewise, *hitRaReR* *(6.4.2.2)* functions as a reflexive of transitive *RiReR*
(*gileax* 'shaved [trans.]' : *hitgaleax* 'shaved [intrans.]'), while in

---

[164]   BAUER – LEANDER (1922: 270 and *passim*) call the Biblical Hebrew perfect
tense "Nominal".

opposition to intransitive *RiReR* or other patterns it has (inchoative) aspect content: *'amad* 'stood' : *hit'amed* 'put himself into a standing position' and *neemad* 'came to a halt'. The relationship between voice and aspect is typologically significant (cf. *coucher* : *se coucher*; *sitzen* : *sich setzen*).

The contiguity of voice and aspect[165] emerges primarily from the fact that all transitive verbs that admit of a passive (and even some intransitive positional verbs[166]) have a stative passive participle, while the existence of a time-characterized (*5.4*) fientive passive participle is warranted only for the class of "strong" (*6.4.2.2*) verbs[167]:

active participle (aorist)	stative pass. part.	fientive pass. part. (aorist)
RoReR *soger* 'closing, close(s)'	*RaRuR* *sagur* 'closed'	*nVRRaR* *nisgar* 'being/is closed'
meRaReR *mešalem* 'paying, pay(s)'	*meRuRaR* *mešulam* 'paid'	—
maRRiR *mazmin* 'inviting, invite(s)'	*muRRaR* *muzman* 'invited'	—

While the missing fientive passive participle (aorist) of *meRaReR* can, in many cases, be supplied by the fientive participle (aorist) of the intransitive-reflexive formation (*mištalem* 'being paid'),[168] no such possibility is obvious for the 'causative' formation *maRRiR*.

[165] The recognizance of the importance of this contiguity is based on H. J. POLOTSKY's teaching.
[166] Such as *šaxuv* 'occupying a lying position', *yašuv* 'occupying a sitting position', *raxuv* 'occupying the position of a rider', *samux* 'leaned to, close to'; also: *lamud* 'experienced', *lavuš* 'dressed' (for the history of these verbs as to development of transitivity see *6.4.2.2*), *savur* 'convinced' (in view of *sover* 'being of the opinion (that)').
[167] And for "verbs of motion" (i.e. change of position); e.g. *mukam* 'is (being) erected', *moovar* 'is being transferred', *muxnas* 'is being introduced', *muval* 'is being transported'.
[168] ROSÉN 1956b: 141–3; 1962a: 273.

A sentence such as 'The guests are being invited' is, as it stands, with no further expansions, not translatable by an Israeli Hebrew passive construction.

We may recall here that the stative-passive participle does not function as a verbal tense: a sentence having such form as a predicate is, for all intents and purposes, a nominal one (*Ha-kesèf mešulam* 'The money is paid': *Ha-kesèf haya mešulam* 'The money was paid'). This underlines again that a contrast of nominality versus verbality conveys a stative versus fientive purport. The almost nonverbal character of the *meRuRaR* pattern is further emphasized by the fact that very frequently it functions not as a part of an inflexional verbal, but of a derivational nominal paradigm (*zakan* 'beard': *mezukan* 'bearded'; cf. *1.5.3, 6.1.2*), just like the *-ed, -atus, -ωτός*, etc. adjectives in English, Latin, Greek, etc., respectively.

While it is self-evident that the directly denominative, consequently voice-devoid, *meRuRaR* adjective can have no cursive-fientive value, we have to qualify, in one respect, earlier statements (ROSÉN 1956b: 140–1; 1962a: 126) on the (con)stative value of the weak passive verbal adjectives *meRuRaR, muRRaR* (p. 181) in view of the material collected by MIRKIN (1968: 150–2), which tends to show that the stative content of a weak passive participle can be overridden by a time- or circumstance-positioning adverbial:

> *Ha-davar mevucaa*   'This (thing) is carried out'
> *Ha-davar mevucaa hayom*   'This is (being) carried out today'

The parallelism with English, where the insertion of *being* is possible, but not necessary, in the fientive expression, is obvious: the cursive value is imparted to the English passive by the adverbial modification. With passive participles, the stative : fientive contrast can be expressed either paradigmatically, as in Israeli Hebrew strong passives or the two German passive constructions

$$Ha\text{-}ša\grave{a}r \quad \begin{vmatrix} sagur \\ nisgar \end{vmatrix} \quad \text{'Das Tor} \begin{vmatrix} ist \\ wird \end{vmatrix} \quad geschlossen\text{'},$$

or else, where no morphological distinction is practicable, by the presence or absence, respectively, of a temporal or quasi-temporal modification:

$$Ha\text{-}nerot\ mudlakim \begin{vmatrix} — \\ ba\text{-}\,er\grave{e}v \end{vmatrix} \quad \text{'The candles are lighted} \begin{vmatrix} — \\ in\ the \\ evening \end{vmatrix}^{169}$$

---

[169]   The situation is different for "verbs of motion" (cp. note *167*).

Still, the marked term of the binary constrast is, in this case, the stative one, since *Ha-nerot mudlakim ba-'erèv* may, like Engl. *The candles are lighted in the evening*, also stands for Germ. *Die Kerzen* sind *am Abend angezündet.*

The stative passive participle being essentially nominal (adjectival), the mechanism described will not be valid in syntactical positions which an Israeli Hebrew adjective cannot occupy (in particular in a position preceding the grammatical subject, a feature of arrangement characteristic for Biblical Hebrew); in such positions, which, by themselves, characterize the participle as verbal, cursive-fientive value will apply: *Metuxnenèt* (feminine singular passive participle of *t-xn-n* 'plan') *gam mirpesèt-tacpit.* 'Also an observation terrace is being planned.' (newspaper item on improvements for an airport).

Another aspect distinction contiguous with voice is the already mentioned use of the strong *nVRRaR*-pattern and its base alternants (*6.4.2.2*), which has passive function in contrast with transitive actives, to express inchoativity[170] in relation to intransitive actives; the inchoative term has time dimension, although it seems not to occur in the "potential" (future) tense:

Ha-pcu'im	*šaxvu* *niškvu* *šoxvim* *niškavim*	*'al-ha-'arèc*
'The injured	lay came to lie lie come to lie	on the ground'

---

[170] Presented as feature of children's language (cf., however, *1.4.2*) by PERETZ (1943: 298) and AVINERY (1946: 169); considered as an aspectual Yiddishism by BLANC (1965: 190–7) (cf. *2.3.2*); attempts at historical explanation: BEN-ḤAYYIM (1953: 60–5; cf. ROSÉN 1953a: 14); *nax(ᵃ)leyti* translated 'ich bin *er*krankt' already in ROSENBERG (1900: 89), a usage probably inspired by Dan 8.27 (*neḥěleyti yåmi·m wå'åqu·m*). For the sake of showing the plausibility of the process it may be permitted to quote active ψύχει 'it is cold' (Herodotus 3.104.3) versus middle ψύχεται 'it becomes cold, it grows cold' (Herodotus 4.181.4).

These relations have classical forerunners: active *šamaa* 'heard' is correlated to the *NVRRaR*-formation *nišmaa* in two senses, 'was heard' and 'obeys', the latter of which may be considered as non-stative in comparison with the active; even more obvious in post-biblical transitive (!) *nizkar* 'remembered' (or 'was mentioned') versus *zaxar* 'kept in mind'.

In this opposition which is limited to colloquial style,[171] time-dimensional inchoativity is to time-dimensional stativity what time-dimensional cursivity is to time-devoid stativity: *neemad* can be regarded as the fientive term of the aspect opposition. Its aorist (present participle) is a verbally characterized form (*nVRRaR* is in contrast with a stative nominal *RaRuR*; cf. above), while its counterpart (*'omed*) is not; therefore, again, the fientive-cursive term is more verbal than the stative one; it may sometimes even be opposed to a perfect participle of the regular (*RaRuR*) formation[172]: *šaxuv* '(being in a) prostrated (position)', but this will then be synonymous with the "active" aorist participle (*šoxev*) apart from the fact that the latter can have both "general" time reference and *hic-et-nunc* reference, the stative only the latter.

These relations must be old; they can be seen also in the classical (and therefore not specifically colloquial) *'avud* 'lost' and *neevad* 'getting lost'[173] versus *'oved* 'lost' (>IH 'getting lost'). If an active strong transitive verb may have a zero object (*2.7.4*), such as *'ocer* 'holds back, brakes (trans.)' or *'ocer* + Ø 'brakes a vehicle', then the zero-object syntagm can be reinterpreted as intransitive, and the *nVRRaR*-formation, consequently, as inchoative: *neecar* 'comes to a stop' : *'ocer* 'stops (while riding a vehicle)'.

Lastly, we have to deal with the oppositions of the type *halax* 'went' : *haya holex* 'used to go'. Semantically, the latter is not an iterative (only the addition of expressions such as *bexol-paàm* 'every time', *le-'itim krovot* 'frequently', or subordinate clauses of com-

---

[171] We may assume that this is connected with the fact that *'amad* 'stood' continues the Biblical Hebrew meaning 'stood' of this verb, and not the most likely Aramaizing sense of postbibilcal Hebrew ('rose'); a similar situation prevails for *šaxav* (but also in Israeli Hebrew, e.g. *šaxav lišon* 'went to bed (to sleep)'). The opposition *haya* 'was' : *nihya* 'became', currently found in familiar colloquial style, is already Biblical.

[172] Cf. note *166* above concerning *yašuv* etc.

[173] Classical, but in current usage commonly replaced by *holex le-'ibud* (literally 'goes to loss'); *neevad* is common for 'was lost' (past).

parable temporal purport would lend iterativity to the expression
thus formed), but a habitual preterite; these forms, composed of
the "remotive" (preterite) *haya* and the participle, e.g. *holex*
(normally immediately following the former in ordinary style),
exists neither for the aorist nor for the "potential" (future) tense.

While it can be stated that the aspectual value of habitualness
obtains in sentences modified by explicit indications of past time
(*Ba-šana še-'avra haya ba' le-'itim yoter krovot* 'Last year he used to
come more frequently'), it will be of interest to discuss the environments in which this "compound remotive" (Rosén 1962a: 227–8)
has other values, and what categorial contiguities thereby develop.

Except in some morphologically delimitated environments, the
compound remotive has a modal content of 'non-actuality' (*Bim-
komi lo haya'ose zot* 'In my place, he wouldn't have done it') which
may be overcharacterized in apodoses pertaining to protases introduced by *lu* or *'ilu* 'if (unfulfilled)', or *lule* 'if . . . not (unfulfilled)'
(*Lu'amartì zot, ma haya'one?* 'Had I said that, what would he have
replied?').

In some cases, the compound remotive contains *haya* 'was' as a
real auxiliary; these cases are, in principle, those in which homophony (whether inherited or the result of phonemic mergers; cf.
p. 138 [I, V]) prevails between the "remotive" (preterite) and a corresponding "aorist" (present) form, e.g.

Hu	*haya*	*gar bi-yrušalayìm*	'He live	-d	in Jerusalem'
	—			-s	

The auxiliary is not required, and hardly used, for the marking of
the preterite sense, where the latter is adequately denoted by a
sentence modifier (e.g. *'eštakad hu gar bi-yrušalayìm* 'Last year, he
lived in Jerusalem'), so that a distinction of the habitual from the
temporal content of the compound tense would appear already
safeguarded thereby (since the 'habitual' sense obtains in past-
characterized sentences, see above); but this neat division is further
underlined by the fact that the nonaspectual (that is, temporal)
purport of the tense is limited to cases in which the aspectual value

of the resulting expression is already determined by the lexical properties of the verb: the opposition between the compound remotive
and the "aorist" (present) tense is of temporal value only with non-
punctual verbs (ROSÉN 1958a: 16–7 = 1966a: 22–3; 1962a: 227–8).
We have therefore:

Biconsonantal strong verbs (3rd person singular[174] homophonous in
aorist and remotive)

Durative verbs:

Hu gar bi-yrušlayìm   versus   *Hu haya gar bi-yrušalayìm*
'He lives in Jerusalem'   '... lived ...'

                and consequently   *Hu haya gar bi-y., 'ílu...* '...
                                           would live[175] ..., if (unfulfilled)'

Hu xay be-šekèt   versus   *Hu haya xay be-šekèt.* '...
'He lives in pace'   lived ...'
                and consequently   *Hu haya xay be-šekèt, 'ílu* ...
                                           '... would live ..., if ...'

Point verbs:

'oreax ba' 'A guest is coming[176]' versus *'oreax haya ba'* '... would
          'A guest has come'   come' (unfulfilled or habi-
                                                tual)

Ha-no'em kam 'The speaker is rising' versus *Ha-no'em haya kam* '...
               'The speaker rose'   would rise'

nVRRaR-pattern (3rd person singular masculine homophonous in
aorist and remotive)

Durative verbs:

---

[174]   Masculine and feminine; for the latter see *3.7.5* and note *73*.
[175]   In all these examples, *haya* + participle also conveys a modal content of
"past unfulfilled", '... he would have lived...', etc.
[176]   The "aorist" (present) of perfective verbs has no strictly *hic-et-nunc*-
reference to the act expressed by the verbal content and approaches a *tempus
instans*-purport, as shown. This may be considered as inherently characteristic
of the aspectual value, and a slavism need not be assumed. Cf. *7.3.2.*

Passive:

Ha-davar nexšav le-moʾil   versus   *Ha-davar haya nexšav lemoʾil*
'This (matter) is considered useful'   '... was considered ...'

                   and consequently   ... *haya nexšav le-moʾil, ʾilu ...*
                   or (inverted order)   ... *nexšav haya ...*
                                         '... would be considered, if ...'

Deponent:

Hu nilxam lemaàn ha-cedèk   versus   *Hu haya nilxam lemaàn ha-cedèk*
'He fights for justice'   '... would fight ...'
                       Past tense supplied by active form:
                       Hu laxam lemaàn ha-cedék '... fought...'

Point verbs:

Passive:

Ha-serèt kvar nigmar   versus   *Ha-serèt haya kvar nigmar.*
'The movie picture is already   'The movie picture would al-
coming to an end' (literally: ready be over'
'being completed'), '... is
over'

Deponent:

Ha-ʾoreax nixnas   versus   *Ha-ʾoreax haya nixnas*
'The guest is coming/going in',   '... would come/go in'
'The guest has come/gone in'

It would appear that habitualness and durativity are incompatible,[177]

[177] In fact, it would seem that habitualness has replaced durativity as the content of the *haya*+participle form. In postbiblical Hebrew, no doubt under Aramaic influence (cf. ROSÉN 1969: 103–4 note 14), the formation of the tenses of the lexically durative verbs was vested in the participle, which could have predicate status either in a nominal clause or else in a tense-marked copula clause in which the copula verb could be in either one of the two (inherited) Biblical Hebrew verbal tenses (perfect: imperfect). It is this new situation, arisen out of the emergence of periphrastic tenses and the ensuing possibility of creating a ternary tense category in the durative verb, that has to be regarded as the point of departure for the current tense system. Through addition of durativity, it must have been easy to reinterpret a contrast 'perfect durative : imperfect durative' as 'past : future'. Whether the restriction, in Israeli Hebrew, of the non-periphrastic form to the "remotive" (past) tense can be explained as a result of this process, I feel unable to discuss. At any rate, the difference between 'he used to come' and 'he came' can be expressed in Israeli Hebrew with refer-

but not habitualness and inchoativity. In fact, the double involve-
ment of the *nVRRaR* pattern with aspect (as a verbal form that has
undergone partial tense-merger due to homophony as well as a
marker of inchoativity) yields the interesting possibility of expressing "habitual inchoativity" : *haya neemad* 'used to stop short'.

It is obvious that this can occur only with strong intransitive
verbs, which do not constitute a morphosyntactic class of any
numerical strength. We do not, therefore, consider it necessary, at
the given stage of development, to assign the terms *inchoative* and
habitual to two different categories. On the basis of introspection, I
would even venture to contend that *haya neemad* is categorially
ambiguous: (1) 'used to stop short', (2) 'would (in a given unfulfilled condition) stop short'.

The compound remotive is, in its aspectual function, another
case of the "renewed" expression of aspect by means of a periphrastic construction with the verb 'to be' (RUNDGREN 1963: 68), but the
appearance of the participle in this context seems specific to the
historical development of Hebrew; the contiguity of aspectual and
modal contents, especially noticeable in the Hebrew compound remotive, is, however, also found in the aspect "renewal" processes of
other Semitic languages (RUNDGREN 1963: 70–3). At any rate, it is
obvious that in view of the nature of the periphrastic constructions and their congruity with copula sentences, the aspectual term
that contrasts with the simply narrative or "event" tense is again
formally characterized by its more nominal features.

7.2.2 Person-sex

The most adequate disposition of the members of the PERSON-SEX
(*5.1.1-2*) category will be by binary subdivision. The first dichotomy

---

ence neither to present nor to future time; but since the same is true for Western
languages (at least as concerns the future), the situation in Israeli Hebrew may
be typology-conditioned. – In certain archaizing styles of current narrative
prose (intimately linked with the stylistic predilections of S. Y. AGNON), the
periphrastic tense has no aspectual value, but can serve as mood- and aspect-
uncharacterized descriptive, and even narrative tense form; here, however,
a "periphrastic future" also occurs occasionally.

has to account for the difference between person-sex unmarked forms and those in which person or sex (or both) are marked: the unmarked form is characterized only by a number morpheme (*holxim* 'one goes') and corresponds to the Western European *on* or *man* 'person'; it will be discussed in more detail later.

The marked forms may be subdivided by the next dichotomy into those in which person only (not sex) is characterized; these are the forms of the "locutory" person (or persons): *halaxtì* 'I went' or *halaxnù* 'we went'. In these forms, sex is not syntactically operative: *'ani medaber* 'I (a male) speak' and *'ani medaberèt* 'I (a female) speak'. The last dichotomy concerns those forms in which sex is marked (in addition to person) and syntactically operative: here the division is between the "allocutory" ("second") and the "delocutory" (third) persons; sex marking of the second person forms is fully preserved and not threatened (at least not in the singular) in spite of the harsh typological contrast thereby called into being between Israeli Hebrew and the European language type.

The full integration of the expression of the "indefinite agent" (*on*, *man*) in the person category is typically Western European (Fr. *on*, Germ. *man*, and Engl. *one* are substitutes for agent pronouns) and therefore typologically significant (ROSÉN 1969: 104). Its principal means of expression in the verbal domain has been inherited from postbiblical Hebrew: *mevarxim* (< *mbàrki·m*) 'one blesses'; recalling that sentences with participial predicates (*mevarxim* is an "aorist" = present participle in the gender-unmarked ("masculine") plural form) have, in postbiblical Classical Hebrew, durative purport (cf. note *177*), it must be underlined that this Classical point of departure for the Israeli Hebrew indefinite-agent form has originally the value of a "general instruction" ('one shall bless'); this type of content has been abandoned in current language, and the form class of the "indefinite agent" has been extended to all tenses (*berxu* 'one blessed', *yevarxu* 'one will bless'). However, in the paradigm of person morphemes, the -*u* suffix, which here occurs in both the remotive and the potential tense, is the unmarked member of the person as well as of the gender (sex) category: *berxu* is of common gender, *yevarxu* is optionally of common gender (with a

stylistically elevated alternant for the feminine plural); cf. form
relations such as: *barex* (imp.sg.) : *barxu* (imp.pl.); *tevarex* : *tevarxu*
(potential tense, 2nd pers. m., sg.: pl.) (common, but with stylistically elevated alternant, homophonous with that of the 3rd
person plural). Consequently, the form used in the remotive and
potential tenses for the indefinite agent person is categorially
marked for number only, precisely as the one used in the aorist
tense.

In adnominal person, the *on*-form again is part of the paradigm
of personal suffixes: *ha-lev nišbar* 'one's heart breaks' (cf., in more
detail, *7.1.2*). The "definite article" *ha-* which carries the content
of '*on*' in the appurtenantive relation, can only be replaced by one
of the person suffixes (such as *lib-i* 'my heart'); it cannot be maintained in addition to the expression of person (as, e.g., in *ha-mnora*
'the lamp' versus *ha-mnora šel-i* 'my lamp', literally 'the lamp of
mine'), since the type *ha-lev*, in which *ha-* = 'one's' excludes all
nouns denoting non-inalienable objects (*7.1.2*), and direct suffixation of the pronoun is, in contrast to the *šel*-syntagm, the marker of
inalienability (*2.6.3*): *ha-* is consequently, in spite of its different
positional properties, a member of the person-sex category.

7.3 VERBAL CATEGORIES

7.3.1 Voice

VOICE is a purely verbal category. While every stem type of the verb
(*6.4.2.2*) has a regular action-noun formation coordinated to it,
which, however, is voice-indifferent, so that the action nouns of
transitive verbs belong in each case to a pair of active-passive sub-
stem-types, e.g. *hazmana* to both *hizmìn* 'invited' and *huzman* 'was
invited', and it is only syntactically that active or passive function
can be assigned to the action noun (ROSÉN 1958a: 148–61 = 1966a:
160–73; 1957: 335–40; 1962a: 254–9): *hazmana šel-xaverim* 'invitation of friends' versus *hazmanat-xaverim* 'friends' invitation, invitation of friends'; it follows that the first mentioned term of the

opposition is the marked one (as active). Special noun patterns are assigned as action nouns to verbal stem types normally functioning as passives only in cases in which no active counterpart exists ("deponent verbs"; e.g.: *he'adrut* 'absence' in view of *needar* 'was absent', a "strong" passive pattern, cf. *6.4.2.2*; or *histaklut* 'contemplation' in view of *histakel* 'contemplated', an intransitive-reflexive pattern, *7.3.4*) or where the passive stem type is semantically and functionally removed from the active morphological counterpart (e.g. *himac'ut* 'presence, *(das) Sich-Befinden*' in view of *nimca'* '*se trouva, befand sich*' which also constitutes the (strong) passive of *maca'* 'found', but 'the fact of a thing being found' would be expressed by the voice-indifferent action noun *mci'a* in a suitable syntactic construction; see above).

It is very important to distinguish for our purposes between the passive counterparts of "weak" verbs (*6.4.2.2*), in which the active–passive correlation is morphologically expressed by the substitution of *u* for another stem vowel (*sidru* 'arranged (pl.)' : *sudru* 'were arranged'; *hizmanti* 'I invited' : *huzmanti* 'I was invited')[178] and originally functionally different formations which, while essentially serving other purposes, can express, in opposition to active stem types of transitive verbs, a passive content (cf. *7.2* for the *hitRaReR* formation, *6.4.2.2* for the *nVRRaR* formation). The former exist only as part of a transitive verb paradigm (in the sense stated in *7.3.4*), while the latter can exist independently of a morphologically correlated active-transitive formation. We consequently have to admit, for Classical as well as contemporary Hebrew, the existence of a class of "deponent" verbs,[179] such as *histakel* 'looked' (*hitRaReR*-type), or the *nVRRaR*-types *nixnas* 'entered', *nizhar* 'was careful', *nilxam* 'fought' (active formation *laxam* synonymous; cf. *7.2.1*), *nil'a* 'became tired' (quasi-synonymous active formation obsolete).

[178] Only traces can be shown to have survived of a prebiblical strong passive formation (parallel to an Arabic formation) in which the same *u*-alternation obtains.
[179] The Israeli Hebrew deponents do not, however, behave (as the Indo-European deponents do) as directly transitive verbs (i.e., they never govern the *'et*-case ["accusative"; *7.1.4*]).

In cases in which such "deponents" occupy a paradigmatic position facing a pair of morphologically correlated active-passive forms, an extension of the voice category occurs, such as:

nixnas 'entered'   versus *hixnís* 'made enter' : *huxnas* 'was made to enter',
nizhar 'was careful' versus *hizhír* 'warned' : *huzhar* 'was warned'

as a result of which the two extreme terms *(nixnas : huxnas)* are interpreted as constituting a conceptually contrastive pair within the "nonactive" domain of the voice category, say "intransitivity without implication of agent" *(nixnas)* versus "intransitivity with agent implied" *(huxnas)*. Cf. also *neelac* 'was forced (by circumstances)' : *'ulac* 'was forced (by a powerful human agent)' in view of *'ilec* 'forced', and *neetak* 'moved away (intr.), got displaced' : *hootak* 'was moved away, was displaced' in view of *heetík* 'moved away (trans.) displaced' (ROSÉN 1955a: 239).

In what appears to be a development within Israeli Hebrew, the value thus obtained by the "left" term of the tripartite opposition (that is, 'undergoing the effect of a real or virtual action without implication of agent') can by expansion be transferred even to strong passives *(nVRRaR)* that are part and parcel of an active-passive correlational pair. This transfer, however, applies only where the strong passive form is characterized by some modality (which includes the negative modality); thus we have from *manaa* 'avoided':

> *nimnaa* 'is avoided (by some agent)' versus
> *nimnaa be-kalut* 'is easily avoided (by some agent)',
>   'is easily avoided (whether there is an agent or not)'
> *bilti-nimnaa* (cf. *6.4.2.1*) 'not avoided by any agent'

One might say that *nimnaa* is the passive of *N* (some agent) *monea* 'N avoids', while *nimnaa be-kalut* or *bilti-nimnaa* are passives of *mon'im* 'one avoids' (indefinite agent; *7.2.2*). Thus the *bilti-nimnaa*-type can be considered as the outcome of non-implication of agent, characteristic of the status of *nixnas* : *huxnas*, while purely semantically, of course, its best interpretation would be one of admissivity ('unavoidable'; ROSÉN 1955a: 238). Cf. also: *Ha-šaàr nisgar be-kalut* 'the door shuts easily'; *Ha-šaàr lo nisgar* 'the gate does not shut' (i.e. cannot be shut); *ha-masmer lo nixnas* 'the nail does not go in' (i.e. cannot be made to go in); *ha-davar mistader* (*hitRaReR*-type) 'the matter is being settled' : *ha-davar mistader be-kalut* 'the matter is easily settled' (i.e. can be easily settled), etc. The contrast *ha-šaàr nisgar* 'the gate shuts' : *ha-šaàr nisgar be-kalut* 'the gate shuts easily' matches (typologically?) those quasi-reflexive European constructions *(voix pronominale)* that include passivity in their functions, such as *das Tor schließt sich : das Tor schließt (sich) leicht* and *la porte s'ouvre : la porte s'ouvre facilement*. Likewise: *ha-kerèš nišbar* 'the board breaks, *la planche (se) casse*' : *ha-kerèš nišbar be-kalut* 'the board breaks easily, *la planche (se) casse facilement*'. For unmodified admissivity, which is not expressible by the *nVRRaR* stem-type, the innovated (*4.3.5*) *RaRiR* admissive participle is a convenient substitute:

fientive:	*nišbar*	*nišbar*	*lo nišbar*
	'is being broken'	'breaks'	'does not break'
stative (7.2.1):	*šavur* 'broken'	*šavir*	*bilti-šavir*
		'breakable'	'unbreakable'[180]

7.3.2 Tenses

The conceptual relations between the three Israeli Hebrew TENSES (*medaber* 'talk(s)' : *yedaber* 'will (shall) talk' : *diber* 'talked'; cf. 6. 4.2.2) are, in certain statable conditions, relations of time, in others of modalities of reality. Except for the receding (*7.3.3*) imperative, which has morphologically to be included in the "potential"

---

[180] The *RaRiR* participle occurs mainly with conceptually negative modifications (*bilti-kari'* 'illegible', *lo kari'* 'not legible', *be-koši kari'* 'hardly legible'), not with *be-kalut* 'easily' and the like.

("future") tense as its person-unmarked subform, no modal contents are inflectionally expressed: mood proper is a syntactical category in Israeli Hebrew.[181]

The contiguity of temporal and modality purport in the Israeli Hebrew tense system calls for a revision of the terminology employed to name the tenses. Since the one proposed in ROSÉN (1962a) has not been unqualifiedly welcomed, either as creating pedagogical difficulties, as hyperscientific, or else inspired by foreign models (cf. ALSTER-THAU 1964, OTTEWELL 1963), it may be legitimate to accompany a brief statement on the "use of the tenses" by an attempt at justifying the terms suggested.

The tense formed with a participle in predicative status is unmarked for time as well as for modality. It is the very nature of a sentence without a finite verb (8.4.2) that creates this unmarkedness; time-modality marking can be accorded to a sentence by either addition of an otherwise content-void finite verb form (such as *haya* 'was', p. 214: *moše medaber* 'Moses talks', *moše šam* 'Moses is there', *'ani šam* 'I am there' : *moše haya medaber* 'M. would talk' (7.2.1), *moše haya šam* 'M. was there, would be there', *hayití šam* 'I was there, would be there'), or else by replacing the participle by a time-modality and person-sex marked verbal form (*'ata medaber* 'you (m.sg.) talk' : *dibartà* 'you (m.sg.) talked').

The range of reference of the participle as verbal tense is so wide that considering it as the unmarked form is amply justified; this is not, however, a property of the verbless sentence pattern, which has more limited reference (*hic-et-nunc* and unspecified "general" time). The participial tense (ROSÉN 1962a: 31) has time reference including the speaker's present (*'ani 'oxel* 'I am eating', *'ani nosea 'axšav le-tel-'aviv* 'I am going to Tel-Aviv now', *'ani lomed 'anglit me'az šnat šišim ve-xameš* 'I have been studying English since (the year)

---

[181] Cf. p. 231 (*Moše yelex* 'Moses will go' versus *Yelex Moše* 'let Moses go, eat Moyses'). – The suggestion of a "jussive" mood composed of *še-* (subordinative particle Fr. *que*) and a potential tense form (PERETZ 1943: 297; W. CHOMSKY 1957: 198; BAR-ADON 1959: 238; 1966) cannot be accepted: *še-yavo'* 'may he come' is not a morphological entity; like its functional and formational French counterpart *qu'il vienne* it is freely separable into its components: *še-moše yavo'* 'que Moïse vienne'.

[nineteen-] sixty-five'), but also acquires time indication from an adverbial complement referring either to subsequent time (*ba-šana ha-ba'a 'ani gomer 'et-ha-limudim* 'I am finishing my education next year') or to past time (*'etmol 'ani metayel ba-rxov; 'et-mi 'ani pogeš? 'et moše* 'Yesterday I walk up and down the street; who do I meet? Moses'). It is in particular this last class of uses, including one of the nature of a descriptive historical present (restricted to the first person?) which emphasizes the unmarkedness of this tense.

The term AORIST proposed for this tense is *prima facie* appropriate on the strength of ἀόριστος χρόνος meaning 'unmarked tense'; it is (due to some stretch of interpretation of the Greek term) so employed mainly in linguistic descriptions of non-Indo-European languages,[182] of which I would here quote in particular Turkish, where this name is given to what is commonly considered the *zeitloses Präsens* (in contrast to the morphologically different *hic-et-nunc* present), but can also be used in narrative prose as some kind of historical present. In Hebrew, the term *aorist* has been adopted as the designation of the Biblical prefix-tense *(yedaber)* to which the Israeli Hebrew "potential" ("future") is the morphological successor; so, for instance, BAUER – LEANDER (1922: 269–70). The terminological shift between Biblical Hebrew and Israeli Hebrew grammar corresponds, in fact, to a functional one: in the two-tense system of Biblical Hebrew (where the participle had nominal, not verbal features), the "aorist" (that is, in that context, the prefix tense) was indeed the unmarked tense; it had, *inter alia*, referential values of *zeitloses Präsens* as well as gnomic uses, and in certain conditions, narrative purport. It may be a residue of this situation, that in certain (idiomatically determined) expressions, the prefix tense is in Israeli Hebrew employed in the 'herewith' situation (*Koinzidenzfall*; KOSCHMIEDER 1945: 26–34): *'avakeš* 'I request' (idiomatically for 'please' with following object), *'agid lxa* 'I tell you' (idiomatically like 'let me tell you', contrasting the suppletive

---

[182] KNOBLOCH says in his *Sprachwissenschaftliches Wörterbuch*, s.v. *Aorist*: "Bei außerindogermanischen Sprachen wird 'Aorist' [. . .] für eine unbestimmte, vom einfachen Stamm des Verbums aus gebildete Verbalform ohne Zeitbezug [. . .] verwendet" (KNOBLOCH 1961-: 144).

aorist *'ani 'omer lxa* 'I am telling you', which is not 'coïncidential').
The loss by the prefix tense of the narrative purport in postbiblical
Hebrew (*6.4.2.2*), combined with the shift of unmarkedness to the
new participial tense (p. 185) made the prefix tense what it is in
Israeli Hebrew. It would, however, appear that this decisive step
was completed only within the history of revived Hebrew: an
examination of the sample texts in ROSENBERG (1900) indicates with
sufficient clearness that the prefix tense was at that time the expressional means for "general time" values as well as (in conjunction
with adverbial time indicators such as *mide-paàm be-faàm* 'from
time to time') for *hic-et-nunc* ones, while the participial tense was
largely excluded from the latter use, which was, however, inherent
in nominal sentences along with *Zeitlosigkeit*.

The assessment of the intrinsic values of the other verbal tenses
has to be based on their functions with respect to time as well as to
modality. The best illustration of these features can be given by the
paradigm of tenses in conditional clauses:

(1) *'im moše šomea mašèhù, hu mesaper li* 'If Moses hears something, he tells me'
(2) *'im m. šamaa m., (hu) siper li* 'If M. heard s., he told me'
(3) *Lu m. šamaa m., (hu) haya mesaper li* 'If M. had heard s., he
would have told me'
(4) *'im m. yišmaa m., (hu) yesaper li* 'Should M. hear s., he will
tell me'

The 'unfulfilled : potential' opposition (3) : (4) corresponds, in the
protases, to a tense contrast, in which the prefix tense constitutes
the potential term; the unfulfilledness of (3) is apodotically expressed
by the periphrastic tense *haya mesaper* (*7.2.1*), overcharacterized
by *lu* 'if (unfulfilled)' (which can, however, in lower style, be replaced by modally neutral *'im* followed by the periphrastic tense
form). The contrast between (1) and (2) is purely temporal. On
considering

(5) *'im m. yišmaa m. ve-lo yesaper, ta'iti* 'Should M. hear s. and
doesn't tell, I have been mistaken',

it becomes evident that in conditional clauses, there is no temporal contrast between the suffix tense and other tenses. (Cf. ROSÉN 1962a: 71–2.)

The prefix tense has also volitive purport: *yišmaa moše* 'let Moses hear; *que Moïse écoute*' and *tišmaa* (2 pers. m.sg.) 'please, listen; *écoute donc*' (on the relation of this form to the imperative *šmaa*, *7.2.3*, cf. *8.4.2*). This volitional content is never an "unfulfilled" one; cf., for instance, volition sentences introduced by the "optative" particle *halevay še-*:

> *Halevay še-moše šamaa 'et-ze!* 'I wish M. had heard that. I wish M. would hear this (implying: but I do not believe, or am not sure he will).' Cf. ROSÉN 1962a: 79–80)

> *Halevay še-moše yišmaa 'et-ze!* (stylistically lower than the use of the "remotive" tense) 'I wish M. would hear this (implying: I believe, or at least hope, he will).'

The term POTENTIAL for the prefix tense suitably combines, I think, the modal and temporal values of this form. The term REMOTIVE is intended to imply remoteness from the speaker's situation, in time (being a past tense) as well as in reality (excluding interpretation as real or as potentially occurring).[183]

---

[183] The Israeli Hebrew tense system is too poor to permit a sequence of tenses; such would necessitate, at least in part, the existence of special "relative tenses" that would have only "relative" (not "absolute") time reference. A: a result, seemingly "ungrammatical" sentences, such as *hi tavo' 'etmol* 'she will come yesterday' may become "grammatical" by syntactical inclusion ("embedding"): *Xikiti 'etmol kol-ha-yom, ki xašavti še-hi-tavo' 'etmol*, the English equivalent of which contains a "relative" tense subject to the sequence of tenses: 'I waited all day yesterday, because I thought she would come yesterday.'

7.3.3 Appeal (categorial relations of the imperative)

APPEAL is here tentatively proposed as the name of a binary verbal category, one of whose terms is the IMPERATIVE. While the value of the imperative is already adequately circumscribed if not by the meaning of its name, at least by the implications generally attached to it in grammars, the assessment of its categorial status presents some difficulty, since it cannot be ranged under moods (firstly, because it does not extend over the range of tenses and secondly, because mood is syntactically expressed; cf. 7.3.2, 8.4.1) nor under tenses (because the imperative is not a dimension crossing that of person, being only "allocutory"; cf. 7.2.2).[184]

The imperative is characterized by sex and number: *daber* 'speak' (unmarked), *dabru* '*idem*, sex-unmarked pl.', *dabri* '*idem*, f.sg.', with an archaic f.pl. *dabernà*; these forms are identical with the potential ones but for the person prefix with which the potentials are equipped (and which the imperative does not need, since it is void of person content): *tedaber* 'you will speak (sg., unmarked for sex)', *tedabri* '*idem*, fem.', etc.

The imperative is not negatable. While '*al-tedaber* is an appropriate translation of 'don't speak', it does not contain the imperative, but its categorial counterpart, the 2nd person of the potential and, moreover, is part of a complete person-number paradigm, that of the volitive mood (8.4.2) which is negated by prohibitive '*al* (and not by the negative *lo* of other moods):

---

[184] Even JESPERSEN encountered some difficulty in placing his treatment of the imperative: while ascribing to it (JESPERSEN 1911-: 7.623) modal status ("will-mood"), he detaches the discussion of it from that of the moods and incorporates it in the section to which the imperative morphologically belongs, following the treatment of the infinitive with which it is homonymous, if not identical (JESPERSEN 1911- : 4.89), introducing the paragraph on the imperative: "This section is placed here for convenience' sake, though the imperative is no verbid. The form of the Imperative is the same as the Infinitive, i.e. the crude or common form of the verb." We take the same position in attaching the imperative to the treatment of the tenses, since morphologically it is part and parcel of the potential tense.

(ʾal-ʾᵃdaber (arch.)	ʿne loquar')	ʾal-nedaber ʿne loquamur'
ʾal-tedaber (m.)	ʿne loquaris'	
ʾal-tedabri (f.)		ʾal-tedabru ʿne loquamini'
ʾal-yedaber (m.)	ʿne loquatur'	
ʾal-tedaber (f.)		ʾal-yedabru ʿne loquantur'

Basically, the contrast between the imperative and (the 2nd persons of) the potential is one of emotional value ("appeal"), the latter implying more a 'wish', the former a 'request' or even 'command'; however, we are here confronted with an opposition that is neutralized as much as it is maintained (in statable conditions, of course), the potential occurring as the "archi-term representative" in the environment of neutralization. This situation led, in earlier studies of Israeli Hebrew to a very widespread notion that the imperative is replaced (in "spoken Hebrew" or in "children's language") by the "future" tense. Still, wherever both terms prevail (cf. below), the contrast is clear and lucid.

The menace to the categorial existence of the Israeli Hebrew imperative stems, it seems, from two sources, of which, while both are typological, one is syntactical and the other phonological: firstly, negatability of the imperative is a basic trait of the European *Sprachbund*, and the Israeli Hebrew imperative is in contradiction thereto; secondly, the nature of the imperative as "the crude or common form of the verb" (JESPERSEN 1911- 4: 89), that is the shortest possible one, a feature that is deeply anchored in many language types, is not always realizable in Israeli Hebrew, and one might very well say that it is only where such realization is feasible (e.g. *kúm* 'rise' : *takúm* 'you will rise') that the existence of the imperative is still systemically supported.

The categorial status of the imperative as the counterpart of the second person of the potential is reflected by the fact that morphologically it doubtless represents a second person potential deprived of the initial syllable that contains the person morpheme *t-*: *tedaber* : *daber*; *takúm* : *kúm*. This is amply corroborated by (in part substandard) analogical innovations such as *šan* 'sleep' (class. *yšan*, potential *tišan*, class. *t·i·šan* /tiyšan/ [ROSÉN 1952a: 9; 1955a: 112; recalled by BAR-ADON 1962: 761; cf. ROSÉN 1962a: 131]), *pol* 'fall down' (BH *npōl* [nfōl], pot. *tipōl*<BH *t·ip·ōl*), *škav* 'lie down' (BH *škab* [šxav], pot. *tiškav*), *kanes* 'come in' (pot. *tikanes*), etc. In principle, the imperative. the "unmarked" (m.sg.) one in particular, as the "shortest" form of the verb, is supposed to have one syllable less than the otherwise identical

corresponding potential; this is especially impracticable in those cases in which the potential is formed by deletion of *h-*, that is in the *Hif'il* and *Hitpa'el* stem types (*6.4.2.2*): a relation such as *tagiš* 'you will serve (food)' – *hageš* 'serve!' is systemically unsupported, and neutralization is the likely and (in average style) the observable result (*tagiš li bevakaša* 'serve me, please'); furthermore, the monosyllabicity of the "unmarked" imperative of the "strong" type (*6.4.2.2*), as in *kum* 'rise' or *kra* 'read', cannot be preserved where the inadmissibility of an initial consonant cluster makes the reduction of the number of syllables impossible (*ršom* 'take a note in writing' is phonetically disyllabic ([rᵉšom]) and so is its potential counterpart *tiršom*, which consequently "represents" the imperative in neutralization position and functions both in the sense of 'take a note!' and in the one of 'you will take a note').[185]

It is only in these cases of neutralization that the Israeli Hebrew potential has come to "replace" a classical (or stylistically elevated) imperative as the syncretistic expression of any kind of "appeal", including that of a request or a command.

7.3.4 Valence

VERBAL VALENCE, by which we mean the status of a verb as being intransitive or related to an explicit or implicit[186] object, is by virtue of this definition a borderline category between inflexion and syntax. It has, in the range of inflexion, a nominal counterpart, status (*7.1.5*), since transitivity or intransitivity of a verb is related to the status of its action noun versus its complement (*7.1.5, 7.3.1*). The terms of valence (interpretable, according to the syntactical nature of each case, as intransitive, transitive, causative, reciprocal,

---

[185]   This restriction (in average style) of the distribution of the imperative forms in terms of morphophonemic conditions has been established in ROSÉN (1955a: 216–9) on the basis of observation, of a questionnaire, and of a sampling of dialogue portions in current literature; it is matched by the sampling of children's usage in BAR-ADON (1959: 237–8). There is no reason to reconsider it (objections have been raised by other scholars orally, never in writing). (Anecdotical corroboration: switchboard operators, putting you through to a temporarily occupied extension, say *tamtin bevakaša* 'wait, please', then *daber* 'speak', never *hamten* or *tedaber*.)

[186]   By *implicit object* we mean, primarily, a zero object, such as in *hu šote* 'he drinks (implied: alcoholic drinks)', which must not be considered as intransitive (cf. *2.7.4*).

and the like) are morphologically materialized by the verbal stem types (*6.4.2.2*) and are thereby contiguous with voice (*7.3.1*) and aspect (*7.2.1*) that are also in part materialized by these same morphological entities.

In the realm of these semantic and, in a certain respect, transformational relations, it will be of importance to ascertain which one of the terms participating in an opposition constitutes the motivating one; it will depend thereon, whether a relation is considered as derivation of an agentless passive (*7.3.1*) from a transitive verb or, inversely, as transitivization (causativization) of an intransitive one. While, for instance, the *Pi'el* : *Hitpa'el* relation has to be interpreted as being motivated by the *Pi'el (nika)* in *nika* 'cleaned' : *hitnaka* 'cleaned himself', the inverse will be true for *histader* 'got settled' : *sider* 'settled', while in some cases some doubt as to the correct direction of motivation may persist (*hitkarev* 'approached', *kerev* 'brought close to').

Implication of an object, that is REFLEXIVITY, is the exclusive and inherited function of the *Hitpa'el* stem form in opposition to any other transitive stem form of the same root: *hitraxec* 'washed (himself)' : *raxac* 'washed (trans.)'. It is the common Semitic function of *t*-characterized stems, and all other syntactico-semantic uses of the *Hitpa'el* must be considered as derivable from it.

In one class of verbs, this derivation has been brought about in a syntactic calquing process from Slavo-Yiddish, where the morpheme of reflexivity (Russ. -ся, Yidd. *zix*) has, with plural verbs, the secondary function of RECIPROCITY (GARBELL 1931: 51). This resulted, in Israeli Hebrew, in the interpretation of inherited *Hitpa'el* forms of "reciprocal" reference (*t·itrā'u* 'you shall see each other', and cf. *4.4.3* on *way·itrōṣṣu*) as expansions of reflexivity; reciprocal *Hitpa'els* (which must imply, by nominal plurality or by adjunction of a complement with *'im* 'with' the double-track action expressed by them; ROSÉN 1962a: 273) are a rather productive class in Israeli Hebrew: *hem hitxabku* 'they embraced', *ha-zug hitxabek* 'the couple embraced', *hu hitxabek ita* 'he embraced her' (literally 'with her'; cf. *er umarmte sich mit ihr*). Likewise *hitnašku* 'kissed (pl.) each other', *hitxatnu* 'married (pl., intrans.)', *hitvakxu* 'argued', *hitkatvu* 'exchanged letters', *hityaacu* 'conferred (pl.)', *hitxavru* 'be-bame friends' (*6.1.2*), etc. (cf. also COHEN – ZAFRANI 1968: 92).

The intransitive aspect of reflexivity places the *Hitpaʿel* in the position of an intransitive form opposite the almost exclusively transitive *Piʿel* (*hitgala* : *gila* 'revealed himself' : 'revealed' > 'became overt' : 'made overt'), and hence, by interpretation of the intransitive as agentless passive, in the position of a passive of the *Piʿel* (cf. p. 000): *hitgala* : *gila* > 'was discovered' : 'discovered' (ROSÉN 1962a: 273). This passive will, however, almost generally remain incapable of being accompanied by the expression of the agent, a circumstance which fostered the increased use of a collateral stem form (only in the remotive tense) of otherwise identical purport, but capable of agent-complementation, the *Nitpaʿel*, inherited from postbiblical Hebrew and, by its initial *ni-*, reminiscent of the intrinsically passive *Nifʿal* stem: *'amérika nitgalta 'al-yde-kolúmbus* 'America was discovered by Columbus', *Ha-mišlaxàt hitkabla be-misrad ha-sar* 'The delegation was received at the minister's office' versus *Ha-mišlaxàt nitkabla 'al-yde-ha-sar* 'The delegation was received by the minister' (ROSÉN 1962a: 274).

Reinterpretation, by inversion of the transformational direction, of the intransitive-passive : transitive relation as TRANSITIVATION or CAUSATIVITY is a forgone conclusion: *histayem* 'terminated (intrans.)' : *siyem* 'terminated (trans.)' > 'came to an end' : 'caused to come to an end'; *hitbarex* 'underwent a blessing' : *berex* 'blessed, caused to undergo a blessing'; *hitbašel* 'cooked (intrans.), *bouillit*' : *bišel* 'cooked (trans.), *fit bouillir*'; *hištana* 'changed (intr.)' : *šina* 'caused to change'; etc. (cf. ROSÉN 1955a: 239; 1962a: 273; 1966a: 289).

Reinterpretation of the *Piʿel* : *Hitpaʿel* relation as transitivation or causativity with the latter stem type as motivating term was facilitated by the previous existence of a transitivation relation (*Qal* : *Hifʿil*) within the framework of the stem types, so that the *Piʿel* : *Hitpaʿel* relation could be integrated into a ready-made correlational frame. This integration was further facilitated by the fact that the *Piʿel* : *Hitpaʿel* relation could fill a *case vide* in the stem system, since the *Hifʿil* served as causative formation in opposition to the *Qal* only, so that *Qal* : *Hif ʿil* and *Hitpaʿel* : *Piʿel* became equipollent pairs.

The transformational relation between the *Qal* and the *Hif ʿil* is an inheritance from Biblical Hebrew. It operates on a simple rule of assigning the grammatical subject of the motivating sentence the status of a direct (*ʾet-*, *7.1.4*) object in the motivated one (ROSÉN 1962a: 280): *Yosef caxak* 'Joseph laughed' → *Yaakov hicxík ʾet-yosef* 'Jacob made Joseph laugh'. Full application of this rule would create the twofold occurrence of a direct object in a transform in which the "kernel" is a transitive construction: *Yosef ʾaxal ʾet-ha-tapuax* 'Joseph ate the apple' → *Yaakov heexíl ʾet-yosef ʾet-ha-tapuax*. However, while Bibilical Hebrew does not restrict the use of these constructions[187] (*way·alb·ēš ʾōto· ʾet-ham·ʿi·l* 'and he made him wear the coat' *Gen* 8.6; cf. ROSÉN 1966a: 290), Israeli Hebrew avoids them (except for the one verb *heexíl* just quoted) by depriving the "transformed" agent of its direct-object status and assigning to it the status of an indirect object in the *le*-case (§ *7.1.4*): *Yosef zaxar ʾet-ha-ʾinyan* 'Joseph remembered the matter' → *Yaakov hizkír le-yosef ʾet-ha-inyan* 'Jacob reminded Joseph of the matter' (ROSÉN 1962a: 282–3). Double transitivity of the causative *Hif ʿil* is fully achieved: the constructions with these verbs are integrated in the generally valid pattern of doubly transitive verbs, in which the object *rei* is in the "accusative" (*ʾet-*), the object *personae* in the "dative" (*le-*), e.g. *Yaakov natan le-yosef ʾet-ha-sefèr* 'Jacob gave Joseph the book'. Each of these two newly established objects has independent status: *Yaakov hizkír le-yosef* 'Jacob reminded Joseph' is as grammatical as *Yaakov hizkír ʾet-ha-ʾinyan* 'Jacob mentioned the matter'. As a consequence, in a passive transformation of sentences of this type, the grammatical subject is the one which occupies the "direct" object position in the active form: *Ha-ʾinyan huzkar le-yosef* 'The matter was mentioned to Joseph[188], while in Biblical Hebrew syntax, any one of the apparent two objects could take the grammatical subject position in the passive sentence.

---

[187] These sentences do not contain a double complement (RUBINSTEIN 1970a: 148–9), but have the constituents 'Jacob caused' + 'Joseph eats the apple'; *Yaakov heexíl ʾet-yosef* is possible, but not a sentence which omits *ʾet-yosef* while maintaining *ʾet-ha-tapuax* as the single object; cf. RUBINSTEIN (1970a: 149).

[188] However, there is some reluctance to employ this type of transformation, so that quite a few causative verbs derived from transitive ones are devoid of passive forms, such as *her'a* 'made see, showed' and *hodia* 'made know, informed'.

7.3.5 Extrasystemic (surviving) distinctions, lexicalizations

Discussion of voice, aspect, and valence by no means accounts exhaustively for the functions of Israeli Hebrew verbal stem relations. There are inherited pairs, showing relations that are no longer productive (such as transitivation by the *Pi'el* versus the *Qal* (*lamad* 'learned' : *limed* 'taught'), or intensification (*kafac* 'jumped' : *kipec* 'jumped up and down')). There are lexicalized pure derivational values, such as the use of the *Hif'il* as denominative factitive formation with motivating adjectives[189] (*gadol* 'large' → *higdil* 'enlarged'); likewise, the use of the *Pi'el* as the general denominative formation from nouns (*6.1.2*), which includes, in inherited items, the value of 'dealing with the object designated by the base noun' in a "negative" or "privative" sense inherent in the specific object designated (*klipa* 'peel [noun]' : *kilef* 'peel [verb]'), while in other cases, the opposite function of 'supplying with the object designated by the base noun' is productive (*mxona* 'machine' : *miken* 'automate [verb]'). Lexicalization of specialized values is also the only way to describe the ever-increasing use of the *Šif'el* pattern, which, although etymologically nothing other than the Akkadian causative (analogous to *Hif'il* by virtue of a rare *h-* : *š-* correspondence) penetrated via Talmudic Aramaic, serves as a secondary causative (factitive) of specialized, and very often, technical sense: *xazar* 'came back' : *hixzìr* 'brought back' : *šixzer* 'reconstituted, reconstructed'; *'avad* : 'worked', *'evèd* 'serf' : *heevìd* 'made work' : *šiabed* 'made a serf of, subjugated'; *kaful* 'double, multiple' : *hixpìl* 'doubled' : *šixpel* 'multicopied' (COHEN – ZAFRANI 1968: 93; cf. *4.4.1* for the terminological specialization of lexical doublets of Aramaic origin).

---

[189]   Israeli Hebrew adjectives are originally participles of qualitative verbs (*5.7.1*); *Hif'il* forms such as *higdil* are, from the point of view of Biblical Hebrew, just as deverbative as BH *ho·di·aʾ* or IH *hicxík*; they have *'et-* government, since the base verb (in terms of Biblical Hebrew) is intransitive. *Hif'il* verbs derived from adjectives are, in Israeli Hebrew, ordinarily transitive or intransitive (*šaxor* 'black' : *hišxìr* 'became black' or 'made black'), while their Biblical Hebrew counterparts are basically and commonly intransitive with collateral transitive usages developing in some cases (e.g. *higd·i·l*).

For all these reasons, it is the verbal stem and not the verbal root that constitutes the syntactically and semantically operative lexical entity in Israeli Hebrew. As has been demanded (ROSÉN 1955a: 104) and carried out for a part of the Hebrew vocabulary in the glossary of ROSÉN 1962b, an Israeli Hebrew dictionary should list the verbal as well as the nominal entries according to the stems and not by the root, which is, however traditional in Arabic, and later in Semitic, lexicography, no longer a useful practice.

8 SYNTACTICAL CATEGORIES

8.1 THE SENTENCE

8.1.1 Forms of sentences

While Israeli Hebrew syntax is presented in ROSÉN (1966a: 197–264) as constituting a variety of about twenty SENTENCE PATTERNS, RUBINSTEIN (1968: 54) assigns to "the entirety of the sentences in the [Hebrew] language" the form "NP + PP" (i.e. noun phrase plus predicate phrase). Both these attitudes, the one implying that the various sentence patterns are not reducible to fewer structures, let alone one structure, and the other one, implying that the generativist rewriting of 'sentence' as 'noun phrase plus verb phrase' is inapplicable to Hebrew, coincide to show that Israeli Hebrew represents a type of language in which not all sentences can be "derived" from one basic structure formula. 'PP' is not an entity describable or cataloguable in terms independent from sentence structure; for the purposes of Hebrew, the use of PP rather than of VP (verb phrase)[190] only implies that every sentence has a "predicate", however this may be conceived, in addition to another constituent which is a noun, a noun phrase, or a noun phrase substitute.

While unable to see what sensible meaning can be ascribed to a notion of 'predicate phrase' other then constituting a sentence part that is addi-

---

[190] The use of "NP + PP" in generativist writing does not imply an abandoning of the earlier "NP + VP" notion, since PP is only an abbreviated notation of "Auxiliary + VP", so that after "extracting" the "auxiliary" (time?) element from the sentence constituents, what is meant by "NP + PP" is still "NP + VP". There is, furthermore, no implication that NP is necessarily not the "logical" predicate.

tional to a noun phrase, RUBINSTEIN would obviously be right if he restricted his statement to saying that any sentence consisting of more than
one element (that is, not such as *Slixa!* 'Pardon!', *Ken* 'Yes', *Lo* 'No', and
Bevakaša 'Please') contains at least one constituent variable that is a
noun phrase, while the variety of other constituents depicts the variety
of grammatical sentence patterns, which the syntactician has to describe.

*8.1.2 Constitution of a sentence: concord sentences, and concordless
sentences*

What makes an Israeli Hebrew sentence containing a noun phrase
a sentence is either (1) that the constituent additional to the noun
phrase belongs to a certain word class, e.g. to that of adverbs
(*kan* 'here'+*šulxan* 'table' yield *Kan šulxan* 'Here is a table'), or
(2) that the constituent additional to the noun phrase agrees with
the latter in gender, number, and, where applicable, person (*ha-
šulxan* (m.sg.) 'the table'+*yafe* 'beautiful (m.sg.)' yield *Ha-šulxan
yafe* 'The table is beautiful'). We may rightly assume the (sometimes
only one existing) noun phrase to be the motivating term of the
concord relation, the other term (whether nominal or verbal)
to be concord-motivated (ROSÉN 1965: 78–80). Considering sentences of the type 'noun phrase+adverb' (*Kan šulxan* 'Here is a table')
as nominal sentences (RUBINSTEIN 1968: 150–60), however devoid
of concord, is a time-honoured procedure, but not very rewarding:
an assumption of the existence of concordless nominal sentences
would lead one to expect to find concordless verbal sentences, which
do not exist, and, on the other hand, one might hesitate to ascribe
to adverbs more verbal or more nominal nature – they have neither.
Lastly, we might encounter unsurmountable difficulties in an attempt
at classing the sentence type *Yosef haya lo kesèf* 'Joseph had money' (*5.5.1–3*) as either verbal or nominal: while the sentence
undeniably contains a verb, the principal concord relation (and
facultatively the only one) applies not to the verb, but to other constituents of the sentence (*Yosef – lo;* m.sg.); it is precisely for these
reasons concerning the particular structure of the *casus pendens*
sentences (*5.5.2*) that we have introduced the notion of 'verboids',

but it would hardly make sense to introduce one of verboid sentences as well.

It is, therefore, more advisable to use as the criterion for the first
classificatory dichotomy of Israeli Hebrew sentences not verbless-
ness, but CONCORD; reserving the term *nominal sentences* for verbless
sentences with concord (ROSÉN 1966a: 227–54), we first divide all
sentence patterns into CONCORDLESS ones, and the rest, which will
be classified, on a second level, as either verbal or verbless (nominal).

Concordless sentences do not necessarily contain a noun phrase.

There is a hierarchical aspect in this kind of division, since morphological constraints come to apply only on the second level of
classification. Sentences of the first class (the concordless ones) are
"simpler" than the rest; this has not unimportant implications
concerning language teaching: a presentation of all sentence patterns in an order in which the concordless ones come first, and those
with the largest number of concord features and other constraints
last, is at the same time pedagogically "graded" (ROSÉN 1966a:
206–7); obviously, verbal sentences will occupy a relatively late
position in a well-devised teaching program of Israeli Hebrew.[191]

8.1.3 Variables and invariables

In a description of patterns, it must be stated which of the elements
of each pattern are VARIABLE and which are INVARIABLES. The latter
neither motivate concord, nor are they motivated by it, nor, as a
rule, are they subject to zeroification. If we state that in a sentence
such as *Yeš le-yaakov makom* 'Jacob has a place' (*8.1.4* [II]), *makom*
and *yaakov* are variables (*Yeš le-yosef makom* 'Joseph has a place';
Yeš le-yaakov kesèf 'Jacob has money'), we imply at the same time
that *yeš le-* is not a "word" in Israeli Hebrew, that is, not a means
of "naming", at least not in the same sense as *yosef, yaakov, makom,*

---

[191]   The progression of sentence patterns in ROSÉN (1962a) is from concordless
sentences (p. 12) to imperative constructions (p. 17) and other concordless
verbal sentence types (p. 27); verbal sentences are introduced last (p. 31).
OTTEWELL (1963: 256–7) finds this progression parallels the order of stages in
"the generative grammar of a child's language" (literature quoted there).

or *kesèf*.[192] Certain elements may occur as variables (that is, as a representative of a substitution class) in one pattern, while constituting an invariable part of another; e.g., the pronominal element *h-* of *hu* (m.sg.), *hi* (f.sg.), *hem* (m.pl.), and *hen* (f.pl.) is an invariable (the copula) of the pattern in *Yayìn hu yakar* 'Wine is expensive', while it is a representative of the class of determinated nouns in *Hu šote* 'He drinks'. Such apparent inconsistencies are, it would appear, the result of the syntactic history of Hebrew.[193]

8.1.4 The sentence patterns

In the following formulaic presentation of Israeli Hebrew sentence patterns, the invariables are explicitly stated as linguistic forms, while the variables are represented by self-explanatory abbreviated symbols indicating the word classes (parts of speech) established in chapter 5. It is implied that in each word class its legitimate substitutes and expansions are subsumed, so that e.g. IMP will stand not only for 'impersonal' as such, but also for 'impersonal phrase', N – not only for a noun, but also for a noun phrase, a substitute of a noun, and a substitute of a noun phrase; cf. *2.7.3* and, in detail, ROSÉN (1966a: 264–5, 276–9). This list closely

---

[192] This is, of course, not transferable to other languages. Engl. *has*, for instance, in *Jacob has money* is a variable: *Jacob gets money*.

[193] *Hu·'* did not function, in all likelihood, as a copula in Biblical Hebrew nonverbal sentences. In asyndetic sentences containing *hu·'* in addition to two nominals in the "nominative", the nominal immediately preceding *hu·'* is the logical predicate of the sentence, while the other nominal should be considered the extrapositional logical subject: *šeba· p·àröt haṭ·ōbōt* ('the seven good cows') *šeba· šàni·m* ('seven years') *hēn·à* (3 pers.f.pl. pronoun) = 'the seven good cows are seven years' (*Gen* 41.26) (*šàni·m* 'years' is the logical predicate); *hãlo·m 'ehàd hu·'* 'it is one single dream' (ibid.) (*'ehàd* 'one' is the logical predicate, the "*interpretans*"); also where *hu·'* is placed between the two nominals: *lo' yàšu·b 'el|'ereṣ miṣrayim* ('he shall not return into the land of Egypt'), *w'aš·u·r hu·' malk·o* ('but the Assyrian (*'aš·u·r*) shall be his king') (*Hos* 11.5). Cf. ROSÉN (1966a: 244–5; 1970: 115–9; the Israeli Hebrew usage of the pattern N+*hu*+ +N as "copula clause" with nondesignation of any one of the nominal constituents as logical predicate coincides with the traditional interpretation (or syntactical understanding) of Biblical verses of that structure, while linguistic analysis deviates (cf. *4.1.2*).

14

follows, in formulation as well as in the graded enumeration of the patterns, ROSÉN (1966a: 209–64), where full statements are made on the syntagmatic features, order of constituents, history, and stylistic properties of each one of the patterns.

(I) ADV+N   'ADV+is/are+N'

Concordless[194]   (ROSÉN 1966a: 209; RUBINSTEIN 1968: 150–60)

Kan šulxan   'Here is a table'
Ha-ʾinyan kax   'The matter is thus'

(II) $ADV(LOC/TEMP) + \begin{vmatrix} yeš \\ ,eyn \end{vmatrix} + N$ 'There is/are $\begin{vmatrix} — \\ no \end{vmatrix} + N + ADV$'

Concordless   (ROSÉN 1966a: 210–1; RUBINSTEIN 1968: 199–203)

ʾaxšav ʾeyn kan mayim   'There is no water here now'

(III) $ADV + \begin{vmatrix} yeš \\ ,eyn \end{vmatrix} + le\text{-}N_1 + N_2$ '$N_1 + $ has/have $+ \begin{vmatrix} — \\ no \end{vmatrix} + N_2 + ADV$'

Concordless   (ROSÉN 1966a: 212–6; RUBINSTEIN 1968: 204–7)

Maxar yeš le-dodi hizdamnut   'My uncle has a chance tomorrow'

(IV) $ADV + ze + \begin{vmatrix} N \\ ADJ(m.sg.) \end{vmatrix}$ 'That's $+ \begin{vmatrix} N \\ ADJ \\ ADV \text{ in relative clause} \end{vmatrix}$'

---

[194] Concordlessness is correlated with the nonrepetition of categorial dimensions in the constituents of the sentence (cf. XII); e.g. an adverb and a noun have no categories in common. With the exception of pattern (which we have, consequently, termed *appositional*), duplication of a category entails its concord.

Concordless; colloquial   (Rosén 1966a: 216–7; Rubinstein 1968: 74–8)

Ze tov   'That's good'
Ze yladim   'That's children'
Káxa ze yladim   'That's how children are', 'That's how it is with children'

(V) ADV+IMPERS (*le*-N)[195] 'N+AUXILIARY+INF+ADV' +INF[196]

Concordless. Grammatical depend- (Rosén 1966a: 218–22;
ence between N and the INF- Rubinstein 1968: 167–70)
group as well as within the latter

'axšav mutav lexa lalexèt   'Now you had better go'
Kan 'alenù[197] *lehafsik*   'Here we must stop'
Laxen keday laxem lehitya'ec[198]   'This is why you should rather consult with each other'

Laxen keday lexa lehitya'ec   'This is why you should rather
   'im[198] *xaverxa*   consult with your friend'

(VI) *Na*+INF   'Will you please INF'

Concordless. Grammatical depend- (Rosén 1966a: 223)
encies due to verbal government ap-
ply within the INF-group. Formal
style

Na lehaavir.   'Please transfer'

[195] On N = Ø 'one', see 7.2.2.
[196] The INF-group (potentially) contains an ADV, which is separate from the sentence-constituent ADV; see Rosén (1966a: 205, 218, 222, 225 etc.). Rubinstein (1970b) keeps the two ADV's apart by terming one "sentence modifier", the other "predicate modifier".
[197] The class IMPERS + *le*- includes (as a portmanteau morpheme) the preposition *'al*-.
[198] *Lehitya'ec* belongs to the class of *pluralia tantum hitRaReR* verbs (7.3.4) which accounts for the plural "agent" following *le*-.

14*

(VII) IMPERATIVE ($+na$)   IMPERATIVE+please

Concordless, but selection of IMPERATIVE form in view of person addressed. Not negatable (*7.3.3*).   (ROSÉN 1966a: 224–5)

  Šev na   'Sit down, please'

VIII) ADV$+$N$+carix+$INF[199]   'ADV$+$N$+$ has to INF'

Concord between N and *carix*. INF-group subject to verbal government.   (ROSÉN 1966a: 225–6)

  'axšav 'anaxnù crixim lif'ol miyad   'Now we have to act immediately'

(IX) ADV$+$N$+$FIN.VB   'ADV$+$N$+$FIN.VB'
(Verbal Sentence)

Concord N–FIN.VB. Order of precedence pertinent for expression of "mood" (*8.4.1*). VB-group subject to valence and case government.   (ROSÉN 1966a: 227–30, 255–7); (RUBINSTEIN 1970a, 1970b)

  'az 'axlu ha-yladim po.   'At that time, the children were eating here'

(X) $N_1 + ADV + \left|\begin{matrix} ADJ \\ N_2 \end{matrix}\right|$ '$N_1 +$ is/are $+ \left|\begin{matrix} ADJ \\ (a)\ N_2 \end{matrix}\right| + ADV$'

(Nominal Sentence)   (Classificatory)

Concord N_1-ADJ, and if N_2 movable, also N_1-N_2. Strict and complicated constraints apply to the N_1-N_2 sentences according to the relative position occupied by N_1 and N_2, respectively, N_2 on a scale of "specific refer-   (ROSÉN 1966a: 230–40; RUBINSTEIN 1968: 60–1, 142–6). Constraints insufficiently stated by RUBINSTEIN (1969: 60–1), because applied to copula sentences (pattern below) on the assumption that nominal sentences (pattern X)

[199]   See note *196*.

ence" including (in that order) *mi* 'who', demonstratives, personal pronouns, anthroponymics, determinated appellatives, *ma* 'what', demonstrative adjectives (p. 156), undeterminated appellatives modified by an anaphoric (*7.1.2*), and finally, unmodified undeterminated appellative nouns. Cf. p. 222.

can be "derived" from copula sentences by deletion of the copula. Cf. also COHEN–ZAFRANI (1968: 257–8).

Yayin kan zol
Yosef nahag
'axšav kulanù talmidim
Mi 'ata?
'axšav ha-baaya kesèf

'Wine is cheap here'
'Joseph is a driver'
'Now we are all students'
'Who are you?'
'Now the problem is money'

$$(XI) \ N_1 + 3 \text{ pers.pron.}(h\text{-}) + \begin{vmatrix} N_2 \\ ADJ \end{vmatrix} + ADV$$

$$\text{'}N_1 + \text{is/are} + \begin{vmatrix} \text{(the)}N_2 \\ ADJ \end{vmatrix} + ADV\text{'}$$

(Copula Sentence)

(Identificatory)[200]

Gender-quantity concord N_1–3 pers.pron. Person-sex-number concord pers. pron. – N_2.

Status of N_1 or, respectively, N_2 as subject or predicate, respectively, very frequently recognizable from position of the nouns on "specific reference" scale (see under pattern X; details ROSÉN (1966a: 241–5)[201]; RUBINSTEIN (1968: 60–146); ROSÉN (1962a: 52).

Yosef hu ha-menahel
'ani hu hamelèx
Mi hi kan ha-mora?
Ze-hu ze

'Joseph is the director'
'I (and nobody else) am the king'
'Who is the (lady-)teacher here?'
'This is it'

---

[200] The opposition 'classificatory' : 'identificatory' (pattern (X) : pattern (XI)) is neutralized in conditions in which the "nominal sentence" is not admissible due to the restrictions applying to it (see above and p. 222)
[201] Cf. note *193*.

(XII) $N_1 + ze + \begin{vmatrix} \text{ADJ (m.sg.)} \\ N_2 \end{vmatrix} + \text{ADV}$ $\quad$ 'N$_1$+that's+$\begin{vmatrix} \text{ADJ} \\ \text{a/the N}_2 \end{vmatrix}$
$\qquad\qquad\qquad\qquad\qquad\qquad\qquad$ + ADV'

(Appositional Copula $\qquad$ (Commenting)[202]
Sentence)

Derivable from pattern (IV) by $\qquad$ (ROSÉN 1966a: 245-55)
assigning to N_1 the status of an extrapositional subject (N_1 frequently
refers to a 'situation' also expressible
by a nominalized sentence taken up
by *ze*)
Concordless. Colloquial unless as a
sentence-part question.

Glida ze tov hayom $\qquad$ 'Ice cream (i.e. eating ice cream)
$\qquad\qquad\qquad\qquad\qquad\qquad$ that's good today'

Ma ze bišvili – ciyonut? $\qquad$ 'Zionism – what is that to me?'
$\qquad\qquad\qquad\qquad\qquad\qquad$ (JESPERSEN 1937: 45)

Káma ze xamiša dólar? $\qquad$ 'How much is (that,) five dollars?'

(XIII)$N_1 + h\text{-}y\text{-} + \begin{vmatrix} N_2 \\ \text{ADJ} \end{vmatrix} + \text{ADV}$ $\quad$ 'N$_1$+*be* (other than $+ \begin{vmatrix} N_2 \\ \text{ADJ} \end{vmatrix}$
$\qquad\qquad\qquad\qquad\qquad\qquad\qquad$ present
$\qquad\qquad\qquad\qquad\qquad\qquad\qquad$ indicative) $\qquad$ +ADV'

(Verbal copula sentence)

Derivable from pattern XI $\qquad$ (ROSÉN 1966a: 259–61; RUBINSTEIN
(Copula sentence) by substituting $\qquad$ 1968: 118–9)
a form of the verb 'to be' (radical
h-y-) for the nonverbal copula.

Person-sex-gender-number concord
$N_1 - h\text{-}y\text{-}$ in addition to concord
applying to copula sentence. Per-
son sex-concord *h-y- –* N_2.

Yosef haya ha-menahel $\qquad$ 'Joseph was the director'
'ani hayiti hamelèx $\qquad$ 'I was the king'
Mi hayta kan ha-mora? $\qquad$ 'Who was the (lady-)teacher
$\qquad\qquad\qquad\qquad\qquad\qquad$ here?'

---

[202] The opposition 'comment' : 'identification' + 'classification' is neutraliz-
able in cases in which patterns X and / or XI are not admissible (cf. note *200*);
ROSÉN (1966a: 245–55).

Ze haya ze   'That was it'
Ha-mefaked hayiti 'ani   'The commander was me', 'It was I who was the commander'

(XIV) ADV+*(lo)* h-y-+*(le-)*N$_1$+N$_2$

(Verbal existential sentence)

Derivable from patterns II–III, XVII by substitution of *h-y-* 'to be' for *yeš*, or of *lo h-y-* 'not to be' for *'eyn.*

Concord *h-y-* – N$_1$ in addition to concord prevailing in underlying pattern. (But cf. *5.5.3.*)

'az lo hayu kan mayim   'There was no water here then'
Maxar tihye le-dodi hizdamnut 'My uncle will have a chance tomorrow'

	Pattern I
	Pattern IV
(XV) *h-y-*+	Pattern V
	Pattern VIII
	Pattern X
	Pattern XII

(Auxiliated sentence)

Derivable as shown. Analogous derivation from verbal sentence (IX) in aorist tense (with same auxiliary *h-y-*) yields sentence in compound remotive tense (*7.2.1*). Derivation from nominal sentence (X) coincides with verbal copula sentence (XIII)[203]

(ROSÉN 1966a: 257–9; RUBINSTEIN 1968: 116–20)

[203] Cf. RUBINSTEIN (1969: 83).

Concord h-y- – N_1 additional
to concord (if any) in underlying
pattern.

Kan haya šulxan (I)	'There was a table here'
Ze hayu yladim (IV)	'That was children'
Kan haya 'alenù lehafsik (V)	'Here we had to stop'
'axšav ('anaxnù) hayinù crixim lif'ol miyad (VIII)	'Now we had to act immediately'
Mi hayità 'ata? (X)	'Who were you?'
Káma ze haya – xamiša dólar? (XII)	'How much was (that), five dollars?'
'az hayu ha-yladim 'oxlim po (IX)	'At that time, the cildren used to eat here'

(XVI) $Láma + le\text{-}N_1 + ADV + N_2$ 'What use + do(es) N_1 have for $N_2 + ADV$'

Concordless. Stylistically marked
as colloquial. Rhetorical question.

Láma li 'axšav kesèf?   'What do I need money for now?'

(XVII) $\begin{vmatrix} yeš \\ 'eyn \end{vmatrix} + le\text{-}N + INF.INT + ADV$

'N + has'
$\begin{vmatrix} & & \text{thing} & \\ & \text{some} & \text{body} & \\ & & \text{time} & + \text{to INF} \\ & & \text{place} & + \text{ADV} \\ & \text{no} & \text{purpose} & \\ & & \ldots & \end{vmatrix}$

INF.INT = an INF-group, one of   (Rosén 1966a: 262–3)
whose elements is an interrogative
of goal, time, place, purpose, etc.,
not placed at the beginning of the
sentence

Concordless. Verbal government
applies in the INF-group.

Pronouncedly colloquial[204]

[204] Garbell (1930: 71) considers the negative construction ('*eyn*...) as primary according to Slavic models, and the affirmative one derived from it by contrast.

Yeš le-yosef ma laasot 'axšav   'Joseph has something to do now'
'eyn le-yosef 'éfo laševèt   'Joseph has no place to sit'
Lo haya li 'et-mi lišloax (XIV)   'I had nobody to send'[205]

(XVIII) $\left|\begin{matrix} yeš \\ 'eyn \end{matrix}\right| + be\text{-N} + kede\text{-INF}$ 'N is $\left|\begin{matrix} - \\ not \end{matrix}\right|$ enough to INF'

No concord. Verbal government   (ROSÉN 1966a: 264)
in INF-group.

Elevated style.

   'eyn ba-ze kede-lesapek 'oti   'This is not enough to satisfy me'

8.1.5 Mutual inderivability of sentence patterns; pattern meanings

It is essential to underline that these patterns cannot be derived from each other, beyond what has been stated, by substitutions, deletions, rewritings, or otherwise, so as to substantially reduce their number. On the surface, one would be tempted, for instance, to consider

(1) *Kan šulxan* 'Here is a table' (I)

as a result of the deletion (zeroing) of *yeš* in

(2) *Kan yeš šulxan* 'There is a table here' (II),

but then, is this any more meaningful than a mere technicality? The constraints that apply to the formation of a sentence of pattern II do not apply, in part, to one of pattern I; e.g., while a determinated noun cannot precede *yeš* in pattern II, it can precede

---

[205] Sentences of this pattern are not derivable from Pattern III by substitution of N by an INF-group. Such derivation would yield, e.g., *Ma yeš le-yosef laasot 'axšav?* (with obligatory extraction of the interrogative from the INF-group and with interrogative sense) 'What has Joseph to do now?' It is the pattern that assigns the non-interrogative meaning to the otherwise interrogative element.

ADV in pattern (I), so that *Ha-šulxan kan* 'The table is here' is not derivable from a sentence containing *yeš* between its two constituents. Furthermore, while ADV in pattern II can be zero, e.g.

(3) *Yeš šulxan* 'There is a table',

it cannot be deleted, of course, in pattern I. Consequently, considering pattern I as a subtype of pattern II, would mean nothing else than replacing the set of dependencies ("rules") that applies to (II) by a new set,that is replacing one pattern by another. Semantic considerations are also to be taken into account: Sentence (1) is only a statement of location, not of existence, while sentence (2) can be both. These are only some of the considerations which apply to patterns I and II.

Considering pattern III, one might ask, why

(4) *La-dira yeš šloša x^{a}darim* 'The apartment has three rooms' (III),

since we also have

(5) *Ba-dira yeš l-a šloša x^{a}darim* 'She has three rooms in the apartment'

should not be of analogous pattern structure with

(6) *Ba-dira yeš šloša x^{a}darim* 'There are three rooms in the apartment' (II),

considering that *le-* and *be-* are (as prepositions) of otherwise equal categorial status, and that a noun prefixed by a preposition can be considered a legitimate substitute of ADV:

(7) *Kan yeš šloša x^{a}darim* 'There are three rooms here'.

But it is not only the semantic remoteness of the two pattern meanings (II) and (III) that prevents us from considering (III) as a particular case of a more general type (II), and not only the fact that we have assigned a special status (as verboid, section *5.5*) to the element *yeš le-* that is constitutive of pattern III. It is above all the fact that the set of descriptive statements that applies to substitutions by overt or covert (zero) elements in pattern III is different from that which covers pattern II. Consider the following sentences which overtly differ by a replacement of the preposition *le-* by the preposition *'al-*:

(8) *Li yeš smixa* 'I have a blanket' (III)
(9) *'alay yeš smixa* 'There is a blanket over me' (II).

Primarily, exchanging *le-* for *'al-* is no legitimate substitution, since the two are not members of the same category, but mutually compatible:

(10) *Li yeš 'alay smixa* 'I have a blanket over me'

Secondly, consider the effects of deleting *yeš* in (8) and (9):

(11) *'alay smixa* (same meaning as (9))
(12) *Li smixa* 'For me a blanket (please)!',

since, as we shall state in more detail below (*8.4.3*), deletion of *yeš* from a sentence of pattern III, whose N is not expanded, has a modal (mostly volitive) effect, at least in ordinary style, an effect that is totally absent from deletion of *yeš* in pattern II. Consider further the application to (8) and (9) of an otherwise legitimate and common substitution rule, namely the replacement of N by INF; with (8) this is freely possible as long as the constitutive invariables *yeš* or *'eyn* are maintained:

(13) *Li yeš laasot ši'urim* 'I (not you) have homework to do'
(14) *'eyn li ši'urim laasot* 'I have no homework to do'.

In (9), however, N cannot be replaced by INF unless *yeš* is deleted

(15) *'alay laasot ši'urim* 'I have to do homework';

since it would be illogical to consider this a variation of a pattern whose constitutive and identificatory element *(yeš)* is obligatorily nonapparent, we must forcibly assign it to a separate pattern V. Patterns II, III, and V are, consequently, discrete syntactic structures.

Pattern XVI, whose stylistic characterization has been mentioned, can be formally derived from pattern III after application of the modally significant deletion of *yeš* (see above):

(16) *Láma yeš li carot?* 'Why do I have troubles?' (II)
(17) *Láma li carot?* 'Why should I have troubles?',

but then, while for pattern II the modal value of the *yeš*-deletion takes effect only in the presence of unexpanded N's (Rosén 1966a: 213; Rubinstein 1968: 205–6) and is not stylistically marked, e.g.:

(18) *Le-yosef yeš yadayìm xazakot* 'Joseph has strong hands'
(19) *Le-yosef yadayìm xazakot* (same meaning as (18)),

the opposite is true for pattern XVI:

(20) *Láma li mxonit xadaša?* 'Why should I have a new car?',
'What use do I have for a new car?'

It would, therefore, be impracticable to consider a sentence of pattern XVI simply as one of pattern III, in which the ADV-category is represented by *láma* 'why'.

A pseudo-problem is posed by the nominal sentences (pattern X) and the copula sentences (XI): are the former derivable from the latter by deletion (or replacement by zero) of the pattern-characteristic invariable copula? While the copula sentences and the copula-less nominal sentences have been represented here, as well as already in Rosén (1966a: 233–45), as two discrete patterns, Rubinstein (1968: *passim*) speaks of one single pattern of "equation sentences" which basically includes a pronominal copula replaceable by $\emptyset$. There is no disagreement concerning the basic facts:

In most texts [206], a clear semantic contrast is expressed by the opposition $\emptyset$: *hu* (RUBINSTEIN 1968: 82)

which is exemplified as follows (the English translations are RUBINSTEIN'S):

(21) *Ha-'ec gavoah* 'The tree is high'
(22) *Ha-'ec hu gavoah* 'The tree is a high one'
(23) *Ha-p'ula pšuta* 'The action is simple'
(24) *Ha-p'ula hi pšuta* 'The action is a simple one'[207]

This matches our characterization of the nominal sentences (21, 23) as semantically classificatory, of the copula sentences as semantically identificatory (22, 24). If this is accepted, one will not easily subscribe to derivation of (21) from (22) by a transformation without semantic impact. It is furthermore agreed that the possibility of replacing the pronominal copula by zero (or 'nothing'?) depends upon certain properties of the nominal components of the sentence; RUBINSTEIN (1969: 121-5) lists these properties in terms of the sentence being made up of two nouns, each of which is either determinated or undeterminated, with specific conditions applying to each possible combination (such as 'determinated noun + undeterminated noun'); while this is, in principle, correct, it is not refined enough, and we have based our present discussion on my earlier, more shaded "scale of specific reference" (ROSÉN 1966a: 230-3), on which *determinated* and *undeterminated noun* are only two out of a dozen terms of grading necessary to arrive at a quasi-exhaustive description of the possibilities of constructing (copula-

---

[206] RUBINSTEIN (1969: 82, 121) assigns also stylistic value to the selection of the pronominal copula, of course where it is a variant of what he considers the 'zero' copula.
[207] Sentences (22) and (24) may also be rendered the same way as (21) and (23), respectively. RUBINSTEIN neglects the question of markedness (see below, p. 223).

less) nominal sentences, that is to delimit the cases in which a distinctive opposition between nominal sentences and copula sentences can exist. However, irrespective of what refinement of the scale is necessary to yield an adequate grammatical description, it had not been contested by RUBINSTEIN that the "omission" of the copula was "admissible" only in certain stated environments; in all other environments, neutralization in favour of the copula sentence takes place. We are confronted here, consequently, with two contrastive terms; none of them can be legitimately considered a "transformation" or "derivation" of the other, any more than 'past' can be considered a transformation of 'future'. Furthermore, the zeroification of ADV is freely possible in the copula sentence:

(25) *Laxen safran hu pakid* 'For this reason, a librarian is (the same as) a clerk'
(26) *Safran hu pakid* 'A librarian is a clerk'.

However, omission of the explicit ADV destroys the nexus in certain types of nominal sentences, such as the pendant of (25):

(27) *Laxen safran pakid* 'For this reason, a librarian is a clerk'

but striking out *hu* from (26) would yield no longer a sentence, but a sentence part (*safran pakid* 'a clerical librarian', i.e. 'a librarian who is a clerk', with *pakid* 'clerk' as apposition to *safran*). The structural nonidentity of the nominal and copula sentences is, consequently, additionally emphasized by the different syntagmatic behaviour of each of the two patterns. Finally, certain features of absence of concord between the nominal constituents of the two patterns discussed makes the construction of a sentence according to any one of them impossible (e.g., neither a nominal nor a copula sentence can be constructed of the constituents $N_1 = yosef$, $N_2 = 'ata$ 'you (m.sg.)'), and an appositional copula sentence (pattern XII) subsidiarily takes their place to express 'Joseph – that's you' *(Yosef ze 'ata)*.

We find it expedient to state explicitly what we consider the consequence of these deliberations: rather than being a unique shape of
structure with two transformable variables (such as NP+VP; and
I will not go into the question of whether there are languages in
which a sentence is, in truth, such a unique shape of structure), an
Israeli Hebrew sentence is, as every linguistic form, a materialization of an intersection of dimensions, one (or more) of which is the
category (or categories) constituted by the variable constituents,
and one the category of the sentence patterns. The specific intersection of these categories represented by every materialized sen-
ence yields its linguistic meaning.

8.2 THE CATEGORY OF PREDICATION

Since the same two nominals (nouns and/or adjectives) can be
joined in quite a few cases in a nexus according to more than one
of the binominal patterns (nominal sentence, copula sentence, appositional copula sentence), these patterns constitute the terms of a
SYNTAGMATIC CATEGORY, namely that of PREDICATION, which can
be established for these patterns and the verbal copula sentences
derived from them (XIII, XV). (It is noteworthy that Israeli Hebrew
is a language in which types of predication are formally distinguishable, and for which notions such as 'analytic' or 'synthetic sentence'
are not purely, or merely, extralinguistic or "logical".) The mutual
relations of the members of this category have to be semantically
interpreted, and the purports of "classification", "identification',
and "comment", respectively, have to be assessed.
   Concerning the first two, it must be stated at once, that theirs is a
"weak" opposition, in the sense that the use of the unmarked term
(i.e., in most environments, pattern X, 'classification') is so severely
restricted by grammatical conditions ("scale of specific reference",
8.1.4 (X); deletion of ADV, *8.1.5*) and the environments of stylistic
variation with the unmarked term (RUBINSTEIN 1969: 121) are so
numerous, that comparatively very few types of instances are left
of semantic opposition.

A clear type of opposition, in which the "identificatory" pattern is the marked term, is represented by *'ani ha-melèx* 'I am the king' ('but not the prince' as well as 'but not somebody else who might be considered king') versus *'ani hu ha-melèx* 'I (and nobody else) am the king'. While in this type of "descending specificity" (the personal pronoun ranks almost highest on the "scale of specific reference"), the determinated noun is the term of "lower specificity", it appears that where the determinated noun is the term of "higher specificity", it might be the classificatory term which is marked (examples on p. 221): *Ha-'ec gavoah* 'The tree is high' versus *Ha-'ec hu gavoah* (same meaning, or) 'The tree is a high one'. (The latter term is "more identificatory" than the former.)

The semantic implications of the opposition 'comment' versus 'identification'/'classification' can be seen from these examples:[208]

Appositional copula sentence	Nominal or copula sentence
Rívka ze tov 'Rebecca is all right', 'C'est bon, Rebecca', ('Whatever is implied by naming Rebecca – is good')	*Rívka (hi) tova* 'R. is good. R. is all right' 'R. est bonne'
Ha-mxir ze 'esèr lirot 'The price is ten pounds' (which is a lot of money), 'Le prix c'est dix livres'	*Ha-mxir (hu) 'esèr lirot* 'The price is ten pounds' (No further comment implied) 'Le prix est dix livres'
Gvarot ze šam 'Ladies – that's there'	*Gvarot (hen) šam* 'Ladies are there'
Tip ze mugbal 'Tipping is restricted'	*Tip hu mugbal* 'A tip is limited'
Ha-kafe ze 'ani 'I am the coffee'[209] 'Le cafe c'est moi'	*Ha-kafe hu 'ani*[210]

[208] Selected from ROSÉN (1966a: 247–54), where more examples of relevance are discussed.
[209] In ROSÉN (1966a: 251), this sentence is paraphrased as follows: "The person who ordered the coffee which you served is me." An analogous "restaurant" situation is invoked by BOLINGER for the English sentence *I'm the soup*: "Spoken in context at the cashier's counter in a restaurant it is normal: *You've got us confused: you're charging me for the noon special; the man in front of me was the noon special; I'm the soup.* Included in the semantic range of *I* is whatever the speaker finds it practical to *associate with* [my italics; H.R.] himself" (BOLINGER 1968: 38).

Ma ze pakid? 'What's that [*sc.*
to me,] a clerk?'

Ma hu pakid? 'What is a clerk?'

Mi ze yosef? (literally 'Who is
that – Joseph?') 'What does
Joseph amount to?'

Mi (hu) yosef? 'Who (of those
addressed) is Joseph?'

8.3 NEGATION

8.3.1 Predication negation and specific negation

NEGATION is either PREDICATION-NEGATION[211] or SENTENCE-PART
NEGATION referring to any one of the sentence constituents: *'ani lo
mitnaged le-hacaatxa* 'I don't object to your proposal' versus *Lo 'ani
mitnaged le-hacaatxa* 'It is not I who objects to your proposal'.
Negation referring to an element of a sentence constituent (such
as the governed object of a verbal part of the pattern) implies a
nonnegated alternative: *'ani mitnaged lo le-hacaatxa* (, *'éla le-
hacaato*) 'I object not to your proposal (, but to his)'. Negation of a
total category included in the sentence – whether constitutive thereof (such as ADV) or belonging to one of its constituents (such as
quantity of a nominal element) – entails the use of a pronoun of
SPECIFIC NEGATION (ROSÉN 1962a: 211–3) particular to that category,
e.g. of *'af* for countable (*7.1.3*), *šum* for any type of quantity:

> *'eyn kan 'af talmid*   'There is no(t any) student here'
> *'eyn kan šum talmid(im)* 'There is/are no student(s) here'
> *'eyn kan šum kesèf*   'There is no money here'.

---

[210] "Imagine a fantastic story (or play) in which 'Coffee' is one of the *dramatis
personae* (in personification)" (ROSÉN 1966a: 251); the sentence could then be
uttered by an actor who plays this part; the sentence is also usable if "in a given
group of persons the word *kafé* metaphorically denotes someone described by
certain features; cf. for instance *bul-ha-'ec* ('log of wood', idiomatically 'stolid
fool') *hu 'ani* (and not another person)".

[211] Sentence content negation is not distinguished in Israeli Hebrew from
predication negation: *lo* is an equivalent of *no* or *nein* as well as of *not* or *nicht*.

15

The formal properties of specific negation will be discussed below, pp. *8.3.2–3*.[212]

While predication-negation of existential sentences ("existence" pattern (II) and "possession" pattern (III); *8.1.4*) is effected by lexical means (replacement of *yeš* by *'eyn*), sentence part or specific negation is not different in these sentences from that in others:

> *Yeš li lo vradim, 'éla cipornim* 'I have not roses, but carnations'
> *Yeš li vradim lo yafim*   'I have roses that are not beautiful' (literally: ... not beautiful roses).

A tendency observable in the thirties in certain ethnic groups (GARBELL 1930: 70) to treat the existential sentences, for the purposes of negation, just as all others (that is, to use *lo yeš* rather than *'eyn*) and thereby to arrive at uniform expression of negative content by *lo*, may now be considered as entirely abandoned.

While there consequently remains a variety of negators in Israeli Hebrew (to *lo* and *'eyn* add *'al* in volitive sentence patterns; cf. *7.3.3*), the limits of their use do not correspond to those of Classical Hebrew, where the predication-negator of all nonverbal sentences was *'eyn*. The shift of distribution (cf. GARBELL 1930: 70) arose out of the fact that sentences with participial predicates (that had been originally subject to the syntax of nominal sentences) came to be regarded as verbal (*5.4*) or that participles of qualitative verbs became to be included in the new part of speech, the adjectives (*5.7*). Consequently, Israeli Hebrew *'ani lo yodea* 'I don't know', *Ze lo tov* 'That is not good' are nonclassical, and in "educated" style they are replaced by sentences including *'eyn* (and not *lo*), such as *'eyn 'ani yodea* or *'eyn ze tov*. Since the inception of revived Hebrew speech, accepted grammar has been extremely sensitive to just this type of deviation from classical usage, which constituted in the minds of most orthoepists (together with another feature of negative expression to be discussed in the next paragraphs, *8.3.3–4*) the one most typical characteristic of the "new spoken Hebrew language". As a matter of fact, most adult speakers, who would make

---

[212] Since the means of expressing specific negation is nominal (a pronoun), negation of a category expressed by a verbal part of speech constitutes a problem in Israeli Hebrew. A type of expression of unexplained origin, with an infinitive preposited to the finite verb, has been developed for this purpose in substandard speech: *Lir'ot* (inf. 'to see') *lo ra'iti* ('I saw') *'oto, 'aval dibartì 'ito ba-télefon* 'I did not see him, but I talked to him on the phone'.

no noticeable effort to write classicizing style, would refrain from using, even in nonliterary writing, verbal expressions of the type *'ani lo yodea*, while being much more permissive towards their own usage as regards the adjective-predicate type *ze lo tov*. This is fully justified by classical syntax, since where not predication-negation, but sentence-part negation prevails, the last quoted sentence would be consistent with classical syntax exactly as, e.g., *'eyn ze tov*.[213]

8.3.2 Pronouns of specific negation;
"double" negation

The PRONOUNS OF SPECIFIC NEGATION (e.g. *šum-* 'any', *klum* 'anything', *le'olam* 'ever', *'af-paàm* 'any time'; cf. ROSÉN 1962a: 211–3) occur

(1) in verbal sentences with a negated verb (*Lo ra'itì klum* 'I saw nothing'; *'al tagid klum* 'Don't say anything'),

(2) following *bli-* 'without' (*Ba'tì bli klum* 'I came with nothing'; *Bli-šum-safek ze naxon* 'Without any doubt, this is correct'),

(3) otherwise with no explicitly negative cooccurring, in average style (*Šum davar* 'Nothing' (*davar* 'thing') as a reply to a question (such as *Ma lakaxtà?* 'What did you take?').

The third usage presents the second grave problem concerning negation (cf. *8.3.2*) faced by classicizing purism, since it is contended that in an expression such as *šum davar* negation is unexpressed (*Šum davar lo* is recommended instead); this view is based (a) on the classical usages of *šum* and *klum*, and presupposes (b) that an "indefinite" (but not negative) purport of *šum-* etc. can be algebraically "extracted" from sentences of type (1) and (2), where an explicitly negative element is present in addition to the pronoun of specific negation.

The class of pronouns of specific negation is an open class, in the sense that expressions preponderantly used in negative contexts

---

[213] Classicizing normative grammar neglects the fact that *'eyn* is only a predication negation and has always resorted to rules according to which, in sentences other than in the remotive ("past") or potential ("future") tenses, the negator *'eyn* has to be used "instead of" *lo*. However, an adequate statement of the classicizingly required stylistic replacements of *lo* by *'eyn* has to be based on the syntactic status of the element to be negated (ROSÉN 1962a: 157–8).

acquire, starting from popular usage, the syntactic behaviour of pronouns of specific negations, that is negative meaning in sentences of type (3), and mainly in one-word sentences: *'adayìn* 'Not yet' (cf. *Hu lo ba' 'adayìn* 'He hasn't come yet'). Clear stylistic differences prevail: *Me'olam* 'Never (in the past)' is of lower stylistic level than *Me'olam lo*. These developments indicate that the pronouns of specific negation have acquired their negative purport through "contagion" contracted in the sentences of type (1) and (2).

8.3.3 "Double" negation

While this situation bears obvious resemblance to French usage (ROSÉN 1952a: 23–4), there are too many and too important structural differences between the Israeli Hebrew and the French phenomenon to permit us, in view of the lack of historical contact between the two languages, to consider the Hebrew development as an internal or "natural" development like the French one. These differences are:

(1) The French specific negators are in part of negative origin (e.g. *nul*; cf. ROSÉN 1958c: 75);

(2) the "absorption" by *rien, personne* and their kin, of negative purports is concomitant with the loss of negative value by the accompanying *ne* (with only residuary negative function,[214] as in *Il ne peut venir* 'He cannot come'), as a consequence of which a combination of, e.g., *ne + nul* cannot be considered synchronically as doubly negative;

(3) nonspecific (i.e., predication) negators (*pas, plus*) have similar syntactic behaviour (*Je ne peux pas* 'I can't'; *Je ne peux plus* 'I can't any more'), but in "elliptic" sentences, they join the fully negative *non* rather than dropping the denegativized *ne* (*Moi non plus* 'Me neither'; *Aimez qu'on vous conseille, et non pas qu'on vous loue* 'Be fond of people's advising you, but not of their praising you' (GREVISSE)), so that their negativity becomes doubtful.

I should, therefore, be now inclined to accept the view (GARBELL 1930: 71–2; ALTBAUER 1964: 4) that more significance must be attached to the Slavo-Yiddish parallel, e.g. (Russian)

Я[I] ничего[II] не[III] хочу[IV]   'I want nothing'
'ani[I] lo[III] roce[IV] klum[II]

---

[214] Accordingly, Israeli Hebrew has nothing corresponding to French low-style *Je sais rien*.

Что[I] хочешь[II]? – Ничего[III]   'What do you want?' – 'Nothing'
Ma[I] 'ata roce? – Klum[III]

Я не хочу   'I don't want to (*or* it)'
'ani lo roce

Contrary to the situation in French (which cannot match Я не хочу by *Je ne veux*), the full verbal sentences are not only etymologically doubly negative (also by synchronic etymology due to the double occurence of the *n*-element), but also functionally analysable as such. In the minds of multilingual speakers of Israeli Hebrew, a status must have been accorded to *klum* similar to that of ничего, and verbal or existential sentences containing it must have been "felt" as being DOUBLY NEGATED. This leaning on Slavic was, in all likelihood, neither direct nor exclusive, but rather supported by Yiddish, in which exactly the same type of phenomenon is carried over from Middle High German. The acquisition, by *klum* and its group, of negative value is, therefore, another case to show that Slavisms are often Yiddish-supported if they penetrate fully into revived Hebrew (cf. *2.3.2*).

8.3.4 "Redundant" negation

Once the existence of doubly negated sentences was stabilized in Israeli Hebrew, other apparently REDUNDANT or "illogical" USES OF THE NEGATOR *lo*, which had weak antecedents in inherited language, could be perpetuated, where it could be supported by Slavic or Slavo-Yiddish analogies:

(1) The construction of 'neither–nor' sentences with redundant verb (or existence-word) negation when in initial position (ROSÉN 1962a: 293): *'al-tagid zot lo le-yosef ve-lo le-yaakov* 'Don't tell that either (literally 'neither') to Joseph or (literally 'nor') to Jacob'; *'eyn hayom ba-šamayim lo koxavim ve-lo yareax* = На небе нет сегодня ни луны ни звезд = *Il n'y a ni lune ni étoiles dans le ciel aujourd'hui* 'There are (literally 'aren't') neither moon nor stars in the sky today'.

(2) Generalizing (enclitic) *-lò* in relative clauses (*3.7.3*): *mašèlò* = что-нибудь 'no matter what' with enclitic second component containing ни.[215]

---

[215] This "redundant" negator *lo* was identified already by GARBELL (1930: 70) as Slavo-Yiddish. ALTBAUER, while accepting the hypothesis in BLANC (1965) of a Yiddish influence, traces it directly to analogous colloquial constructions in Slavic, that "strengthened the original tendency in Hebrew" (ALTBAUER 1964: 2).

8.4 MOOD

8.4.1 Order properties

MOOD is a syntactical category[216] whose members contrast by the ORDER properties (relative position of sentence variables) of verbal sentences, verbal copula sentences, and possessional sentences. According to what sentence pattern enters the order opposition, the purport of the modal characterization is different.

To describe the processes involved, it must be stated in advance that the uncharacterized and emphasisless position of a finite verb in a nonsubordinate statement is the "second" place, with the grammatical subject preceding: *Yosef nasaa'etmol le-Tel-'Aviv* 'Joseph went to Tel-Aviv yesterday'. While this is a common feature in numerous languages (not, however, in Biblical Hebrew), the coincidence with contemporary German is remarkable in that, in a stretch of text of nonliterary prose, the sentence parts occupying the first (pre-finite-verb) position would be those that occupied the same position in a corresponding German text. A sampling of current daily newspapers yields the result that a sentence part other than the grammatical subject that occupies the first position in a nonsubordinate verbal sentence with statement purport, creates a content link with either the foregoing or the subsequent sentence; this is in keeping with what has been observed in contemporary German prose (FOURQUET 1938: 26).

8.4.2 Volitivity

As a consequence of what has been stated, there is a pertinent opposition between a nonsubordinate sentence in which a finite verb opens the sentence with the grammatical subject following and one in which the grammatical subject occupies the first position; for a verb in the potential tense, this opposition expresses the con-

---

[216] Mood is not an inflexional category; see p. 194 with note *181*.

trast between VOLITIVITY and statement (ROSÉN 1962a: 71; 1966a: 255–7): *Yosef yevorax 'al-maasav* 'Joseph will be blessed for his acts'; *Yevorax yosef 'al-maasav* 'May Joseph be blessed for his acts'. This opposition is, of course, neutralized where there is no explicit grammatical subject, that is, primarily, in the second persons and first person plural: *Nelex* 'We shall go' or 'Let's go'.

The modal opposition is underlined by the fact that volitive sentences are negated by *'al* (*7.3.3*), while *lo* is excluded from them; the negator also shows that the "inverted" sentence is the marked term of the opposition:

> *'al yevorax yosef 'al-maasav* 'May Joseph not be blessed
> or: *Yosef 'al yevorax 'al-maasav*   for his acts'

> *Yosef lo yevorax 'al-maasav*   'Joseph will not be blessed
>   for his acts'.

In the neutralization position, the negator is the sole indicator of 'volitivity' versus 'statement': *'al nelex* 'Let's not go': *Lo nelex* 'We shall not go'.[217]

8.4.3 Volitivity in possessional sentences

There is an analogous opposition in POSSESSIONAL SENTENCES (pattern III; *8.1.4*) with unexpanded N_2[218]; the modal contrast is

---

[217] Likewise in the second persons: *'al telex!* 'Don't go!' versus *Lo telex* 'You will not go'. This differs strongly from Biblical Hebrew usage (such as in the Decalogue prohibitions: *Lō' t·irṣáḥ* 'Thou shalt not kill' *Ex* 20.13). In Biblical Hebrew, the second person of an (indicative) imperfect preceded by *lō'* stands for a categorial and unconditioned prohibition, while *'al* followed by a second person jussive expresses an interdiction in a given stituation (*'al-t·išp·ku· dắm!* 'Shed no blood!' *Gen* 37.22). Cf. ROSÉN (1970: 112–3).

[218] The 'volitive' : 'non-volitive' opposition in this pattern is based on the distribution of the functions of logical predicate and logical subject in a way that one is vested in one of the 'N' constituents, the other one in the other 'N'. If N_2 is expanded (e.g. *šaloš raglayim* 'three legs'), this distribution may be disturbed by the fact that only the expansory element functions as logical predicate, while the nucleus of N_2 together with N_1 constitute the logical

expressed by replacing *yeš* by Ø (cf. *8.1.5*):

(1)	*La-giborim yeš kavod*	'The heroes have honour'
or	*Kavod yeš la-giborim*	
or	*Yeš kavod la-giborim*	
or	*Yeš la-giborim kavod*	
versus	*Kavod la-giborim!*	'Honour to the heroes!'
or	*La-giborim kavod!*	
(2)	*Yeš li smixa*[219]	'I have a blanket'
versus	*Li smixa!*	'For me a blanket (please)!'
(3)	*Yeš sof la-diburim*[219]	'Talking has an end.'
	Sof la-diburim!	'An end to the talks!'
(4)	*Šalom lxa!*	(Literally 'Peace to you!') Greeting formula

This is corroborated by the use of the negators:

(5)	*'eyn kavod la-bogdim*	'Traitors have no honour'
	'al kavod la-bogdim!	'No honour to traitors!'

This mechanism may be considered analogous to the one based on the "inversion" process in potential tense sentences

---

subject and occur in the "underlying question": *La-šulxan (yeš) šaloš raglayim.* 'The table has three legs', answering *Káma raglayim (yeš) la-šulxan?* 'How many legs has the table?' (ROSÉN 1966a: 212–3; less adequately RUBINSTEIN 1968: 204–7). Consequently, contrary to the example quoted presently, *Kavod gadol la-giborim* 'The heroes have great honour' has no volitive purport; *Šalom rav lxa!* (literally 'Much peace to you!', greeting formula; cf. example (4) below) has, but then since *rav* 'much' is not a freely selectable modifier of *šalom*, but idiomatically invariable, *šalom rav* should not be regarded as an expanded N_2.

[219] Positional variants as in (1), that is to the exclusion of *yeš* in sentence final position.

since *yeš* is excluded from sentence final position of possessional sentences,[220] so that *La-giborim kavod!* may be considered as *La-giborim kavod Ø* with the zero-alternant of *yeš* placed in final position due to modal inversion.

8.4.4 Conjunctive

An inversion process in verbal sentences (again placing the finite verb in a position preceding all other constituents; cf. *8.4.2*) creates a modal correlation (ROSÉN 1966a: 228–30) in all tenses, but for the aorist only in its function as a "historical present"[221] (*7.3.2*): *Ha-sandlar ba' 'el-ha-melèx* 'The cobbler came to the king' is indifferent as to autarky in discourse or being completed by a sequel, but the inverted *ba' ha-sandlar 'el-ha-melèx*, or *ša'al 'oto ha-melèx* 'the king asked him', is marked as preparatory to a necessary sequel: *Ba' ha-sandlar 'el-ha-melèx, ša'al 'oto ha-melèx* 'The cobbler came to the king, *and* the king asked him', or rather 'When the cobbler came to the king, the king asked him'; *Šo'el* (aorist, "historical present") *ha-melèx 'et-ha-sandlar, ('az) hu 'one* '(So) the king asked the cobbler, *and* (then) the cobbler replied'. In this nonintellectual narrative style, the inverted sentence is immediately followed by the finite verb of the sequel sentence, so that the latter can be considered as having its finite verb in 'second' position, the first position being occupied by the inverted sentence, as a sort of "conjoined" clause. We may consequently term this modal feature "CONJUNCTIVE construction".[222]

Other than in narrative prose (in this case, the use of the aorist is excluded), the content of an "inverted" verbal sentence (or,

---

[220] That is with explicit (nonzeroified) N_1; where N_1 is omitted, an "existential" sentence (*8.1.4*) results, from which *yeš* is not excluded in final position: *Kesèf yeš* 'There *is* money; *Geld ist da*'.

[221] Otherwise, sentence initial position of an aorist is practically obsolete; it used to occur, until a generation ago, in the speech of oldtimers, as an imitation of German-Yiddish word order in yes-or-no questions.

[222] In the etymological sense of *con-* versus *sub*-junctive; this terminological usage is found in the grammatical description of some non-Indo-European languages.

rather, of an asyndetic clause) is 'protasis', normally with a "potential" or "injunctive" apodosis: *'amad*[I] *ha-talmid*[II] *be-xol*[III] *ha-bxinot*[IV], *yekabel*[V] *'et-t'udato*[VI] 'If the student[II] has passed[I] all[III] examinations[IV], he will receive[V] his diploma[VI']; '*Hat*[I] *der Student*[II] *alle*[III] *Prüfungen*[IV] *bestanden*[I], *so erhält*[V] *er*[V] *sein Diplom*[VI']. The protatical conjunctive sentence in the potential tense is negated by *lo*, contrary to the inverted volitive sentence which is negated by *'al*: *Lo yaamod ha-talmid be-xol ha-bxinot, lo yekabel t'uda* 'If the student does not pass all his examinations, he will not receive a diploma'.

8.4.5 The history of the syntagmatical expression of mood

Volitive contents are expressed, in Biblical Hebrew, by inflexional means, but the verbal form serving this purpose (the "jussive"; BAUER-LEANDER 1922: 274) is normally placed in sentence initial position; the "inversion" feature described for Israeli Hebrew may be considered inherited. The Biblical Hebrew "jussive" has furthermore, again in sentence initial position, protatical function, if suitably continued by an apodotical sequel: *T·åšet*[I]*-hošek*[II] *wi·hi·*[III]*låylå*[IV] (*Ps* 104.20) 'If Thou layest[I] darkness[II], there is[III] night[IV]', '*Machst du Finsternis, so wird es Nacht*' (BAUER-LEANDER 1922: 274). The Biblical Hebrew perfect (= Israeli Hebrew remotive) enters, as it would appear, this construction in the later layers of BH: *Måṣå'*[I] *'iš·å*[II] *måṣå'*[III] *ṭo·b*[IV] (*Prov* 18.22) 'If (a man) has[I] found[I] a woman[II], he has[III] found[III] a good[IV] thing'; the pattern continues to be very common in postbiblical, primarily rabbinical, style. At the time of revival, it coincided with German, Yiddish, Russian, and probably some other, types of asyndetic conditional clauses.

The study of the expression of modal contents in Israeli Hebrew shows eloquently how the loss of the early inflexional modal distinctions was amply compensated by syntagmatic means of expression, a process highly in keeping with developments in numerous languages; the survival of inherited formal features was made possible through the support of the extra-Hebraic parallelisms.

8.5 SYNTACTIC STATUS

8.5.1 Inclusion; the general subordinative particle

SYNTACTIC STATUS is a binary (below, p. 000) category, by virtue of which every sentence is formally characterized as being either INCLUDED (dependent, subordinate) or not, the former constituting the marked term of the opposition. Syntactic inclusion is expressed by a nominalizing transformation or by the presence, in the included sentence, of the GENERAL SUBORDINATIVE PARTICLE še- (ROSÉN 1962a: 224–8, 256–9), except in protases which are introduced by a suitable conditional conjunction:

> Hu katav 'et-ha-sefèr 'he wrote the book'
> ktivat-hasefèr 'the writing of the book' (included)
> še-hu katav 'et ha-sefèr 'he wrote the book' (included).

Nominalization, which is not feasible for all of the sentence patterns (e.g., existential and possessional sentences are excluded), adequately expresses the nonverbal functions of sentence parts (such as grammatical subject or object) by means of the inflexional categories of nominal status (7.1.5) and case (7.1.4).

8.5.2 Subordinative conjunctions

The še-characterized clauses have nominal status and are consequently subjected to the category of case and other relations prepositionally expressed (7.1.4); their linking to the preceding prepositions frequently requires a preliminary "support" (representing the content of the clause), comparable to ce in Fr. jusqu'à ce que 'until'; e.g. ze or kax in Natxíl[I] ba[II]-ze (or be[II]-xax) še-niš'al[III] š'elot[IV] 'Let's[I] start[I] with[II] (our[III]) asking[III] questions[IV]'. Where such support is not required or not compulsory,[223] a class of SUBORDINATIVE CONJUNCTIONS emerges that are, in effect, nothing other than a conglomerate of a preposition with the subordinator še- in immediate succession; e.g. lifne⌐ 'before' (preposition) in lifne-ha-'ᵃvoda 'before (the) work' versus lifne-še- 'before' (con-

---

[223] Details in ROSÉN (1962: 225–8).

junction) in *lifne-še-'avadnù* 'before we worked'.[224] While the process of formation of subordinative conjunctions is highly productive, the class as such goes back to Talmudic Hebrew and, in effect, to Biblical Hebrew where the subordinate particle *k·i* '*daβ*' is correspondingly used until later *še-* takes over.

8.5.3 Markers of the subordinate clause

It is pertinent in this context to recall the prehistory of Mishnaic *še-*. Syntactically as well as, probably, etymologically this is a direct calque on Aramaic *d·i·* which, sprung from an inflected anaphoric pronoun, early acquired (after loss of inflexion or in its inflexionless uses) the function of a gender-number-indifferent relative pronoun and, subsequently, of a general subordinator. This double function was taken over by postbiblical Hebrew *še-* and preserved by it to this day, so that, for a full understanding of the development of the syntactical functions of *še-*, it is necessary to bear in mind constantly its doublefaced nature.

One of the significant developments (directly calqued on Aramaic *d·i·-*) of the syntactic use of Mishnaic *še-* as a relative pronoun is its occurrence after the interrogative pronominal antecedents *mi* 'who' and *ma* 'what': *Mi ba'?* 'Who came?' versus *mi-še-ba'* 'who ('compound' relative) came' (subordinate). A formal characteristic consequently developed which distinguishes the interrogative *who* '*quis*' or *what* '*quid*' from the ('compound') relative *who* '*qui*' or *what* '*quod*' – and immediately subsequent to the time of revival, the lexical identity of current European interrogative and relative pronouns must have been felt to be reflected in these formal oppositions in Hebrew. As a result, in familiar style, these formal relations were expanded to all of the interrogatives: *matay* 'when?' versus *matay-še-* 'when' (conjunction); and *'éyfo* 'where?' versus *'éyfo-še-* 'where' (conjunction);[225] stylistically more desirable expressions of like purport contain *še-* in its status as a relative: *be-*

---

[224] Israeli Hebrew has no subordinative conjunctions whose source is an interrogative–indefinite adverb of the type *when, quand*; but cf. *8.5.3.*

[225] Cf. also the expansion with generalizing enclitic -*lò* (*3.7.3, 8.3.4*), such as *matay-šè-lò* 'whenever'.

makom še- (*makom* 'place') '*loco quo*'; *(be-)ša'a še-* (*ša'a* 'hour, time') '*tempore quo*'.

The subordinating function of *še-* in conjunction with otherwise interrogative elements became so stabilized that, in informal colloquial style again, *še-* acquired the status of a marker of subordination, however facultatively used, in dependent questions (ROSÉN 1962a: 235), e.g. *Todía li matay še-tagía* 'Inform me when you are going to arrive'. It must be kept in mind that the European type of language considers independent interrogatives, relative (pronouns or adverbs) and dependent interrogatives (such as *where*, *who*; Germ. *wo*, *wer*; Russ. где 'where') almost without exception as a single lexical entity; it is remarkable how Israeli Hebrew could achieve (in one style for the present, but undoubtedly as point of departure for future developments), thanks to the categorial marker *še-*, complete congruence with the content relations prevailing in the substratum languages.

8.5.4 History and typological aspects

Without going into the question of how syntactic status was expressed in Biblical Hebrew, it is obvious that only very rarely the sentence whose status was to be characterized was in itself, and independently from other parts of the utterance, adequately marked. Full marking of a clause as subordinate, and the possibility of identifying it as subordinate or included part of a higher syntactical unit, with shades of semantic relations (such as descriptive, temporal, causal, concessive) fully and unequivocally expressed, was not achieved until after the revival of Hebrew had taken place (ROSÉN 1955a: 128–33). Clauses thus marked forming with the unmarked ones a binary opposition, whose binarity in itself is a far cry from its Biblical antecedents (ROSÉN 1969: 107–8; 1970: 123–6), impart to Israeli Hebrew the faculty of intellectual discourse so integrally a part of the *innere Form* of the current type of European languages. It is this specifically syntactic aspect of content structure more than anything else that places Israeli Hebrew among the Western languages of civilization both now and in future time.

9. BIBLIOGRAPHY

Publications marked ° have no direct bearing on Contemporary Hebrew. Otherwise, * indicates secondary importance.

Aescoly, Aaron Zeaev
*1938 *L'hébreu moderne; leçon inaugurale du cours d'hébreu moderne à l'Ecole Nationale des Langues Orientales Vivantes* (Paris: Geuthner).

Alster-Thau, G.
*1964 Review of ROSÉN (1962a), *Bibliotheca orientalis* 21: 227-31.

Altbauer, Moshé
*1949 "O technice zdrobnień i spieszczeń we współczesnej hebrajszczyźnie" [The technique of diminutive formation and hypocoristics in Contemporary Hebrew], *LPosn* 1: 189-98. [with summary in French]
*1952 "Mi-lšon dayage Yisra'el" [Fishermen's slang in Israel], *Lšonenù la-'am* 3-4: 26-32. [Italian version: "Dalla lingua dei piscatori israeliani", *Bolletino dell'Atlante Linguistico Mediterraneo* 2-3 (1960-61): 169-74]
  1964 "New negation construction in Modern Hebrew", in: *For Max Weinreich on his seventieth birthday; studies in Jewish languages, literature and society* (The Hague: Mouton), pp. 1-5.

Ariel
    Ariel. A quarterly review of the arts and sciences in Israel (Jerusalem: Cultural and scientific relations division, Ministry for Foreign Affairs). [multilingual publication; references are to the English edition]

Avinery, Yitzhak
  1933 *Maḥ"ax hitpatxut ha-lašon ha-'Ivrit* [The course of the development of Hebrew] (Tel Aviv: Atar ~ 1933). [series of earlier articles published in *Lšonenù*]
*1943 "Me-'ikšim le-mišor" [From unevenness to evenness], *Lšonenù* 12: 160-71.
  1946 *Kibuše-ha-'Ivrit be-dorenù* [The conquests of Hebrew in our age] (Merhavia – Ha-Kibbutz ha-Artzi: Sifriat ha-Poalim).
  1964 *Yad-ha-lašon* [The monument of Hebrew] (Tel-Aviv: Yezre'el). [linguistic thesaurus in alphabetic arrangement]

Bachi, Roberto A.
*1955 "A statistical analysis of the revival of Hebrew in Israel", *Scripta Hierosolymitana* 3: 179-247. [Hebrew version: *Lšonenù* 20 (1956): 65-82; 21 (1957): 41-68]

Bar-Adon, Aaron
1959 "Lšonam ha-meduberèt šel-ha-yladim be-Yisra'el" [The spoken language of Israeli children 1: The verb] (Jerusalem). [Ph. D. thesis; mimeographed]
*1962 "Analogy and analogic changes as reflected in Contemporary Hebrew", in: *Proceedings of the Ninth International Congress of Linguists* (Ed.: Horace G. Lunt) (= *Janua linguarum, series maior* 12) (London – The Hague – Paris: Mouton 1964), pp. 758–64.
*1963 "Lšono ha-meduberèt šel-ha-dor ha-ca'ir be-Yisra'el" [The colloquial language of the young generation in Israel], *Ha-Xinux* 35: 21-35.
*1966 "New imperative and jussive formation in Contemporary Hebrew", *JAOS* 86: 410–3.
Bar-Hillel, Yehoshua
1956 "He 'arot methodologiyot li-ysodot ha-morphologia" [Methodological remarks on the foundations of morphology], *Lšonenù* 21: 127–38.
Barles, A.
1937 "Li-sfat ha-yladim" [On childrens' language], *Lšonenù* 8: 185–90.
Bauer, Hans – Pontus Leander
°1922 *Historische Grammatik der hebräischen Sprache des Alten Testamentes* 1: *Einleitung, Schriftlehre, Laut- und Formenlehre* (Tübingen: Max Niemeyer).
Bendavid, Abba
1965 *Lšon-ha-Mikra' u-lšon Xaxamim²* [Biblical Hebrew and Mishnaic Hebrew] (Tel-Aviv: Dvir).
Ben-Ḥayyim, Zeev
1953 *Lašon 'atika bi-mci'ut xadaša* [An ancient language in a new setting] (= *Lšonenù la-'am* 4.3–5, fasc. 35–7).
1955 "La-theoria šel-ha-'Ivrit kfi-še-hi meduberèt" [On the theory of Hebrew as it is spoken], *Tarbiz* 24: 337–42.
Ben-Yehuda, Eliezer
1908–1959 *Milon ha-lašon ha-'Ivrit ha-yšana ve-ha-xadaša* [Dictionary of the ancient and modern Hebrew language]. [title also: *Thesaurus totius Hebraitatis et veteris et recentioris*], 16 vol.; vols. 10–16 by N. H. Tur-Sinai [Torczyner] (using the late BEN-YEHUDA's slip collections); first volumes published Berlin, later reprinted and additional volumes added (Jerusalem: The Ben-Yehuda Foundation); variously reprinted in Tel-Aviv and New-York.
Bergsträsser, Gotthelf
1928 *Einführung in die semitischen Sprachen* (München: Max Hueber).
Blanc, Haim
1953 Review of WEIMAN (1950), *Word* 9: 87–90.
1954 "The growth of Israeli Hebrew", *Middle Eastern affairs* 5: 385–92.
*1956a "Dialect research in Israel", *Orbis* 5: 185–90.
1956b "A note on Israeli 'psycho-phonetics", *Word* 12: 106–13 [cf. S.Z. KLAUSNER 1955)]
*1956c "La-ysod ha-'Araviy še-ba-dibur ha-Yisr'eliy" [On the Arabic element in Israeli speech], *Lšonenù la-'am* 6.53: 6–14; 6.54–5: 27–32; 6.56: 20–6·
1956d Review of ROSÉN (1955a), *Language* 32: 794–802.

1957a "Hebrew in Israel: trends and problems", *Middle East journal* 11: 397–409.
1957b "Ketà šel-dibur 'Ivriy-Yisr'eliy" [A passage of Israeli-Hebrew speech], *Lšonenù* 21: 33–9.
1964a "Israeli Hebrew texts", *Studies in egyptology and linguistics in honour of H. J. Polotsky* (Ed.: H. B. Rosén) (Jerusalem: Israel Exploration Society), pp. 132–52.
1964b *Intensive spoken Israeli-Hebrew* (Washington: English Language Services). [mimeographed booklet accompanying prerecorded tapes]
1965 "Some Yiddish influences in Israeli Hebrew", in: *The field of Yiddish; studies in language, folklore, and literature* 2nd collection (Ed.: Uriel Weinreich) (The Hague: Mouton), pp. 185–201.
*1968 "The Israeli koine as an emergent national standard", in: *Language problems of developing nations* (Ed.: J. A. Fishman *et alii*) (Somerset, N. J.: John Wiley), pp. 237–51.

Bloomfield, Leonard
°1933 *Language* (New York: Henry Holt).

Bolinger, Dwight
°1967 "Apparent constituents in surface structure", in: *Linguistic studies presented to André Martinet on the occasion of his sixtieth birthday* (Ed.: A. Juilland) (= *Word* 23) (New York: Linguistic Circle of New York 1969), pp. 47–56.
°1968 "Judgments of grammaticality", in: *In honour of Anton Reichling on the occasion of his seventieth birthday* (Eds.: W. S. Allen – S. C. Dik *et alii*) (= *Lingua* 21) (Amsterdam: North Holland Publishing Company), pp. 34–40.

Chomsky, William
1957 *Hebrew: the eternal language* (Philadelphia: Jewish Publication Society of America).
*1958 "Toward broadening the scope of Hebrew grammar", *Jewish quarterly review* 49: 179–90.
*1962 "The growth and progress of Modern Hebrew", in: *Studies and essays in honour of Abraham A. Neuman, president, Dropsie College for Hebrew and Cognate Learning, Philadelphia* (Eds.: M. Ben-Horin – B. D. Weinryb – S. Zeitlin) (Leiden: Brill), pp. 106–27.

Choueka, Yaacov
*1964 "Nituax mechanographiy šel-ha-morphologia ha-'Ivrit: 'efšaruyot ve-hesegim" [A mechanographic analysis of Hebrew morphology: potentialities and achievements], *Lšonenù* 27–28: 354–72.
1969 "Dikduk-ycira formaliy la-mila ha-šemanit be-'Ivrit" [A formal generative grammar of Hebrew noun words] in: *Bar-Ilan volume in humanities and social sciences, decennial volume* 2 (Ed.: M. Z. Kaddan) (Jerusalem: Kiryath-Sepher), pp. 106–28.

Christie, W.
*1931 *The renaissance of Hebrew* (London: Harrison).

Cohen, David
1959 Review of ROSÉN (1955c), *BSL* 47.2: 257–62.
1964 Review of ROSÉN (1962), *BSL* 59.2: 233–4.

*1968 "Les langues chamito-sémitiques", in: *Le langage* (Ed.: A. Martinet) (= *Encyclopédie de la Pléiade* 25) (Paris: Gallimard), pp. 1288–330.

Cohen, David – Haim Zafrani
1968 *Grammaire de l'hébreu vivant* (Paris: Presses Universitaires de France).

Cohen, Henri M.
*1951 *Schets der ontwikkeling van het Hebreeuws tot moderne omgangstaal* (Amsterdam: Joachimstal). [Amsterdam dissertation]

Cohen, Marcel
°1939 "Langues et nations", in: *Mélanges Marcel Cohen* (Ed.: David Cohen) (The Hague: Mouton 1970), pp. 14–28.

Collinder, Björn
°1970 *Noam Chomsky und die generative Grammatik; eine kritische Betrachtung* (= *Acta Universitatis Upsaliensis, Acta Societatis Linguisticae Upsaliensis* NS 2.1) (Stockholm: Almqvist – Wiksell).

Devoto, Giacomo
°1957 "Le sopravvivenze linguistiche latine nel mondo moderno", in: *Travaux du cercle linguistique de Copenhague* 11 (= *Acta Congressus Madvigiani* 5) (Copenhagen: Nordisk sprog- og kulturforlag), pp. 75–88.

Drozdík, Ladislav
°1967 "The structure of multicomponential terms in Modern Written Arabic", in: *Sbornik Filozofickej Fakulty Univerzity Komenského: Philologica* 17 (Bratislava: Slovenske pedagogicke nakladatelstvo), pp. 7–25.

Enoch, Paul – Gadi Kaplan
°1969 "Ha-mahut ha-physikalit šel-ha-hat'ama ba-'Ivrit ha-Yisr' elit"[The physical nature of Israel Hebrew accentuation], *Lšonenù* 33: 208–22.

Epstein, Izhac
1915 *La pensée et la polyglottie* (Paris: Payot).

Eytan, Ely
1950 "Mi-loazit le-'Ivrit [Form foreign languages to Hebrew], *Lšonenù la-'am* 2.11: 21–5; 2.12: 13–7; 2.13: 11–4; 2.14: 20–4; 2.15: 15–23.

Fourquet, Jean
°1938 *L'ordre des éléments de la phrase en germanique ancien; étude de syntaxe de position* (= *Publications de la Faculté des Lettres de l'Université de Strasbourg* 86) (Paris: Les Belles Lettres). [reprinted in part as "Zur neuhochdeutschen Wortstellung", in: *Das Ringen um eine neue deutsche Grammatik* (Ed.: H. Moser) (Darmstadt: Wissenschaftliche Buchgesellschaft 1962), pp. 360–75]

Fraenkel, Gerd
1960 Review of ROSÉN (1958a), *Journal of the American Oriental Society* 80: 142–5.
1966 "A structural approach to Israeli Hebrew", *Journal of the American Oriental Society* 86: 32–8. [review of ROSÉN (1962)]

Frei, Henri
°1960 "Tranches homophones", *Word* 16: 317–22.
°1968 "Syntaxe et méthode en linguistique synchronique", in: *Methoden der Sprachwissenschaft* (Ed.: H. Schnelle) (= *Enzyklopädie der geistes-*

wissenschaftlichen Arbeitsmethoden 4) (München – Wien: Oldenbourg), pp. 39–63.

Garbell, Irene
 1930 *Fremdsprachliche Einflüsse im modernen Hebräisch* (Berlin). [dissertation]
 1955 "The pronunciation of Hebrew in Israel", *Maître phonétique* 104: 26–9.

Garbini, Giovanni
 1964 "Il consonantismo dell'ebraico attraverso il tempo", *Annali del Istituto Universitario Orientale di Napoli*, NS 14: 165–90.

Goshen-Gottstein, Moshe H.
 1951 "Ha-lašon ha-'Ivrit ha-meduberèt ke-nose' le-mexkar" [Spoken Hebrew as a subject of research], *Lšonenù* 17: 231–40.
 *1954 "Balšanut mivnit u-politika lšonit" [Structural linguistics and language policy], *Lšonenù la-'am* 5.43: 17–24.
 1969 *Mavo' la-milona'ut šel-ha-'Ivrit ha-xadaša* [Introduction to the lexicography of Modern Hebrew] (Jerusalem – Tel-Aviv: Schocken).

Gougenheim, Georges
 °1956 Review of GREVISSE (1955), *BSL* 52.2: 77–8.

Grevisse, Maurice
 °1955 *Le bon usage*6 (Gembloux: J. Duculot). [1st edition: (1936)]

Guiraud, P.
 °1956 "Les champs morpho-sémantiques (Critères externes et critères internes en étymologie)", *BSL* 52.1: 265–88.

Gumpertz, Y.G. P.
 1938 "La-mivta' ha-Sfaradiy befi-'oley-Germania" [On the Sefardic pronunciation of immigrants from Germany], *Lšonenù* 9: 99–109.

Halkin, Hillel
 *1969 "Hebrew, as she is spoken", *Commentary* 48.6: 55–60.

Harris, Zellig S.
 1948 "Componential analysis of a Hebrew paradigm", *Language* 24: 87–92.
 °1951 *Methods in structural linguistics* (Chicago: The University of Chicago Press).

Hjelmslev, Louis
 °1963 *Sproget* (København: Berlingske Forlag). [quotations are by page numbers of the French translation: *Le langage* (Paris: Éditions de Minuit 1966)]

Jespersen, Otto
 °1911– *A Modern English grammar*, 7 vol. (London: George Allen – Unwin; Copenhagen: Ejnar Munksgaard).
 °1937 *Analytic syntax* (London: George Allen – Unwin).

Kaddari, Menahem Z.
 *1961 "Li-vdikat ha-metaphora ba-'Ivrit šel-yameynù" [A study of metaphor in Modern Hebrew,] *Lšonenù* 25: 134–44.
 1965 "Al-herkeve šem-toàr ba-'Ivrit šel-yameynù" [Adjectival compounds in Contemporary Hebrew], *Lšonenù la-'am* 16: 195–206.

Klausner, Joseph
 1929 "'Ivrit 'Atika ve-'Ivrit Xadaša" [Ancient Hebrew and New Hebrew], *Lšonenù* 2: 3–21.

1948 "ʾAramismim" [Aramaisms], *Lšonenù* 16: 192–6.
1949 *Ha-lašon ha-ʾIvrit – lašon xaya* [Hebrew – a living language] (Jerusalem: Hebrew Language Council).
1957 *Ha-ʾIvrit ha-Xadaša u-vaayotehà* [Modern Hebrew and its problems] (Tel-Aviv: Masada). [a collection of articles published between 1903 and 1957)

Klausner, Samuel Z.
*1955 "Phonetics, personality and status in Israel", *Word* 11: 209–15. [Cf. BLANC (1956b)]

Koschmieder, Erwin
°1945 *Zur Bestimmung der Funktionen grammatischer Kategorien* (= *Abhandlungen der Bayrischen Akademie der Wissenschaften, philosophisch-historische Abteilung*, neue Folge 25) (München: Beck). [reprinted in: Erwin Koschmieder, *Beiträge zur allgemeinen Syntax* (= *Bibliothek der allgemeinen Sprachwissenschaft 2. Einzeluntersuchungen und Darstellungen zur allgemeinen Sprachwissenschaft*) (Heidelberg: Winter 1965), pp. 9–69]

Knobloch, Johann
°1961– *Sprachwissenschaftliches Wörterbuch* (= *Indogermanische Bibliothek 2. Wörterbücher*) (Heidelberg: Winter).

Kutscher, Eduard Yechezkel
1956 "Modern Hebrew and Israeli Hebrew", *Conservative Judaism* 1956: 28–45.
*1957 "The role of Modern Hebrew in the development of Jewish-Israeli national consciousness", *Proceedings of the modern language association* 2.72: 38–42.

Larish, R.
*1933 "Idiš in Eretz-Yisroeldikn Hebreiš" [Yiddish in Palestinian Hebrew], *YIVO-Bleter* 5: 80–4.

Lewis, G. L.
°1967 *Turkish grammar* (Oxford: Oxford University Press).

Lipschütz, E. M.
1920 *Vom lebendigen Hebräisch; ein sprachgeschichtlicher Versuch* (Berlin: Jüdischer Verlag).
1959 *Ktavim* [Writings] 2 (Jerusalem: Mosad Ha-Rav Kuk).

Lšonenù
Lšonenù (= *Lěšonénu*). A journal for the study of the Hebrew language and cognate subjects (Jerusalem: The Hebrew Language Academy). [Hebrew; from 1966 on, each issue includes English summaries of all articles.]

Lšonenù la-ʾam
Lšonenù la-ʾam. A popular monthly on matters of language (Jerusalem: The scientific secretariate of the Hebrew Language Academy). [Hebrew]

Masson, Michel
1968 "La dérivation dénominale en hébreu israélien" (Paris). [thèse; mimeographed]
*1969 "La composition en hébreu israélien", *Comptes rendus du Groupe Linguistique d'Études Chamito-Sémitiques* 12–13: 106–30.

16*

Medan, Meir
  1955 "'Al 'Ašknazit u-'Sfaradit'" [On Ashkenazic ɪnd 'Sephardic"],
        Lšonenù la-'am 6.60–61: 35–9.
  1969 "The Academy of the Hebrew Language", Ariel 25: 40–7.
Mehlman, I. – Y. Shaked – H. B. Rosén
  1960 A foundation word list of Hebrew (Jerusalem: The World Zionist
        Organization).
Mirkin, Reuven
 *1962 "i- + šmot-p'ula ba-'Ivrit ha-sifrutit ha-xadaša" ['i- with action nouns
        in modern literary Hebrew], Lšonenù 26: 217–9.
  1968 "Miškal mefu'al" [The Mefu'al pattern], Lšonenù 32: 140–52.
Mirkin, Shelomo
        see following entry
Morag (= Mirkin), Shelomo
  1947 "Al-šibuše ha-lašon ve-darxe 'ᵃkiratam" [Depravations of language
        and ways of their eradication], Ha-xinux 1947: 3–22.
  1959a "Planned and unplanned development in Modern Hebrew", Lingua
        8: 247–63.
 *1959b "'asor šel-'Ivrit" [A decade of Hebrew], Lšonenù la-'am 10: 67–94.
  1967 "Uniformitiy and diversity in a language: dialects and forms of speech
        in Modern Hebrew", in: Actes du 10ᵉ Congrès International des Lin-
        guistes, Bucarest, 28 août – 2 septembre 1967 1 (Réd.: A. Graur et alii)
        (Bucarest: Editions de l'Académie de la République Socialiste de
        Roumanie 1969), pp. 639–44.
Morag, Shelomo – Raphael Sappan
 *1967 "Mi-lšon ha-dayagim ve-yorde-ha-yam be-Yisra'el" [The language
        of fishermen and sailors in Israel], Lšonenù 31: 289–98; 32: 308–25.
Motsch, Wolfgang
 °1967 "Können attributive Adjektive durch Transformationen erklärt
        werden?", Folia linguistica 1: 23–48.
 °1970 "Ein Typ von Emphasesätzen im Deutschen", in: Vorschläge für eine
        strukturale Grammatik des Deutschen (Ed.: H. Steger) (Darmstadt:
        Wissenschaftliche Buchgesellschaft), pp. 88–108.
Müller-Ott, Dorothea
 *1965 "Slavische Elemente in der neuhebräischen Wortbildung", Wiener
        Slavistisches Jahrbuch 12: 60–6.
Qrnan, Uzzi
  1964 Ha-cerufim ha-šemaniyim bi-lšon ha-sifrut ha-'Ivrit ha-xadaša, beyixud
        'al-pi ha-prosa šel-X. N. Bialik [The nominal phrase in Modern Heb-
        rew with particular reference to the prose writings of H. N. Bialik]
        (Jerusalem: Hebrew University). [Ph. D. dissertation; Hebrew, with
        English summary; unpublished] [Part 1 published as ORNAN (1965)]
  1965 The nominal phrase in Modern Hebrew 1: Introduction and article
        (= Applied Logic Branch, The Hebrew University, Jerusalem, technical
        report 18) (Bethesda, Md.: Educational resources information center
        No. ED 011–644). [Cf. ORNAN (1964)]
  1968a "Pirke yixud", Maalot 10.1–2: 46–59.
 *1968b "Kaze ve-xazot" [Kaze and kazot], Lšonenù 32: 46–59.

1968c   *Taxbir ha-'Ivrit ha-Xadaša* [Syntax of Modern Hebrew] 1 (Jerusalem: Akademon).
Ottewell, Guy
1963   Review of ROSÉN (1962a), *Journal of Semitic studies* 8: 255–61.
Patai, Raphael
*1954   "The phonology of 'Sabra' Hebrew", *Jewish quarterly review* 44: 51–4.
Peretz, Yitzhak
*1943–44   "Li-lšon ha-yladim ve-ha-'am" [Childrens' and popular language], *Lšonenù* 11 (1943): 296–300; 13 (1944): 58–9.
Piamenta, Moshe
*1961   "Hašpa'at ha-'Aravit 'al xiduše Ben-Yhuda" [The influence of Arabic on Ben-Yehuda's word coinings], *Lšonenù la-'am* 12: 150–8.
Plessner, Martin
*1931   "Modernes Hebräisch", *Orientalistische Literaturzeitung* 34: 803–8.
Price, James D.
*1969a   *The development of a theoretical basis for machine aids for translation from Hebrew to English* (Philadelphia, Dropsie College). [Ph.D. thesis]
*1969b   "An algorithm for generating Hebrew words", *Computer studies in the humanities and verbal behavior* 2: 84–102.
Rabin, Chaim
*1940   "La chute de l'occlusive glottale en hébreu parlé et l'évolution d'une nouvelle classe de voyelles", *Comptes-rendus du groupe linguistique d'études chamito-sémitiques* 2: 77.
*1949   *Hebrew reader* (London: Lund Humphries). [according to pireface completed 1944]
*1958a   *The revival of Hebrew* (= *Israel today* 5) (Jerusalem: Israel Digest).
1958b   "Le-xekèr ha-'Ivrit ha-šifrutit ha-xadaša" [On the study of modern literary Hebrew], *Lšonenù* 22: 246–57.
1969   "The revival of the Hebrew language", *Ariel* 25: 25–34.
*1970a   "The role of language in forging a nation: the case of Hebrew", *The incorporated linguist* 9.
1970b   "Hebrew", in: *Current trends in linguistics* (Ed.: Thomas A. Sebeok) 6: *Linguistics in South West Asia and North Africa* (The Hague – Paris: Mouton), pp. 304–46.
Reiff, J. A.
*1968   *Construct state nominalization in Modern Hebrew* (Philadelphia, University of Pennsylvania). [Ph.D. thesis]
Rieger, Eliezer
1953   *Modern Hebrew* (New York: Philosophical Library).
Rivkay, Y.
1932   "'Al ha-specifiyut ha-lšonit be-fi-yladeynù be-'Erèc-Yisra'el" [Language specificness of Palestinian children], *Lšonenù* 4: 279–94; 5: 73–7, 93–5, 231–42.
Rosén, Haiim B.
*1952a   *Tahʿlixe lašon* [Linguistic processes] 1 (= *Lšonenù la-'am* 3.25).
*1952b   "Remarques descriptives sur le parler hébreu-israélien moderne", *Comptes-rendus du groupe linguistique d'études chamito-sémitiques* 6: 4–7.

*1953a *Tahᵉlixe lašon* [Linguistic processes] (= *Lšonenù la-'am* 3.32).

*1953b "'al-standard ve-norma, 'al tahᵉlixim u-šgi' ot" [Standard and norm, processes and mistakes], *Lšonenù la-'am* 4.38: 3–8; 4.39: 3–7; 4.40–41: 3–11.

°1953c "Remarques au sujet de la phonologie de l'hébreu biblique", *Revue biblique* 60: 30–40.

1955a *Ha-'Ivrit šelanú; dmuta be-'or sitot ha-balšanut* [Our Hebrew lanuage, viewed by linguistic methods] (Tel-Aviv: Am-oved).

1955b Review of WEIMAN (1950), *Tarbiz* 24: 234–7.

*1956a *Tahᵉlixe lašon* [Linguistic processes] (= *Lšonenù la-'am* 6.62).

1956b "*Mefu'al* ba-'Ivrit ha-Yisr'elit" [The *Mefu'al* pattern in Israeli Hebrew], *Lšonenù* 20: 139–48.

1957 "Sur quelques catégories à expression adnominale en hébreu-israélien", *BSL* 53.1: 316–44.

1958a *'Ivrit tova* [Good Hebrew; studies in the syntax of "correct" usage] (Jerusalem: Kiryat-Sepher). [Cf. ROSÉN (1966a)]

*1958b "La lingua ebraico-israeliana", *Il Ponte* 14: 1568–81.

1958c "L'hébreu-israélien", *Revue des études juives* 17: 59–90.

1961a "Syntactical notes on Israeli Hebrew", *Journal of the American Oriental Society* 81: 21–6.

°1961b "A marginal note on Biblical Hebrew phonology", *Journal of Near Eastern studies* 20: 124–6.

1962a *A textbook of Israeli Hebrew*, with an introduction to classical language (Chicago: University of Chicago Press).

1962b "Some possible systemic changes in a Semitic system of language", in: *Proceedings of the Ninth International Congress of Linguists* (Ed.: Horace G. Lunt) (= *Janua linguarum, series maior* 12) (London – The Hague – Paris: Mouton 1964) pp. 827–32.

°1964 "An outline of a general theory of juncture", in: *Studies in egyptology and linguistics in honour of H. J. Polotsky* (Ed.: H. B. Rosén) (Jerusalem: Israel Exploration Society), pp. 153–89.

°1965 "Quelques phonoménes d'absence et de présence de l'accord dans la structure de la phrase en hébreu", *Comptes-rendus du groupe linguistique d'études chamito-sémitiques* 10: 78–86.

1966a *Ivrit tova*² (Jerusalem: Kiryat-Sepher). [Cf. ROSÉN 1958a]

1966b "Composition adjectivale et adjectifs composés en hébreu-israélen", *Compte-rendus du groupe linguistique d'études chamito-sémitiiques* 10: 126–35. [Hebrew version in: *Bar-Ilan Volume in Humanities and Social Sciences, decennial volume* 2 (Ed.: M. Z. Kaddri) (Jerusalem: Kiryath-Sepher), pp. 98–105]

°1968 "Die Grammatik des Unbeegten", *Llinguna* 21: 359–81.

1969a "Israel language policy, language teaching and linguistics", *Ariel* 25: 92–111.

°1969b "La position descriptive et comparative des formes contextuelles en hébreu", *Actes du Congrèl international de lidguistique sémitique et chamito-sémitique, Paris 1969*. [To apper]

*1970 "Retrouver la Bible à travers l'hébreu de nos jours", *Revue d'histoire et de philosophie religieuses* 2: 109–26.

Rosenberg, J.
1900 *Ha-mesiax; hebräische Conversationsgrammatik* (Wien – Pest – Leipzig: Hartleben [ca. 1900]).

Rubinstein, Eliezer
1968 *Ha-mišpat ha-šemaniy* [The nominal sentence] (Merhavia: Ha-Kibuc ha-Me'uxad).
1970a *Ha-ceruf ha-pooliy* [The verb phrase] (Merhavia: Ha-Kibuc ha-Me'uxad).
1970b "Te'ur-hanasu' ve-te'ur-ha-mišpat u-maamadam ha-taxbiriy" [Sentence midifiers and verb modifiers and their position in the sentence], *Lšonenù* 35: 60–74.

Rundgren, Frithiof
°1963 *Erneuerung des Verbalaspekts im Semitischen* (= *Acta Universitatis Upsalensis, Acta Societatis Linguisticae Upsalensis* N.S. 1.3) (Stockholm: Almqvist – Wiksell).

Samuelsdorff, Paul Otto
*1963 "Versuch einer Programmierung des hebräischen Verbs", in: *Erstes Kolloquium über Syntax natürlicher Sprachen und Datenverarbeitung, Saarbrücken, 29–30 April 1963* (Ed.: Hans Eggers *et alii*) (= *Deutsche Forschungsgemeinschaft, Forschungsberichte* 5) (Wiesbaden: Steiner), pp. 28–36.
*1967 "Hebrew-English automatic translation – an empirical approach", in: *Actes du 10e Congrès International des Linguistes, Bucarest, 28 août – 2 septembre 1967* (Red.: A. Graur *et alii*) 4 (Bucarest: Editions de l'Académie de la République Socialiste de Roumanie, 1969), pp. 1011–7.

Sappan, Raphael
1963 *Darxe-ha-slang* [The ways of slang] (Jerusalem: Kiryath-Sepher).
1965 *Milon ha-slang ha-Yisr'eliy* [Dictionary of Israeli slang] (Jerusalem: Kiryath-Sepher).
*1969 "Hebrew slang and foreign loan words", *Ariel* 25: 75–80.

Schramm, Gene M.
°1965 "The chronology of a phonemic change", in: *Symbolae linguisticae in honorem Georgii Kuryłowicz* (Red.: A. Heinz – M. Karaś *et alii*) (= *Polska Akademia Nauk, Oddział w Krakowie, Prace komisji językoznawstwa* 5) (Wrocław – Warszawa – Kraków: Wydawnictwo Polskiej Akademii Nauk), pp. 276–86.

Segal, J. B.
*1958 Review of ROSÉN (1955c), *BSOAS* 21.2: 304–5.

Sivan, Reuven
1961 "Xiduše ha-milim šel-'Eli'ezèr Ben-Yhuda" [Eliezer Ben-Yehuda's word coinings], *Lšonenù la-'am* 12.114–15: 37–77.
*1964 *Curot u-mgamot be-xiduše ha-lašon be-'Ivrit bi-tkufat txiyata* 1: *Ha-poál* [Patterns and trends of linguistic innovations in Modern Hebrew; introduction and part 1: The verb] [Jerusalem, Hebrew University Ph. D. dissertation; Hebrew, with English summary; unpublished]
1966 "Me-xaye ha-milim" [The life of words], *Lšonenù la-'am* 17: 151–5, 245–53; 18: 3–7, 72–6, 99–104, 247–51.

*1969 'Ben-Yehuda and the revival of the Hebrew speech", *Ariel* 25: 35–9.

Spiegel, Shalom

  1930 *Hebrew reborn* (= *Meridian books* JP 27) (Cleveland: World publishing company; Philadelphia: Jewish publication society of America, 1962).

Tarbiz

    Tarbiz. A quarterly for Jewish studies (Jerusalem: The Magnes Press – The Hebrew University). [Hebrew; English summaries included at the end of each issue.]

Téné, David

  *1961 "La phonologie de l'hébreu contemporain selon l'usage d'un unilingue" [Paris, thèse de l'université; unpublished]

  1962 "Ha-mešéx ha-nimdad šel-ha-tnu'ot be-'Ivrit" [The measured duration of the Hebrew vowels], *Lšonenù* 26: 220–68.

  1968 "L'hébreu contemporain", in: *Le langage* (Ed.: A. Martinet) (= *Encyclopédie de la Pléiade* 25) (Paris: Gallimard), pp. 975–1002.

  *1969a "Israeli Hebrew", *Ariel* 25: 48–63

  1969b "L'articulation du signifié de monème en hébreu contemporain", *Word* 25 (= *Linguistic studies presented to André Martinet* 3: *Non-Indo-European linguistics*): 289–320.

Thornhill, R.

  *1951 "The rise of Modern Hebrew", *Durham University journal* 43.3.

Trubetzkoy (= Troubetzkoy), Nikolai S.

  °1939 "Grundzüge der Phonologie", *TCPL* 7: 1–271.

  °1949 *Principes de phonologie* traduits par J. Cantineau (Paris: Klincksieck). [= TRUBETZKOY (1939)]

Tubielewicz, Władysław

  1956 "Vom Einfluß europäischer Sprachen auf die Gestaltung des modernen Hebräisch", *Rocznik Orientalistyczny* 20: 337–51.

Tur-Sinai, N. H.

  1951 "Mi-txiyat ha-lašon ha-'Ivrit u-vaayotehà" [On the revival of Hebrew and its problems], *Lšonenù* 17: 29–36.

  1952 "Modern Hebrew and its problems", *Civilisations* 11: 33–40.

Ullendorff, Edward

  1957 "Modern Hebrew as a subject of linguistic investigation", *Journal of Semitic studies* 2: 251–63.

  °1958 "What is a Semitic language?", *Orientalia* 27: 66–75.

  °1961 "Comparative Semitics", *Studi semitici* 4: 13–32.

Vendryes, Joseph

  °1933 "La mort des langues", in: *Conférences de l'Institut de Linguistique de l'Université de Paris, année 1933* (= *Revue des cours et conférences* 35) (Paris: Boivin), pp. 5–15.

  °1951 "La mort et la résurrection des langues", *Hesperia* 6–7: 79–101.

  °1953 "Pour une étymologie statique", *BSL* 49.1: 1–19.

Vriezen, T. C.

  1956 "De ontwikkeling van het moderne Hebreeuws", *MKNA* 19.3: 119–32.

Wartburg, Walther von

  °1956 *Von Sprache und Mensch; gesammelte Aufsätze*, mit einer Bibliographie der Publikationen des Verfassers (Ed.: K. Baldinger – A. Thierbach) (Bern: Francke).

Wackernagel, Jacob
°1926–28 *Vorlesungen über Syntax*, 2 vol. (Basel: E. Birkhäuser).

Weiman, Ralph W.
1950 *Native and foreign elements in a language; a study in general linguistics applied to Modern Hebrew* (Philadelphia: Russell Press).

Weinberg, Werner
1966 "Spoken Israeli Hebrew", *Journal of Semitic studies* 11: 40–68.

Weinreich, Uriel
1960 "Ha-'Ivrit ha-'Aškenazit ve-ha-'Ivrit še-be-Yidiš, bxinatan ha-geographit" [Ashkenazic Hebrew and Hebrew in Yiddish, geographically examined], *Lšonenù* 25: 242–52; 25: 57–80.

Whatmough, Joshua
°1956 *Language: a modern synthesis* (London: Secker – Warburg).

Winter, Werner
°1965 "Transforms without kernels?", *Language* 41: 484–9.

Zand, M. I.
1965 [Занд, М. И.] "Идиш как субстрат современного Иврита 1: Вводные замечания, фонетика." [Yiddish as the substratum of Modern Hebrew 1: Introductory remarks, phonetics] in: *Семитские Языки* (Ed.: G. Š. Šarbatov) (Moscow: Nauka), pp. 221–45. [with English summary]

Zixronot
Zixronot Vaad-ha-Lašon ha-'Ivrit [Memoirs of the Hebrew Language Council] (Jerusalem). [*Zixronot* is the predecessor of *Lšonenù;* in all, six volumes were published at irregular intervals from 1912 to 1928.]